KB261642

ALL ABOUT JUNIOR TOEFL
[LISTENING]

Pre-intermediate Course

Bansok Junior

ALL ABOUT JUNIOR TOEFL LISTENING (Pre-intermediate Course)

1st edition : Printed in Apr. 15, 2008 (1st impression)

Authors : Naomi Kim, Alan Hahn
Publisher : Mi-soon Ko
Editor in chief : Seung-ju Kang
Editors : Min-jung Kwon, Dam-hee Cho
Marketing Department : Keum-hee Kim
Design : Eun-ryoung Kim
Publisher : Bansok Publishing Company
Address : 87-5 Anam-dong, Seongbuk-gu, Seoul
Registration No. : 9-33
Web site : www.bansok.co.kr
E-mail : bansok@bansok.co.kr
Phone : 02-928-0027
Fax : 02-928-3415

ISBN 978-89-7172-484-2   13740
Printed in Korea

ALL ABOUT JUNIOR TOEFL [LISTENING]

Pre-intermediate Course

Bansok Junior

PREFACE

iBT 토플 시험에서 리스닝 섹션이 차지하는 비중이 여느 때보다 크게 증가했습니다. 문제는 청취력이 짧은 시간 집중적으로 공부한다고 해서 실력이 부쩍 늘어나지는 않는다는 것입니다. 글로 써있을 때는 무슨 의미인지 쉽게 알 수 있는 내용도 원어민의 발음으로 들려주면 무슨 내용인지 도무지 모를 때가 많습니다.

청취력을 향상시키기 위해서는 무엇보다도 매일매일 영어 듣기 환경에 귀를 노출시키고 청취 절대시간을 늘리는 것이 중요합니다. 배경 음악처럼 영어 테이프나 라디오를 틀어 놓고 무의식 중에 귀를 영어에 노출시키는 것도 좋지만, 하루에 일정 시간 이상은 오로지 듣기에만 집중하여 청취 학습을 하는 습관을 들여야 합니다. 듣기 학습은 받아 쓰기와 따라 읽기를 병행하는 것이 최상의 방법입니다. 짧은 문장이라도 원어민이 말하는 것을 반복해서 들으며 받아 적는 연습을 하면 원어민의 발음과 문장의 리듬에 익숙해질 뿐만 아니라 놓치기 쉬운 세세한 발음까지 잡아 내어 문장이 어떻게 구성되는지를 자연스럽게 터득하게 되는 효과도 있습니다.

여러 번 들어도 잘 안 들리는 부분은 스크립트를 보고 원어민처럼 말할 수 있을 때까지 계속 따라 읽으며 외우는 것이 효과적입니다. 다음 단어가 저절로 나올 정도로 따라 읽어 표현이 입에 붙은 문장은 잘 잊혀지지 않습니다. 하지만 아무리 효과적이고 뛰어난 듣기 학습법을 알고 있어도 직접 이러한 방법을 활용하여 공부하지 않으면 아무런 소용이 없습니다. 듣기 공부는 하루도 빼놓지 않고 해야 한다는 것을 기억하고 실천하는 것이 토플 리스닝 시험에서 높은 점수를 받을 수 있는 가장 확실하고 빠른 길입니다.

iBT Listening 섹션 준비의 지침서가 될 본 교재는 기본적인 청취력 향상과 토플 리스닝 정복이라는 두 가지 기본 목표를 가지고 집필 되었습니다. 본 교재는 크게 영어 발음과 영어 리듬 원리를 공부하는 Part I과 유형별로 토플 문제를 공략하는 Part II로 구성되어 있습니다. Part I에서는 혼동하기 쉬운 영어 발음을 구분하고 영어의 리듬에 적응하여 청취력을 향상시키는 훈련을 합니다. Part II에서는 리스닝 섹션의 출제경향을 철저히 분석하여 각 문제 유형별로 최적의 전략과 학습방법을 제시하고 있습니다. 또한 시험에 실제로 자주 출제되는 대화 상황과 강의 주제를 중심으로 지문을 제작하여 실전 시험과의 유사성을 높였으며, 학습 효과를 극대화 하기 위해 난이도가 높은 문제들을 뒤쪽에 배치하여 자연스럽게 난이도를 조금씩 높여가며 공부할 수 있도록 하였습니다. 4주 학습 완성을 목표로 구성된 학습 계획표에 맞추어 본 교재를 차근차근 공부해나가면 부쩍 향상된 청취 실력과 더불어 iBT 토플 시험에 완벽하게 준비된 자신감에 넘치는 자신의 모습을 발견할 수 있을 것입니다.

Naomi Kim, Alan Hahn

CONTENTS

Part I How to listen

Part II Types of Questions

별책 Answer / Script / Explanation

이 책의 구성과 특징

Part I How to listen
Overview

Chapter 1에서는 혼동되는 5가지 발음의 구분, Chapter 2에서는 영어의 리듬을 만들어내는 5가지 요소를 다양한 예를 들어 설명하고 있다.

Activities

Overview에서 설명된 기본적 원리를 다양한 활동을 통해 적용해보고 반복 학습하는 코너이다. mp3를 듣고 문장을 따라 읽기, 혼동하기 쉬운 발음 체크, 문장에서 적절한 단어 찾기 등의 청취 연습을 통해 리스닝에 대한 기본기를 쌓을 수 있다.

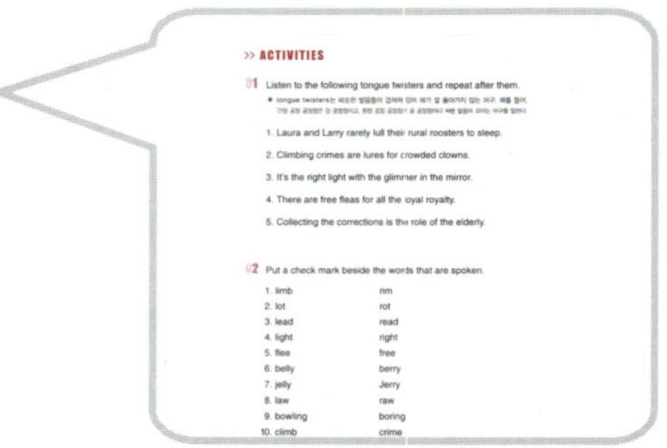

Part II Types of Questions
Overview

각 문제 유형에 대한 소개와 분석이 들어 있으며 문제에 효과적으로 접근할 수 있는 핵심 전략이 제시되어 있다.

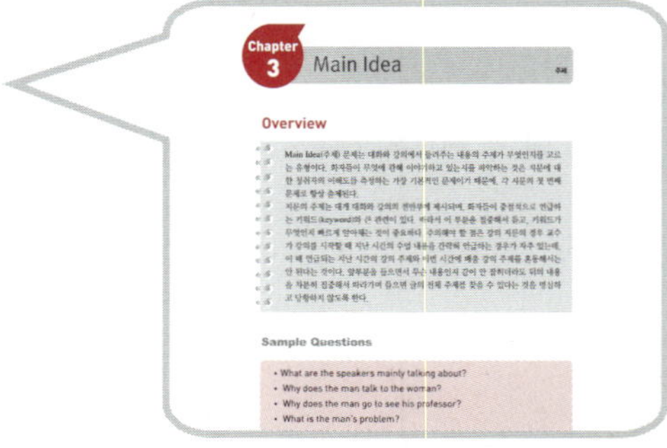

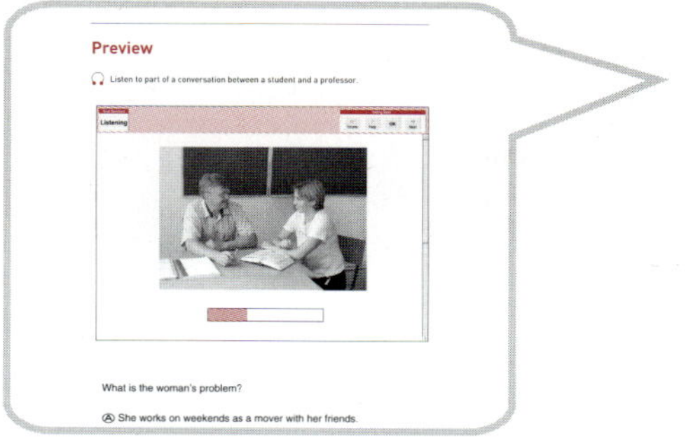

Preview

실제 문제를 풀어보며 앞서 제시된 전략을 적용해보는 코너이다. 문제 접근법과 해결법이 문제 풀이과정과 자세한 해설을 통해 구체적으로 설명되어 있다.

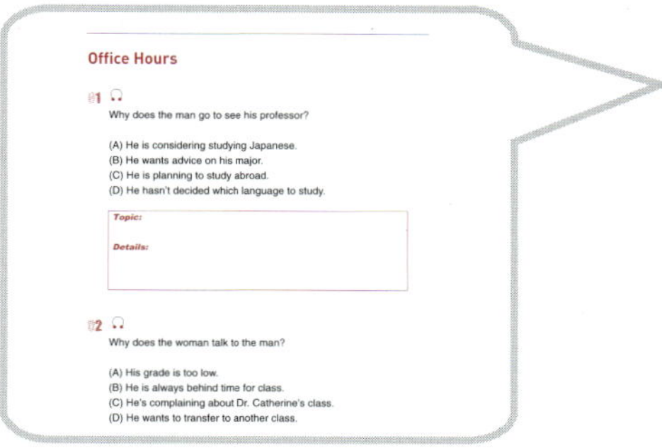

Office Hours / Service Encounters / Lectures

실전보다 짧은 길이의 스크립트를 듣고 문제를 풀어본다. 각 문제 유형을 단계적으로 공략할 수 있도록 난이도가 조정되어 있다. 대화는 문항당 1 문제, 렉쳐는 문항당 2문제가 출제되어 있다.

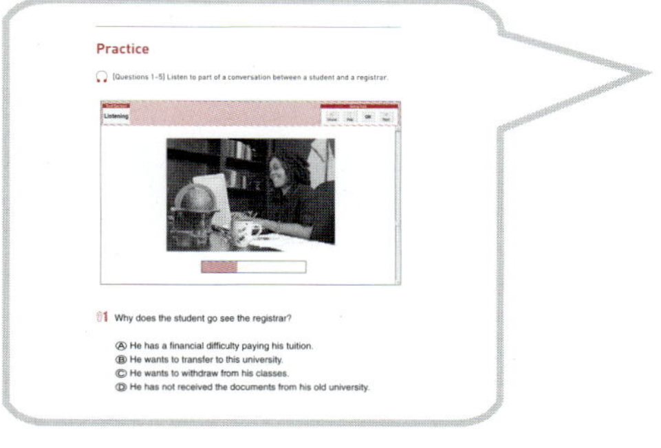

Practice

앞 코너에서 각 문제 유형을 집중적으로 학습한 후 Practice에서는 실전과 유사한 문제를 풀어본다. 실전과 마찬가지로 하나의 스크립트에 모든 문제 유형이 출제되어 있다.

Review

앞서 들었던 스크립트에서 몇 문장을 발췌하여 받아쓰기를 해보고 끊어 읽기를 반복 학습한다.

iBT Listening 특징!

iBT Listening 섹션은 기존 CBT의 짧은 대화 지문이 없어지고 긴 대화 지문과 강의로만 이루어져 있다. 대화와 강의 모두 CBT에 비해 지문이 상당히 길어졌으며 실제 대화와 수업과 같이 말을 하다가 잠시 쉬는 부분이나 머뭇거리는 부분 등, 보다 현실감 있게 구성되어 있다.

1. 2~3개의 파트로 구성된다.
한 개의 파트는 대화(conversation) 1개, 강의(lecture) 2개로 이루어져 있다. 따라서 시험이 2개 파트로 구성되어 있으면 총 2개의 대화와 4개의 강의가 출제되며, 시험이 3개 파트로 구성되어 있으면 총 3개의 대화와 6개의 강의가 출제된다.

2. 대화는 지문당 5개, 강의는 지문당 6개의 문제가 출제된다.
대화는 약 3분간 들려주고, 지문은 약 400~500자로 이루어져 있으며 각 지문당 5개의 관련 문제가 출제된다. 강의는 약 3~5분간 들려주고, 지문은 약 500~800자로 이루어져 있으며 각 지문당 6개의 관련 문제가 출제된다.

3. 대화는 Office Hours와 Service Encounters로 나뉘어져 있다.
Office Hours 대화에서는 학생과 교수가 대화를 나누고, Service Encounters 대화에서는 학생과 사서, 기숙사 직원과 같은 학교 직원이 대화를 나눈다.

4. 강의는 Monologue와 Discussion으로 나뉘어져 있다.
Monologue 강의에서는 교수가 혼자 강의 주제를 설명해나가고, Discussion에서는 학생과 교수의 질의응답으로 강의가 진행된다.

5. Note-taking이 허용된다.
지문의 길이가 상당히 긴 편이므로 Note-taking을 적극 활용하는 것이 좋다.

6. 대화와 강의 환경이 실제 상황과 유사하다.
CBT에서는 화자의 말이 딱딱 끊어지는 느낌이 나고 정형화되어 있었으나, iBT Listening에서는 화자가 말을 하며 머뭇거린다거나 말을 더듬는 등 대화와 강의 상황이 실제와 같이 보다 자연스럽게 이루어져 있다.

7. 다양한 영어권 국가의 발음과 억양을 들려준다.
미국식 화자의 음성 외에도 영국이나 호주식 화자의 음성을 들려준다.

8. 지문의 일부를 다시 듣고 푸는 문제가 출제된다.
화자의 태도나 말한 의도 및 목적을 묻는 문제(stance/function question)에는 헤드셋 표시가 나오고 지문의 해당 부분을 다시 한 번 들려준다.

9. 2점의 배점이 주어지는 문제도 출제된다.
대부분의 문제는 1점짜리 이지만 2점짜리 문제도 간혹 출제되며 배점이 따로 표시된다.

문제 유형		특 징
Basic Comprehension	Main Idea	• 지문의 주제 찾기
	Detail	• 지문에 직접적으로 언급되어 있는 세부 정보를 찾기
Connecting Information	Inference	• 지문에 직접적으로 언급되어 있지는 않지만 지문에 흩어져 있는 정보를 바탕으로 논리적으로 추론할 수 있는 것을 고르거나 결론을 도출하기
	Connecting Information	• 지문에 정보가 어떻게 조직되어 있는지 내용상, 구조상의 전개방식을 이해하고 내용들 사이의 관계를 바탕으로 정보를 연결하기
Pragmatic Understanding	Stance/Function	• 지문에 제시되는 정보에 대한 화자의 입장과 태도를 파악하고 발화 목적과 의도를 알아내기

	화 자		토 픽
Conversation	Office Hours	학생과 교수	• 시험, 성적, 수업 참여도, 과제물, 수업 내용, 현장 학습, 전공 선택, 인턴, 진로 등
	Service Encounters	학생과 학교 직원	• 기숙사 생활, 도서 대출, 교재 구입, 수강 신청, 카페테리아 이용, 학비 납부 및 장학금 신청, 실습실 이용, 학교 행사, 동아리 활동 등
Lecture	Monologue	교수	
	Discussion	교수와 학생	• history(역사학), literature(문학), economics(경제학), political science(정치학), psychology(심리학), film(영화), anthropology(인류학), archaeology(고고학), photography(사진), biology(생물학), astronomy(천문학), geology(지질학), paleontology(고생물학), urban planning(도시공학)

1. 어휘력을 기른다.

시험에 자주 등장하는 토플 수준의 다양한 어휘와 표현(이디엄)을 외워둔다. 글자만 외울 것이 아니라 소리 내어 읽으며 외워서 정확한 표현을 실제 대화 상황에서 써먹을 수 있을 정도로 외운다. 단어와 표현을 외울 때는 정확한 발음을 알아두도록 한다. 발음을 잘못 알고 있으면 의미를 아는 단어라도 제대로 알아 듣기가 힘들다.

2. 많이 듣고 따라 읽는다.

토플 리스닝 교재나 기타 듣기 자료 등을 활용하여 무조건 많이 듣는다. 일주일치 학습량을 하루에 몰아서 듣고 그 다음 주까지 아무 것도 듣지 않는 것보다 매일매일 조금씩 꾸준히 듣는 것이 훨씬 효과적이다. 내용의 이해가 최우선이지만 발음과 억양에도 신경을 집중하고 들으며 따라 읽는 연습을 한다.

3. 들으면서 Note-taking을 한다.

듣기 연습을 할 때 Note-taking을 하는 습관을 기르도록 한다. 키워드의 개념 정리를 시작으로 핵심 내용을 빠르고 체계적으로 적는다. Note-taking은 단순한 받아 적기가 아니라 듣는 사람이 자기만의 방식으로 내용을 간단하게 메모하는 것이다. 시험장에서 들려주는 내용을 놓치는 일 없이 Note-taking을 제대로 활용하기 위해서는 많은 연습이 필요하다. Note-taking을 다 한 후에는 적어 놓은 내용이 스크립트의 흐름과 맥을 같이 하는지 확인해보고 본인이 적은 내용만 보고도 글의 내용을 이해할 수 있는지 확인해본다.

4. 글을 요약하는 연습을 한다.

들은 후 핵심 내용을 재대로 이해했는지 들은 내용을 요약해 보도록 한다. 요약 연습은 Note-taking과 연계하여 해보는 것이 좋다. 메모에 스크립트의 중요 사항이 흐름대로 잘 적혀있다면, 이 메모가 요약의 틀을 짜는 바탕이 될 수 있기 때문이다. 요약할 때는 되도록 들려준 그대로의 어휘나 표현을 사용하지 말고 본인만의 표현으로 바꾸어 나타내본다.

5. 많이 읽는다.

토플 리스닝 강의에 등장하는 지문은 길이도 길뿐만 아니라 다양한 분야의 학구적인 내용을 다루기 때문에 내용 자체도 어려운 편이다. 낯선 분야의 강의 내용을 사전 지식 없이 바로 들으면 무슨 내용인지 이해하지 못할 때가 많다. 따라서 듣기와 더불어 평소에 많은 글을 접하여 읽어 본다.

6. 배경 지식을 늘린다.

토플 시험에 등장할만한 다양한 분야의 글을 읽고 들으며 배경지식을 쌓도록 한다. 특히 시험에 자주 등장하는 토픽은 내용을 간략히 정리해두는 것도 좋다. 대화 파트를 위해서는 영어 회화를 많이 해보고 대

iBT Listening Note-taking

iBT Listening에서는 노트 테이킹이 허용된다. CBT에 비해 지문의 길이가 많이 길어졌지만, 내용이 많아지고 길어진 만큼 지문을 들으면서 내용을 적을 수 있기 때문에 노트 테이킹을 효과적으로 활용하면 더 높은 점수를 받을 수 있는 가능성도 높아졌다. 지문을 들으면서 노트 테이킹을 하면 내용의 전체적인 주제와 전반적인 흐름을 이해하고 세부 정보를 정리하여 기억해내는데 효과적이다. 노트 테이킹을 할 때는 먼저 도입부에 제시되는 글 전체의 주제를 파악하고 이 주제를 전개하기 위해 언급되는 중심 정보와 세부 정보를 간단명료하게 적는 것이 중요하다. 노트 테이킹의 목적은 지문에 언급되는 모든 정보를 얼마나 잘 정리하느냐에 달린 것이 아니라 듣고 적은 내용이 문제를 풀며 내용을 기억해내고 정보간의 관계를 파악하는데 얼마나 도움을 주느냐에 있다. 따라서 내용 이해에 방해가 되지 않는 선에서 노트 테이킹을 해야 하며, 지문을 한 번밖에 들을 수가 없고 들려주는 내용의 양이 상당히 많다는 Listening 섹션의 특성을 고려하여 내용을 효율적으로 받아 적을 요령이 필요하다.

Note-taking 핵심 요령

1. 주제 (main topic)를 먼저 명료하게 적는다.

도입부를 들으면서 핵심어(keyword)를 중심으로 앞으로 전개될 대화와 강의의 주제를 먼저 적는다.

2. 세부 정보를 하위 주제에 따라 구분하여 적는다.

도입부에 대화와 강의의 중심 정보가 나온 후, 그 뒤에는 이 중심 정보와 관련된 세부 정보가 언급된다. iBT Listening에서는 한 지문당 듣기 시간이 상당히 긴 편이므로, 이 세부 정보 역시 하위 주제별로 구분하여 정리해 두어야 한다. 특히 강의를 들을 때는 하위 주제가 전환될 때 이를 알려주는 전환어가 자주 등장하므로 이를 듣고 화제가 바뀌고 있음을 알 수 있다.

3. 가능한 간단히 적는다.

완전한 문장으로 적을 필요는 없다. 구(Phrase)를 사용하여 최대한 간단히 적는다.

4. 약어와 부호를 이용해 적는다.

자주 등장하는 어휘나 표현의 부호와 약어를 충분히 익혀두고 노트 테이킹을 할 때 적극 활용한다. 시간을 절약하는데 도움을 준다.

5. 잘 듣지 못한 부분은 넘어간다.

대화와 강의를 들으면서 알아듣지 못한 부분이나 놓친 부분은 넘어간다. 알아들었다고 해도 앞부분의 내용을 먼저 적다가 잊어버리는 수도 있다. 특히 이런 경우에는 지나간 내용에 집착하게 되는데, 잊어버린 내용을 기억해내려고 하는 동안에도 화자의 말은 계속 되고 있음을 잊지 말아야 한다. 한 번 지나간 부분은 다시 들을 수 없다. 따라서 놓친 부분에 연연해하지 말고 앞으로 들어야 할 내용에 더 신경을 쓴다.

iBT TOEFL 특징

토플은 비영어권 국가의 수험생들의 영어 능력 측정을 목표로 한다. 특히 영어권 국가의 대학 생활과 같은 학술적 환경에서의 영어 사용 능력을 측정하는 데 초점을 맞추고 있다. 학문적 지식이나 컴퓨터 활용 능력을 평가하려는 것이 아니므로 모든 문제는 시험에 제시되는 내용만을 근거로 정답을 골라야 한다. iBT (Internet-based test) 토플은 인터넷을 통해 시험이 치러지며 언어의 네 가지 영역인 읽기(Reading), 듣기 (Listening), 말하기(Speaking), 쓰기(Writing) 능력을 종합적으로 평가한다.

1. Speaking(말하기) 영역이 평가된다.

영어를 읽고 듣고 쓰는 능력에 비해 말하기 실력이 부족한 사람들이 많다는 것을 감안해 iBT 토플에서는 Speaking 영역이 평가된다. 글을 듣거나 읽으면서 이해하는 것으로만 그치지 않고 이해한 내용을 체계적으로 말할 수 있어야 한다.

2. 언어의 통합적(Integrated) 사용 능력이 중요하다.

Speaking과 Writing에서는 말하고 쓰는 독립적 능력 외에, 언어의 통합적 사용 능력이 함께 평가된다. Speaking 영역에서는 강의나 대화를 듣고 말하거나 지문을 읽고 강의나 대화를 들은 후 말하는 통합형 문제가 출제된다. Writing 영역에서는 지문을 읽고 강의를 들은 후 내용을 요약해야 하는 통합형 문제가 출제된다.

3. 문법 실력만을 측정하는 별도의 영역은 없다.

CBT에서는 문법(Grammar) 영역이 별도로 있었으나 iBT에서는 문법 실력만을 별도로 측정하는 영역은 없다. 이는 문법이 언어 구사에 있어 기본적인 요소인 만큼 읽고 듣고 말하고 쓰는 실용적 상황에서의 기본적인 문법 활용을 측정하기 위함이다.

4. Note-taking이 허용된다.

시험 내내 Note-taking을 할 수 있는 별도의 용지가 제공된다. 따라서 평소에 공부할 때도 기억력보다는 이해력과 논리력에 중점을 두고, 시험 중에 Note-taking을 위해 이를 최대한 활용할 수 있도록 충분히 연습해 두어야 한다.

5. Writing 영역의 답안 작성시에는 타이핑만 가능하다.

종이에 답안을 작성할 수 없으므로 능숙한 영자 타이핑 실력이 필요하다. 시험 도중 서투른 타이핑으로 시간을 낭비하는 일이 없도록 시험 전에 많은 연습을 해두도록 한다.

6. 인터넷으로 성적을 확인할 수 있다.

인터넷 기반 시험인 만큼 시험일로부터 15일 후에 인터넷으로 성적 확인이 가능하다.

iBT TOEFL 구성

영역	시간	문항 수	점수	특징
Reading	60~100분	지문 수 : 3~5개 문제 수 : 각 12~14개	0~30점	• 지문은 약 700자로 구성되어 있다. • 일부 지문에는 그림이 등장한다. • 지문의 종합적인 이해를 요구하는 표 채워넣기 문제(Summary, Category chart)가 출제된다.
Listening	60~90분	대화 지문 수 : 2~3개 대화 문제 수 : 각 5개 강의 지문 수 : 4~6개 강의 문제 수 : 각 6개	0~30점	• 대화는 약 400~500자로 구성되어 있고, 강의는 약 500~800자로 이루어져 있다. • 대화는 3분간 들려주고 강의는 3~5분간 들려준다. • 화자의 억양과 발음이 다양화되어 미국식, 영국식, 호주식 발음을 들려준다.
Break (휴식)	10분			
Speaking	20분	독립형 문제 수 : 2개 통합형 문제 수 : 4개	각 문제 : 0~4점 총점 : 0~30점	• 독립형은 개인적 경험을 말하는 문제 1개와 두 가지 선택사항 중 하나를 선택하여 말하는 문제 1개로 구성되어 있다. • 통합형은 지문을 읽고 강의나 대화를 들은 후 말하는 문제 2개와 강의나 대화를 듣고 말하는 문제 2개로 이루어져 있다. • 헤드셋과 연결되어 있는 마이크에 대고 답을 녹음하며, 이는 디지털화되어 채점 기관으로 전송된다.
Writing	55분	통합형 문제 수 : 1개 독립형 문제 수 : 1개	각 문제 : 0~5점 총점 : 0~30점	• 통합형 문제는 먼저 독해 지문을 읽고 강의를 들은 후 강의 내용을 독해 지문과 연계하여 요약해야 한다. • 독립형 문제는 주어진 주제에 대해 개인적 경험이나 생각에 기초하여 글을 작성해야 한다. • 답안은 타이핑으로 작성해야 한다.

iBT TOEFL 시험 등록

1. www.ets.org/toefl 웹사이트를 방문하여 인터넷 접수를 한다. 상시 등록이 가능하며 응시일로부터 최소 7일 전까지 등록을 해야 한다. 응시료는 신용카드로 결제한다.

2. 한미교육위원단으로 전화를 하여 시험을 접수한다. 응시일로부터 최소 7일 전까지 등록을 해야 하며 응시료는 신용카드로 결제한다. 전화번호는 02-3211-1233.

3. 한미교육위원단으로 우편접수를 한다. 등록 신청서(registration form)를 작성하고 수표나 우편환을 동봉하여 보낸다. 응시일로부터 최소 4주 전까지 등록을 해야 한다. 주소는 서울특별시 마포구 염리동 168-15 한미교육위원단(121-874).

4. 응시료는 US $140, 시험일자 변경 비용은 US $40, 취소한 성적 복원 신청 비용은 US $20, 성적 추가 리포팅 비용은 US $17이다.

5. 등록한 시험을 취소하기 위해서는 직접 등록 센터를 방문하거나 웹사이트에 접속하여 절차를 밟아야 한다. 우편으로는 등록 취소가 불가능하다. 응시일로부터 최소 4일 전까지 등록 취소가 가능하며 US $85를 환불 받을 수 있다.

6. 시험 당일에는 반드시 신분증(주민등록증, 운전면허증, 여권 중 택일)을 지참해야 하며 등록 번호(registration number)를 알고 있어야 한다.

7. 시험은 약 4시간 동안 진행되고 두 영역이 끝난 후 10분간의 휴식시간이 주어진다.

8. 성적은 응시일로부터 15일 후 인터넷으로 확인 할 수 있다. 시험 당일에 원하는 4개 기관으로 성적 리포팅이 가능하다.

9. 성적표에는 영역별 점수와 함께 총점이 기재되며 각 영역별로 수험자의 실력을 진단해주는 feedback이 들어있다. 성적표의 유효 기간은 2년이다.

10. 시험 당일 날 시험을 마치면서 성적을 취소할 수 있으며 취소한 성적을 복원하기 위해서는 응시일로부터 10일 이내에 시험주최측에 연락을 해야 한다. 앞서 언급한 대로 성적 복원 신청 비용은 US $20이다.

학습 계획표

	Day 1	Day 2	Day 3	Day 4	Day 5	Day 6	Day 7
Week 1	Ch. 1 1. L/R 발음 ~ 2. F/P 발음	Ch. 1 3. B/V 발음 ~ 4. TH 발음	Ch. 1 5. [æ]와 [e] 발음 ~ Ch. 2 1. Contraction	Ch. 2 2. Liaison ~3. Word Stress	Ch. 2 4.Sentence Stress ~ 5. Pause	Ch. 3 Overview, Preview	Ch. 3 OH, SE
Check							
Week 2	Ch. 3 Lectures	Ch. 3 Practice, Review	Ch. 4 Overview, Preview	Ch. 4 OH, SE	Ch. 4 Lectures	Ch. 4 Practice, Review	Ch. 5 Overview, Preview
Check							
Week 3	Ch. 5 OH, SE	Ch. 5 Lectures	Ch. 5 Practice, Review	Ch. 6 Overview, Preview	Ch. 6 OH, SE	Ch. 6 Lectures	Ch. 6 Practice, Review
Check							
Week 4	Ch. 7 Overview, Preview	Ch. 7 OH, SE	Ch. 7 Lectures	Ch. 7 Practice, Review	복습	복습	복습
Check							

* OH: Office Hours   SE: Service Encounters

Part I | How to listen

발음
Pronunciation

Chapter 1

1. L / R 발음

1. L 발음

[d]나 [t] 발음을 할 때처럼 입 천장의 윗니 바로 뒤쪽으로 혀를 갖다 대고 소리를 낸다. 흔히 우리말의 'ㄹ'과 대응한다고 생각하는데, 꼭 그렇지만은 않다. 단어의 처음에 올 때와 중간에 받침으로 사용될 때, 단어의 끝에 올 때 발음이 미묘하게 달라진다.

leaf [li:f]	love [lʌv]	lake [leik]
Latin [lǽtin]	long [lɔ:ŋ]	listen [lísən]
license [láisəns]	lately [léitli]	lettuce [létis]
lucky [lʌ́ki]	silly [síli]	milk [milk]
Ally [ǽli]	walk [wɔ:k]	world [wə:rld]
full [ful]	fuel [fjú:əl]	missile [mísəl]
mail [meil]	sale [seil]	

2. R 발음

[r] 소리는 우리말에 적절하게 대응하는 소리가 없어 어려운 발음으로 인식된다. 영어를 할 때 발음을 굴려서 말하라고 하는데, 바로 [r]과 관련 있는 이야기이다. [r]을 발음하는 요령은 입을 오므리고 혀를 위로 동그랗게 말아 뒤쪽으로 밀어주며 소리를 내는 것이다. 이 때 혀가 입 천장에 전혀 닿지 않도록 해야 한다. 미국식 표준 영어에서는 [r] 발음을 할 때 혀가 이리저리 움직이지 않지만, 영국식 영어에서는 발음을 하면서 혀가 조금씩 움직인다.

roof [ru:f]	real [rí:əl]	rural [rúərəl]
rainbow [réinbòu]	radio [réidiòu]	reason [rí:zən]
request [rikwést]	road [roud]	rubber [rʌ́bər]
Russia [rʌ́ʃə]	serious [síəriəs]	word [wə:rd]
mirror [mírər]	wrong [rɔ:ŋ]	park [pɑ:rk]
choir [kwáiər]	door [dɔ:r]	rare [rɛər]
car [kɑ:r]	sore [sɔ:r]	

>> ACTIVITIES

01 Listen to the following tongue twisters and repeat after them.
* tongue twisters는 비슷한 발음들이 겹쳐져 있어 혀가 잘 돌아가지 않는 어구, 예를 들어,
'간장 공장 공장장은 강 공장장이고, 된장 공장 공장장은 공 공장장이다' 처럼 발음이 꼬이는 어구를 말한다.

1. Laura and Larry rarely lull their rural roosters to sleep.

2. Climbing crimes are lures for crowded clowns.

3. It's the right light with the glimmer in the mirror.

4. There are free fleas for all the loyal royalty.

5. Collecting the corrections is the role of the elderly.

02 Put a check mark beside the words that are spoken.

1. limb ______	rim ______
2. lot ______	rot ______
3. lead ______	read ______
4. light ______	right ______
5. flee ______	free ______
6. belly ______	berry ______
7. jelly ______	Jerry ______
8. law ______	raw ______
9. bowling ______	boring ______
10. climb ______	crime ______
11. walk ______	work ______
12. flame ______	frame ______
13. lime ______	rhyme ______
14. lift ______	rift ______
15. lock ______	rock ______

03 Listen to the following sentences and circle the right word between the two that are underlined.

1. Carrie was very upset when she realized that she had lost the _lace / race_.

2. The class was surprised to learn that Ronald comes from a _loyal / royal_ family.

3. The lawyer was very proud that he was able to complete the _climb / crime_.

4. Dr. Richard Karras was _elected / erected_ during the last federal election.

5. No one really liked Larry because he always thought he was _light / right_.

04 Listen to the following paragraph and fill in the blank.

When Larry ______ in Alberta, he loved to ______ the range. He ______ left early in the morning and rode until he saw the lovely on his ______. Larry then ______ his horse, Lady, to wait while he ______ into the lake and did several ______. Luckily, the weather is ______ rainy in ______. So Larry could ride and swim every morning. ______ Larry!

2. F / P 발음

1. F 발음

윗니로 아래 입술을 지긋이 눌러주며 소리를 낸다. [f] 소리는 성대가 울리지 않는 무성음으로 발음을 할 때 바람이 빠져 나가는 소리가 들린다. [v] 소리를 낼 때와 입 모양은 비슷하지만, 차이점은 [v] 발음은 소리를 낼 때 성대가 울리는 유성음이라는 것이다. 우리말의 'ㅍ' 소리와 혼동하기 쉬운 발음이지만, 우리말의 'ㅍ'에 대응하는 발음은 [p]이다. 둘의 차이점을 구분하여 많이 발음을 해보아야 차이점을 명확하게 알 수 있다.

face [feis]	fan [fæn]	fine [fain]
freedom [frí:dəm]	fat [fat]	furnish [fə́:rniʃ]
fulfill [fulfíl]	favorite [féivərit]	France [fræns]
life [laif]	afar [əfá:r]	TOEFL [tóufəl]
safety [séifti]	defeat [difít]	cafeteria [kæ̀fitíəriə]
phantom [fǽntəm]	philosophy [filásəfi]	telephone [téləfòun]
photograph [fóutəgrǽf]	phosphor [fásfər]	

2. P 발음

윗입술과 아랫입술이 붙어 있다가 입술이 벌어지며 소리를 낸다. [f] 발음과 마찬가지로 성대가 울리지 않고 바람이 빠져 나가며 나는 무성음이다. [b] 소리와 입이 벌어지는 원리는 같지만, 차이점은 [b] 발음은 소리를 낼 때 성대가 울리는 유성음이라는 것이다. 우리말의 'ㅍ'에 해당하는 발음이라고 생각하면 된다.

pet [pet]	pea [pi:]	pig [pig]
pie [pai]	peach [pi:tʃ]	punish [pʌ́niʃ]
punch [pʌntʃ]	pupil [pjú:pəl]	pardon [pá:rdn]
Pulitzer [pjú:litsər]	apart [əpá:rt]	couple [kʌ́pəl]
happy [hǽpi]	Japan [dʒəpǽn]	department [dipá:rtmənt]
cap [kæp]	gap [gæp]	hop [hɑp]
map [mæp]	pop [pɑp]	

01 Listen to the following tongue twisters and repeat after them.

1. Jeffery plans to pick up a leaf for his faithful wife.

2. The professor professed that professional proficiency would be preferred.

3. Peter Piper picked a peck of pickled peppers.

4. They failed to fulfill their promises to perform a perfect play without faults.

5. Phoebe laughed at an awful photograph of her nephew's falling off a fence.

02 Put a check mark beside the words that are spoken.

1. fine ______	pine ______
2. feel ______	peel ______
3. often ______	open ______
4. fork ______	pork ______
5. defend ______	depend ______
6. suffer ______	supper ______
7. few ______	pew ______
8. chief ______	cheap ______
9. cuffs ______	cups ______
10. fry ______	pry ______
11. coffee ______	copy ______
12. ferry ______	Perry ______
13. fast ______	past ______
14. fare ______	pare ______
15. fair ______	pair ______

03 Listen to the following sentences and circle the right word between the two that are underlined.

1. Perry had a _file / pile_ of papers on his purple desk.

2. The bus _fare / pare_ has been raised again.

3. Frank told his father that he didn't want him to _fry / pry_.

4. The children went to the washroom to wash their hands before going to _suffer / supper_.

5. Pam was upset because the _coffee / copy_ machine was out of order again.

04 Listen to the following paragraph and fill in the blank.

> Last Friday, Fiona _________ like going to a poppy ______ for a change of ______. The wind felt wonderful on her ______, and birds ______ by, fluffing their _________. She felt like she was _________ out on a blanket of soft clouds, but she was soon _________ by hailstones and her _________ ended.

3. B / V 발음

1. B 발음

[b] 소리는 윗입술과 아랫입술이 붙어있다 떨어질 때 성대를 함께 울려서 내는 유성음이다. 발음을 하면서 목에 손가락을 갖다 대면 진동이 울리는 것을 느낄 수 있다. 우리말의 'ㅂ' 소리를 낼 때와 비슷하다.

bee [biː]	big [biɡ]	bye [bai]
beach [biːtʃ]	bunch [bʌntʃ]	battle [bǽtl]
basalt [bəsɔ́ːlt]	ballad [bǽləd]	buoyant [bɔ́iənt]
bomb [bɑm]	robbery [rɑ́bəri]	problem [prɑ́bləm]
symbol [símbəl]	tube [tjuːb]	breakthrough [bréikθrùː]
reimburse [rìːimbə́ːrs]	rugby [rʌ́ɡbi]	web [web]
job [dʒɑb]	subscribe [səbskráib]	

2. V 발음

[b] 소리와 마찬가지로 성대가 울리면서 소리가 나는 유성음이지만, 발음 원리는 다르다. [f] 소리를 낼 때처럼 윗니로 아랫입술을 살짝 눌러주는데, 성대가 울릴 때 살짝 눌린 아랫입술이 간지러울 정도로 함께 진동이 울린다. [b]와 [v]는 같은 유성음이지만 서로 다른 입 모양을 통해 소리가 달라지므로, 이 미묘한 소리의 차이를 인지하고 연습을 많이 해보아야 발음이 좋아지고 청취력도 향상된다.

value [vǽljuː]	vaccine [vǽksi(ː)n]	valid [vǽlid]
vain [vein]	vine [vain]	vault [vɔːlt]
vista [vístə]	vessel [vésəl]	save [seiv]
invention [invénʃən]	avoidance [əvɔ́idəns]	starvation [stɑːrvéiʃən]
previous [príːviəs]	live [liv]	revolution [rèvəlúːʃən]
heavy [hévi]	preserve [prizə́ːrv]	obsessive [əbsésiv]
prove [pruːv]	revolve [rivɑ́lv]	

>> ACTIVITIES

01 Listen to the following tongue twisters and repeat after them.

1. Those bins are for Bill Beal's beans.

2. Black block background, brown block background.

3. The batter with the butter is the batter that is better.

4. Rugby's brother bought and brought her back some rubber baby-buggy bumpers.

5. The big black bug bit the big black bear, but the big black bear bit the big black bug back.

02 Put a check mark beside the words that are spoken.

1. biking _____		Viking _____	
2. ban _____		van _____	
3. banish _____		vanish _____	
4. bet _____		vet _____	
5. bent _____		vent _____	
6. bow _____		vow _____	
7. bail _____		vail _____	
8. best _____		vest _____	
9. base _____		vase _____	
10. balance _____		valance _____	
11. ballet _____		valet _____	
12. Bali _____		volley _____	
13. buy _____		vie _____	
14. boys _____		voice _____	
15. bury _____		very _____	

03 Listen to the following sentences and circle the right word between the two that are underlined.

1. Sally put the flower in a _base / vase_ that her boyfriend brought for her.

2. It is difficult to keep the family and work in _balance / valance_.

3. Dinosaurs _banished / vanished_ from the geological record about 65 million years ago.

4. I _bet / vet_ she hasn't finished her final project yet.

5. Ally invited all of her classmates to her _ballet / valet_.

04 Listen to the following paragraph and fill in the blank.

Ugly Betty is my __________ television show __________ on ABC. Betty works at a __________ company as an assistant to her boss Daniel. Everyone __________ Betty is not __________ and can never __________ in the fashion industry. However, Betty is the only one __________ and __________ in the building.

4. TH 발음 💿

1. [θ] 발음

[θ]와 [ð] 소리를 낼 때 혀의 위치는 거의 비슷하나, 유성음이냐 무성음이냐에 따라 차이가 난다. 무성음인 [θ] 소리를 낼 때는 혀를 윗니와 아랫니 사이에 끼워 넣고 혀 끝이 입 밖으로 나오게 한다. 혀를 윗니와 아랫니 사이에 갖다 댈 때부터 바람 소리가 나가며, 소리를 내면서 내밀었던 혀를 다시 입 안으로 당겨 넣는다. [s] 발음과의 차이는 [s]를 발음할 때는 혀가 입 속에 있다는 것이다.

three [θriː]	third [θəːrd]	thunder [θʌ́ndər]
thought [θɔːt]	theater [θí(ː)ətər]	thesis [θíːsis]
thermometer [θərmámitər]	theology [θiːálədʒi]	Thanksgiving [θǽŋksgìviŋ]
theft [θeft]	ether [íːθər]	philanthropy [filǽnθrəpi]
stethoscope [stéθəskòup]	pathetic [pəθétik]	South [sauθ]
North [nɔːrθ]	faith [feiθ]	youth [juːθ]
worth [wəːrθ]	health [helθ]	

2. [ð] 발음

[ð] 소리를 낼 때 역시 혀를 윗니와 아랫니 사이에 끼워 넣고 혀 끝이 입 밖으로 나오게 한다. [ð]는 유성음이라 성대가 울리면서 소리가 나온다. [ð] 소리 역시 발음을 하면서 내밀었던 혀를 다시 빠르게 입 속으로 당긴다. [d] 발음과의 차이는 [d]를 발음할 때는 혀가 입 속에 있다는 것이다.

than [ðæn]	this [ðis]	that [ðæt]
there [ðɛər]	whether [hwéðər]	thy [ðai]
either [íːðər]	clothing [klóuðiŋ]	although [ɔːlðóu]
mother [mʌ́ðər]	gather [gǽðər]	Southern [sʌ́ðərn]
Northern [nɔ́ːrðərn]	weather [wéðər]	soothe [suːð]
seethe [siːð]	sheathe [ʃiːð]	loathe [louð]
teethe [tiːð]	worthy [wə́ːrði]	

01 Listen to the following tongue twisters and repeat after them.

1. Rather than loathing their mothers, soothe their fathers.

2. Bathing in the bays is soothing to those teething brothers.

3. Ether either makes Thor writhe or seethe.

4. Nothing is worth thousands of deaths.

5. Thursdays are thirsty days for lethargic Ruth and Thelma.

02 Put a check mark beside the words that are spoken.

1. thing _____	sing _____
2. thin _____	sin _____
3. father _____	fodder _____
4. there _____	dare _____
5. those _____	doze _____
6. breath _____	breathe _____
7. breathing _____	breeding _____
8. bath _____	bathe _____
9. thick _____	sick _____
10. thaw _____	saw _____
11. moth _____	moss _____
12. think _____	sink _____
13. path _____	pass _____
14. myth _____	miss _____
15. thigh _____	sigh _____

03 Listen to the following sentences and circle the right word between the two that are underlined.

1. The weeds in the garden were _breathing / breeding_ like rabbits.

2. Roy G. Mathers is often _soothed / sued_ by his clients.

3. I _thought / sought_ you'd come to my birthday party.

4. Professor Smith did not believe Thomas' essay to be _worthy / wordy_.

5. _Moth / Moss_ is considered a harmful pest in many areas in the world.

04 Listen to the following paragraph and fill in the blank.

> Three _________ were sleeping under a tree when _________ woke to the sound of _________. One of the thugs said that he _________ the weather was changing and it would soon rain. The other two were _________ and didn't want to move. Rather than wait for his companions, the first thief left the other two _________. He decided it was not _________ getting wet in the _________. And off he went.

5. [æ]와 [e]발음

1. [æ] 발음

[æ]와 [e] 발음은 소리로만 들으면 거의 비슷하게 들려 구분이 힘들기 때문에, 입으로 직접 소리 내어 많이 발음해보아야 차이점을 알 수 있다. [æ] 소리를 낼 때는 입을 옆으로 늘리듯이 벌리고 턱을 아래로 내리면서 발음한다. 혀가 턱을 아래로 밀어내는 것처럼 입 모양을 만들며 소리를 내본다. 우리말의 '애'와 비슷하다.

apple [ǽpl]	adverb [ǽdvə:rb]	answer [ǽnsər]
hat [hæt]	aunt [ænt]	hamburger [hǽmbə̀:rgər]
task [tæsk]	basket [bǽskit]	ladder [lǽdər]
sandwich [sǽndwitʃ]	Paris [pǽris]	Manhattan [mænhǽtn]
language [lǽŋgwidʒ]	cancel [kǽnsəl]	plan [plæn]
contact [kántækt]	contrast [kántræst]	imagination [imæ̀dʒənéiʃən]
outstanding [àutstǽndiŋ]	Pandora [pændɔ́:rə]	

2. [e] 발음

[e] 소리를 낼 때는 [æ] 소리를 낼 때보다 턱이 상대적으로 덜 내려간다. 아래의 단어들을 듣고 따라 해보며 [æ] 발음과의 차이를 알아보자.

desk [desk]	end [end]	edge [edʒ]
essay [ései]	episode [épəsòud]	step [step]
sense [sens]	gem [dʒem]	next [nekst]
pencil [pénsəl]	test [test]	memory [méməri]
evidence [évidəns]	technology [teknálədʒi]	credit [krédit]
bread [bred]	development [divéləpmənt]	resolution [rèzəlú:ʃən]
profession [prəféʃən]	question [kwéstʃən]	

01 Listen to the following tongue twisters and repeat after them.

1. Matt never had less capital than several checks ago.

2. Rather than settling Al and Ellie's debts, Fran just laughed and left.

3. Dennis and Kent can't dance because they're dense dancers.

4. Dan's den is a sad shed back of Beck's badly built bed and breakfast.

5. Clem's clams went up Betty's back and tampered with her temper.

02 Put a check mark beside the words that are spoken.

1. than _____	then _____
2. bat _____	bet _____
3. mat _____	met _____
4. bland _____	blend _____
5. gas _____	guess _____
6. ladder _____	leather _____
7. pat _____	pet _____
8. pack _____	peck _____
9. past _____	pest _____
10. dad _____	dead _____
11. mad _____	med _____
12. pan _____	pen _____
13. mass _____	mess _____
14. last _____	lest _____
15. dan _____	den _____

03 Listen to the following sentences and circle the right word between the two that are underlined.

1. The girls *sat / set* their purses down on the table.

2. Rachel bought a *pat / pet* from the store for her grandmother.

3. When Max saw the woman, he *laughed / left*.

4. I was *sanding / sending* an email when my dad arrived.

5. Many farmers have used agrochemicals to control *past / pest* populations.

04 Listen to the following paragraph and fill in the blank.

Pat was so _________ that she made a _________ with Lenny the _________. She bet him that she could get a fat _________ and a wet _________ under her hat. Unfortunately, the fat cat was not Fat Pat's _________, and it sat on the rat. The rat naturally ran away. Poor Fat Pat. She lost her _________.

리듬
Rhythm

Chapter 2

1. Contraction 단축

영어에서는 두 단어를 합친 다음 줄여서 발음하기도 하는데, 구어체 뿐만 아니라 문어체에서도 표준 영어로 표기되기도 한다. 다음 표에 정리되어 있는 단축형들을 듣고 따라 읽어보자.

주어 + be동사	I am → I'm She is → She's He is → He's It is → It's That is → That's	You are → You're We are → We're They are → They're
주어 + 조동사	I will → I'll You will → You'll She will → She'll He will → He'll We will → We'll It will → It'll That will → That'll They will → They'll	I would/ I had → I'd You would/ You had → You'd She would/ She had → She'd He would/ He had → He'd We would/ We had → We'd It would/ It had → It'd They would/ They had → They'd
	I have → I've You have → You've She has → She's He has → He's We have → We've It has → It's That has → That's They have → They've	I would have → I would've I should have → I should've I could have → I could've I might have → I might've
부정형	Is not → Isn't Was not → Wasn't Are not → Aren't Were not → Weren't Do not → Don't Does not → Doesn't Did not → Didn't	Has not → Hasn't Have not → Haven't Will not → Won't Would not → Wouldn't Cannot → Can't Could not → Couldn't Must not → Mustn't Should not → Shouldn't

01 Listen to the following sentences and fill in the blank.

1. _______ it on sale?

2. I _______ seen you in ages.

3. I _______ find my jacket in the closet.

4. _______ better get going now.

5. _______ you there at the party last night?

6. _______ had it with her.

7. _______ it be necessary to bring an umbrella?

02 Listen to the following sentences and fill in the blank.

1. I'll _______ _______ _______ _______ back to the garage.

2. _______ _______ like the spaghetti?

3. _______ _______ _______ charge that to my credit card.

4. I _______ _______ the competition.

5. That's _______ _______ _______ price range.

6. We'll give you a full refund _______ _______ _______ _______ receipt.

7. I _______ _______ _______ here all day.

2. Liaison 연음

원어민들이 영어로 대화하는 것을 들어보면 단어 하나하나가 명확하게 들리지 않는 경우가 많다. 분명 눈으로 보면 아는 단어인데도 말하는 것을 들어보면 무슨 말인지 모를 때가 있는데, 이는 연음 현상의 이해를 통해 해결할 수 있다. 연음 현상은 가까이 있는 단어들이 서로 연결되어 발음되는 것을 가리킨다. 주로 자음으로 끝나는 단어와 모음으로 시작하는 단어가 이어서 발음될 때 연음 현상이 일어난다. 예를 들어 think about it을 들어보면 [씽크 어바웃 잇]이라고 들리지 않고 [씽커바우릿]이라고 들리는 것을 알 수 있다. think의 마지막 자음 k와 about의 첫 모음 a가 연결되어 [커]라고 발음되는 것이다. 다양한 예를 통해 연음 현상을 이해해보고 따라 읽어보자.

a lot of	Go for it!
as easy as pie	Hold on.
get up	I like it.
give up	I made it!
keep up with	Keep at it!
kind of	Not at all.
put it back in	Send her in.
put it aside	What is it?
take off	Cut it out!
wrap it up	Don't let it out.
Get out of here.	

01 Listen to the following sentences and write down the preposition in the blank.

1. The light is _______ .

2. Look _______ you!

3. I'll pick it _______ at a flower shop.

4. I'll catch _______ with you later!

5. Seth ignored my request to send _______ his report.

6. Serena was called _______ to make a speech.

7. You need to know how to put _______ a fire.

02 Listen to the following sentences and fill in the blank.

1. _______ _______ _______ sons is a lawyer.

2. The pen is _______ _______ _______ _______ you.

3. What _______ _______ salad would you like with your soup?

4. She made _______ _______ _______ money last year.

5. I _______ _______ _______ her.

6. You can _______ _______ about our project.

7. I can't _______ _______ _______ him anymore.

3. Word Stress 단어 강세

1음절 이상으로 이루어져 있는 모든 영어 단어에는 다른 음절보다 더 길고 더 음이 높고 크게 발음되는 음절이 적어도 하나는 있다. 이를 단어의 강세라고 하는데, 우리말과 영어의 가장 큰 차이점 중의 하나이기도 하다. Conversation 에는 두 번의 강세가 들어가는데, con-과 -sa-에 한 번씩 들어간다. 이 때, -sa-를 더 강하게 발음해주는데, 이는 -sa-가 주강세이고 con-이 보조강세이기 때문이다. 강세는 영어를 특징 짓는 일부분이고, 이런 단어의 강세를 잘 활용해 강세가 들어가는 부분을 잘 지켜 리듬을 타며 말하면 듣는 사람도 무슨 내용인지 이해하기가 훨씬 쉽다. 다음의 단어들에 강세가 어디에 들어가는지 잘 듣고 따라 읽어보자. 주강세가 들어있는 음절은 대문자로 표기되어 있다.

1. 명사(noun)

PHOtograph	phoTOgraphy	phoTOgrapher	photogRAphic
TEAcher	NEtherlands	Accent	PERfect
INteresting	aBOVE	inforMAtion	volunTEer
empLOyer	emploYEE	Immigrate	immigRAtion

2. 복합명사(compound noun)

앞에 오는 명사에 강세가 있음

NOTEbook	BOOKstore
SAVINGS account	APARTMENT complex
EXPIRATION date	COMMUNICATIONS satellite
SALES department	CUSTOMS duties

3. 동형이의어(homograph)

철자는 같으나 의미나 발음이 다른 단어로, 강세가 어디에 있느냐에 따라 모음의 소리가 바뀜

동사	명사
reCORD	REcord
proCEED	PROceed(s)
proGRESS	PROgress

01 Listen to the following words and draw a line under the stressed syllables.

1. keyboard
2. permit

3. blackboard
4. take out

5. water tank
6. permit

7. tax return
8. present

9. application form
10. sports car

11. sales promotion
12. present

13. reference
14. complicated

15. telecommunications industry

02 Listen to the following sentences and fill in the blank.

1. _______ language
2. _______ system

3. _________ desk
4. _________ form

5. greenhouse ______
6. heart ______

7. daughter in ______
8. ______ penalty

9. ______ margin
10. _________ card

11. food _________
12. generation ______

13. ______ tale
14. ______ food

15. mineral ______

4. Sentence Stress 문장 강세

Word Stress(단어 강세)가 한 단어 내에서 더 강하게 발음되는 음절을 가리킨다면, Sentence Stress(문장 강세)는 한 문장 내에서 다른 단어들보다 더 강하게 발음되는 단어들을 가리킨다. 이러한 문장 강세를 잘 살려 말을 하면 문장이 리듬을 타면서 자연스럽게 흘러간다. 하지만 아무 단어나 강조해서 읽는 것은 아니고, 특히 강조해서 읽어주어야 하는 단어들이 따로 있다. 바로 내용어(content word)이다. 내용어는 문장의 실질적인 의미를 전달해주는 단어들이다. 반면, 기능어(function word)는 문장 내의 문법적 관계를 보여주는 단어로, 관사나 전치사, 대명사, 접속사, 관계사 등이 이에 해당한다. 기능어는 실질적인 의미를 전달해주는 것이 아니기 때문에 짧게 약화되어 발음되는 경향이 강하다. 가령 Drink your coffee라는 문장에서는 drink, coffee가 내용어이고, your가 기능어에 해당한다. 기능어가 빠진 채 내용어만으로도 의미 전달이 가능함을 알 수 있다.

1. Charlotte is a famous architect in Seattle.

2. Kelly is playing the piano in the living room.

3. Meeting different kinds of people is part of our education.

4. Physical fitness is key to improving one's health.

5. The books that are in the library are new.

6. Tommy made an appointment with the doctor on Tuesday.

7. Murder is taboo in most societies around the world.

8. Smoking has been banned in all the bus stops.

9. I received a complimentary ticket to fly anywhere in Europe.

01 Listen to the following sentences and draw a line under the content words.

1. Freedom is a system based on courage.

2. The sad dog walks slowly to his house.

3. Body functioning can be affected by an imbalance of nutrients in the diet.

4. I'm taking a Spanish class for my business trip to Spain.

5. I have a craving for chocolate cake.

6. Poor school attendance is linked to low academic standing.

7. Youth clubs provide teenagers with opportunities for social interaction.

02 Listen to the following sentences and fill in the blank.

1. Many people don't listen to _________ and _________.

2. _________ and _________ end _________ between friends.

3. Shopping at a _________ _________ is _________ and _________.

4. Many of the _________ didn't _________ _________ yesterday.

5. _________ _________ I graduated, I got a job at a law firm.

6. A fierce _________ has been sparked over the issue of human _________ _________.

7. Korea has a rich artistic _________ that goes back _________ of years.

5. Pause 끊어 읽기

원어민들이 영어로 말하는 것을 듣다 보면 띄어 쓰기를 할 때처럼 문장 중간에 잠깐씩 쉬면서 (pause) 말하는 것을 발견할 수 있다. 말하는 도중에 숨이 차서 한 번씩 쉬고 다시 말하는 그런 것이 아닌, 영어의 일부를 차지하는 중요한 규칙이다. 영어를 배우는 사람들이 흔히 하는 실수 가운데 하나가 이러한 pause가 어느 부분에서 일어나는지를 잘 몰라 내용을 제대로 못 알아듣거나 말을 할 때 서투르고 단조롭게 들린다는 것이다. 어느 부분을 속도를 내어 연달아 말하고 어느 부분에서 잠깐 쉬어 말하는지 다음의 문장들을 듣고 살펴보자. Pause가 들어가는 부분은 사선(/)으로 표기되어 있다.

1. 구 (phrase)

1. After class, / they went to a restaurant / to have dinner.

2. Is there any place / to grab a bite / around here?

3. I enjoy reading the books / written by Jane Austen.

2. 절 (clause)

1. Speaking English is fun, / and it is also interesting.

2. Please let me know / if you need anything.

3. I can't believe / she did this to you.

4. I went to the party / 2 hours after Jennifer had left.

5. What Jerry told me / is none of your business.

6. Eric is the only one / I can trust.

01 Listen to the following sentences and draw a slash after a pause.

1. I'll go and check what's wrong.

2. I don't know whether it will rain or not.

3. I stayed up all night studying so that I could get good results.

4. There are neither books nor magazines in the library.

5. Heaven helps those who help themselves.

6. All of my classmates like Ms. Claire who is kind and generous.

7. Because of the heavy snow, many people couldn't get to the work.

02 Listen to the following sentences and fill in the blank.

1. I'll tell you ＿＿＿ ＿＿＿ ＿＿＿ your mother.

2. ＿＿＿ ＿＿＿ ＿＿＿ ＿＿＿, I would not believe what he says.

3. Mikaela needed a friend ＿＿＿ ＿＿＿ she could talk.

4. Do you know ＿＿＿ ＿＿＿ I love you?

5. ＿＿＿ ＿＿＿ ＿＿＿ is not something you can learn at school.

6. ＿＿＿ ＿＿＿ ＿＿＿ ＿＿＿ ＿＿＿ that is prepared when hiring a lawyer.

7. Professor Kim wants to know ＿＿＿ ＿＿＿ ＿＿＿ ＿＿＿ last week.

주제
Main Idea

Chapter 3

Overview
Preview
Office Hours
Service Encounters
Lectures
Practice
Review

Overview

- Main Idea(주제) 문제는 대화와 강의에서 들려주는 내용의 주제가 무엇인지를 고르는 유형이다. 화자들이 무엇에 관해 이야기하고 있는지를 파악하는 것은 지문에 대한 청취자의 이해도를 측정하는 가장 기본적인 문제이기 때문에, 각 지문의 첫 번째 문제로 항상 출제된다.

- 지문의 주제는 대개 대화와 강의의 전반부에 제시되며, 화자들이 중점적으로 언급하는 키워드와 큰 관련이 있다. 따라서 이 부분을 집중해서 듣고, 키워드가 무엇인지 빠르게 알아채는 것이 중요하다. 주의해야 할 점은 강의 지문의 경우 교수가 강의를 시작할 때 지난 시간의 수업 내용을 간략히 언급하는 경우가 자주 있는데, 이때 언급되는 지난 시간의 강의 주제와 이번 시간에 배울 강의 주제를 혼동해서는 안 된다는 것이다.

- 앞부분을 들으면서 무슨 내용인지 감이 안 잡히더라도 뒤의 내용을 차분히 집중해서 따라가며 들으면 글의 전체 주제를 찾을 수 있다는 것을 명심하고 당황하지 않도록 한다.

Sample Questions

- What are the speakers mainly talking about?
- Why does the man talk to the woman?
- Why does the man go to see his professor?
- What is the man's problem?
- What problem does the woman have?
- What is the professor mainly discussing?
- What are the speakers mainly discussing?
- What is the main topic of the lecture?
- What is the lecture mainly about?

Preview

 Listen to part of a conversation between a student and a professor.

What is the woman's problem?

Ⓐ She works on weekends as a mover with her friends.
Ⓑ She might get low grades on her midterm.
Ⓒ She can't attend the study session for the physics midterm.
Ⓓ She is going to her hometown to see her father.

 Listen to part of a conversation between a student and a professor.

M: You wanted to see me?

W: Professor Xavier, I can't make it to your physics review session on Saturday.
학생이 교수를 찾아온 이유: 토요일에 물리학 복습 시간에 참석할 수 없음
Can we talk about some other way to get the information?
대안을 찾고 싶어함

M: You really ought to go. You need to get a good grade on your midterm.

W: I know, but there's a problem. I have to move that day. We've had it scheduled for two months, we've rented a truck, and we've asked our friends to help.

M: I see.

W: So, can I meet with you later, one-on-one?
학생의 제안: 일대일 만남

M: I guess that won't work. The test is on Monday, and I'm going out of town Sunday.
학생의 제안 거절

W: There must be something I can do!

M: Have you considered hiring movers? They aren't expensive, and then you'd be
교수의 제안: 이삿짐 센터 이용
able to come.

W: Well, I'll ask my father about that. I know he's worried about my grades. Maybe he'll lend me the money. Thanks!

남: 나를 보자고 했다고?

여: Xavier 교수님, 저 토요일에 물리학 복습 시간에 참석할 수 없을 것 같아요. 수업 내용에 대한 정보를 얻을 다른 방법이 없을까요?

남: 꼭 참석해야 한단다. 중간고사에서 좋은 성적을 받아야하잖니.

여: 네, 알아요. 하지만 문제가 있어요. 그 날 이사를 해야 하거든요. 2개월 전부터 일정을 잡아 놓았고, 트럭도 빌렸고, 친구들한테 도와달라고 부탁도 했어요.

남: 그렇구나.

여: 그럼, 나중에 교수님과 개별적으로 만날 수 있을까요?

남: 음, 그건 안 될 것 같구나. 시험이 월요일이고, 난 일요일에 여기 없거든.

여: 뭔가 방법이 있어야 해요!

남: 이삿짐 센터를 이용하는 건 생각해보았니? 별로 비싸지도 않고, 이삿짐 센터를 이용하면 수업에 올 수 있을 거야.

여: 음, 아버지께 여쭤보아야겠어요. 아버지도 제 성적에 대해 걱정하시거든요. 이삿짐 센터 비용을 빌려주실지도 몰라요. 감사합니다!

어휘 | physics 물리학 | session 수업 | midterm 중간 고사 | hire 고용하다 | mover 이삿짐 운송업자 |
expensive 값비싼

해설 | 여자의 첫 번째 말에 대화의 주제가 들어 있다.

M: You wanted to see me?

W: Professor Xavier, I can't make it to your physics review session on Saturday.

Can we talk about some other way to get the information?

》 토요일에 물리학 복습 시간에 갈 수 없어서 그에 대한 대안을 찾으려고 교수와 상담을 하는 내용이다. 여자의 첫
문장을 다른 말로 바꾸어 표현한 것이 보기 (C)이다.

해석 | 여자가 가지고 있는 문제는 무엇인가?
(A) 주말마다 친구들과 함께 이삿짐 센터에서 일한다.
(B) 중간고사에서 낮은 성적을 받을지도 모른다.
(C) 물리학 중간 고사에 대비한 공부 모임에 참석할 수 없다.
(D) 아버지를 만나기 위해 고향에 갈 것이다.

Office Hours

01 

Why does the man go to see his professor?

(A) He is considering studying Japanese.
(B) He wants advice on his major.
(C) He is planning to study abroad.
(D) He hasn't decided which language to study.

> **Topic:**
>
> **Details:**

02

Why does the woman talk to the man?

(A) His grade is too low.
(B) He is always behind time for class.
(C) He's complaining about Dr. Catherine's class.
(D) He wants to transfer to another class.

> **Topic:**
>
> **Details:**

Service Encounters

01 

Why does the man talk to the woman?

(A) He missed orientation for new students.
(B) He wants to know how to get to the library.
(C) He arrived on campus late.
(D) He asks the woman to set up his computer.

> *Topic:*
>
> *Details:*

02

What problem does the woman have?

(A) She can't go to the library in other colleges by herself.
(B) She can't reserve the book she's looking for on Monday.
(C) She has not decided the topic of her paper yet.
(D) The book she needs is not available at the library.

> *Topic:*
>
> *Details:*

Lectures

01 

1. What is the professor mainly discussing?

(A) A person has many different roles in modern society.
(B) It is not easy to find a perfect solution to role conflict.
(C) A person's different roles create discord.
(D) Role conflict is related to high accident rates.

2. Which of the following is NOT an example of a social role?

(A) One's job
(B) One's place of residence
(C) One's gender
(D) One's family relations

<table>
<tr><td>Topic:</td></tr>
<tr><td>Details:</td></tr>
</table>

02 🎧

1. What is the main topic of the lecture?

(A) Widespread lake terrains in the Northern part
(B) How thermokarst got its name
(C) The cause of the formation of thaw lakes
(D) The current trend in permafrost's melting down

2. Which of the following is NOT true of thaw lakes?

(A) They are found in the Himalayas and the Swiss Alps.
(B) They are normally not deep.
(C) Rise in global temperature is responsible for their creation.
(D) They tend to contain much salt.

Topic:

Details:

Practice

01 Why does the student go see the registrar?

    Ⓐ He has a financial difficulty paying his tuition.
    Ⓑ He wants to transfer to this university.
    Ⓒ He wants to withdraw from his classes.
    Ⓓ He has not received the documents from his old university.

02 What can be inferred about the student's old university?

    Ⓐ It is far away from his house.
    Ⓑ It is not very efficient because of its size.
    Ⓒ It is quite expensive.
    Ⓓ It has many different courses.

03 Why is the student not able to take upper classes?

(A) His professor wants to check if he took basic courses before.
(B) He finds those classes very difficult to study.
(C) The term for registering for those classes ran out.
(D) Those classes start too early in the morning.

04 In the conversation, the woman suggests several ideas that would help the student solve his problems. Indicate in the table below whether each of the following is one of the ideas suggested by the woman. Click in the correct box for each phrase.

	Suggested	Not Suggested
(A) Make a call to the registrar at the old university		
(B) E-mail the registrar at the old university		
(C) Allow the student to take advanced courses		
(D) Request a fax of the student's records at the old university		
(E) Permit the student to attend classes without paying tuition		

Listen again to part of the lecture. Then answer the question.

05 What does the woman imply when she says this:

(A) The man must handle the problem on his own.
(B) The problem is so irritating.
(C) It is difficult, but the problem can be solved.
(D) The man should talk to other students.

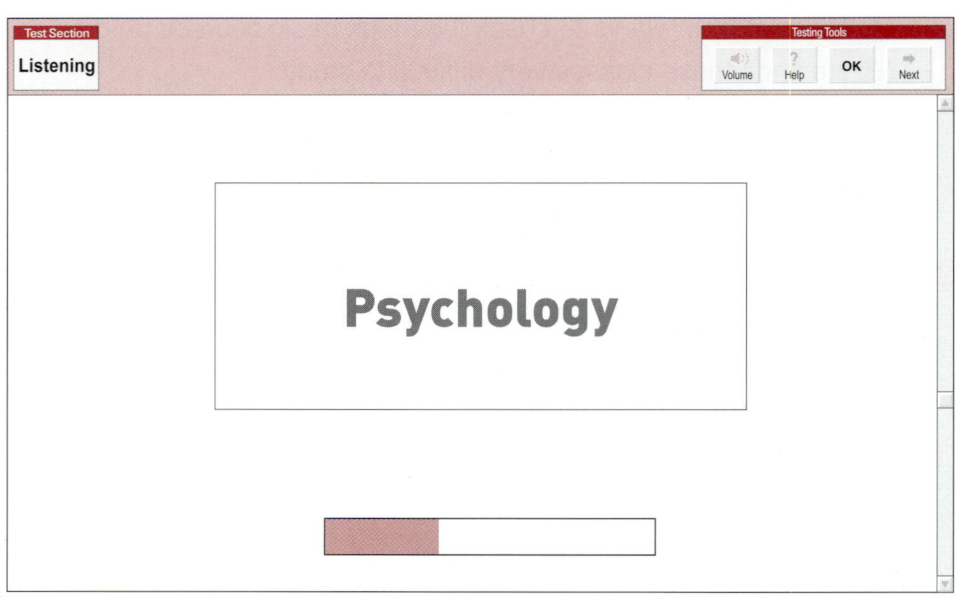

Test Section
Listening
Testing Tools
Volume
Help
OK
Next
Psychology

Test Section
Listening
Testing Tools
Volume
Help
OK
Next

06 What is the lecture mainly about?

Ⓐ How to arouse pleasant emotions
Ⓑ The act of appreciating one's help
Ⓒ Positive rewards
Ⓓ Negative reinforcement

Listen again to part of the lecture. Then answer the question.

07 What does the professor mean when he says this:

Ⓐ He will bring it up again by the end of the class.
Ⓑ He thinks it's not worth discussing at all.
Ⓒ He is not going to talk about it.
Ⓓ He will mention it next time.

Listen again to part of the conversation. Then answer the question.

08 What does the professor mean when he says this:

Ⓐ People want to get praised from their family.
Ⓑ All societies have ways of expressing gratitude.
Ⓒ People like to give hand to others.
Ⓓ Simple rewards may be very effective.

09 In the lecture, the professor discusses positive rewards. Indicate in the table below whether each of the following can be one of those rewards. Click in the correct box for each phrase.

	Yes	No
Ⓐ Well done!		
Ⓑ I appreciate that.		
Ⓒ So what?		
Ⓓ It's very kind of you.		
Ⓔ Mind your own business.		

10 Which of the following are NOT examples of primary rewards?

Ⓐ Water
Ⓑ Residence
Ⓒ Meals
Ⓓ Smile

Listen again to part of the conversation. Then answer the question.

11 What does the professor imply when he says this:

Ⓐ Money may be the most powerful secondary reward.
Ⓑ Money should be used more delicately.
Ⓒ Money has little value because it is only good for primary rewards.
Ⓓ Money exists in all societies around the world.

Review

01 다음 문장들을 듣고, 밑줄에 들어갈 단어를 받아 써보자.

1. If you're _________ ____ business, then you _________ ____ consider Chinese.

2. Well, it _________ that you need to _________ change your work hours ____ take another class.

3. China has become an _________ _________ , and the language will give you a ____ _________ .

4. Well, you could also go to ____ ____ _________ libraries yourself, and borrow the book.

5. I _________ _________ the hospital in the afternoon, and I _________ _________ ____ School afterward.

02 다음 문장들을 듣고, pause가 들어가는 부분에 사선을 그어보자.

1. I'm not sure which language to take for my elective.

2. We need to talk about why you're always late for class.

3. If you arrive on time for Dr. Catheerine's class for the rest of the semester, you might get a better grade.

4. If you don't have your own computer, or it's not set up yet, why not stop by the computer lab in the library?

5. The online catalog says it's checked out.

Part II | Types of Questions

세부사항
Detail

Chapter 4

Overview
Preview
Office Hours
Service Encounters
Lectures
Practice
Review

Overview

- Detail(세부사항) 문제는 대화와 강의에서 화자들이 한 말들 중 세부 정보에 관한 질문에 맞는 답을 고르는 유형이다. 들려주는 내용을 청취자가 얼마나 정확하게 이해하고 있는지를 확인하는 문제다. Detail 문제는 대화에서는 1문항, 강의에서는 2문항 정도가 출제되고 있다.

- 대화에서는 주로 육하원칙, 즉 누가(who), 언제(when), 어디서(where), 무엇을(what), 어떻게(how), 왜(why) 하는지에 관한 문제가 출제된다. 특히 교수가 학생이 가진 문제 해결을 위해 제안하는 것이 무엇인지를 묻는 문제가 자주 출제되는 편이며, 답을 2개 고르는 문제도 가끔 출제된다. 강의에서는 강의 주제에 관한 설명 중 맞는 것과 맞지 않는 것을 고르는 포괄적인 문제와 강의 내용 중 세부적인 사항에 관해 묻는 지엽적인 문제가 함께 출제된다.

- Detail 문제는 지문에 직접적으로 언급되었던 내용을 묻는 문제이기 때문에 답은 이미 들려준 내용 속에 그대로 들어 있다. 하지만 보기 속의 정답은 지문에서 들었던 것과는 약간 다른 표현이 쓰이는 경우가 대부분이다. 이처럼 의미는 똑같이 유지하되 표현을 바꾸어 쓰는 것을 paraphrase(바꾸어 쓰기)라고 한다. 지문에서 들려준 단어나 표현이 그대로 등장한 보기는 오히려 오답일 가능성이 높다는 것을 염두에 두도록 하자.

Sample Questions

- What is ~?
- Why is ~?
- Where will ~?
- Who will ~?
- When will ~?
- How will ~?
- Which of the following is true of~?
- Which of the following is NOT true of~?
- What does the professor suggest the student do? Click on 2 answers.
- What are two reasons for ~? Click on 2 answers.

Preview

 Listen to part of a conversation between a student and a lab manager.

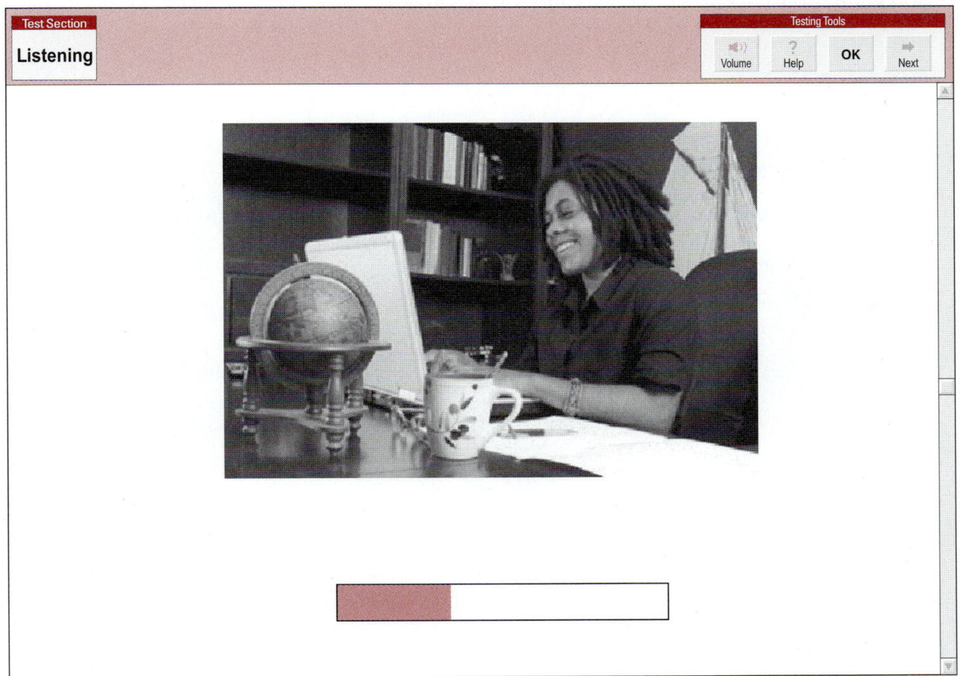

How will the lab manager help the student use the lab?

Ⓐ By e-mailing someone from the registrar's office
Ⓑ By asking his friend from the same class
Ⓒ By lending him the key temporarily
Ⓓ By making a call to the chemistry department

 Listen to part of a conversation between a student and a lab manager.

M: Hi, I need to use the chemistry lab, but it's locked. May I borrow the key?
화학 실험실 사용을 원함　　　잠겨 있음　　주제: 키를 빌리고 싶어함

W: Which class are you taking?

M: Introduction to organic chemistry.

W: All right, and what's your name?

M: My name is Darren Robert.

W: Wait a minute... Hmm, I don't see your name on the roster. Are you a student
명부에 학생의 이름이 없음
at this university?

M: Yes. I was on the waiting list for the class, and a space opened up.
대기자 명단에 올라 있었음　　　　자리가 남
It'll take another day or so to update everything in the computer system.
컴퓨터 시스템에 정보를 업데이트 하는데 며칠 걸림

W: Yes, it is slow sometimes. Would you show me your student ID card?

M: Here it is.

W: Well, we still need something to prove you're in the class.
직원의 요구 사항: 학생이 수업을 듣는다는 걸 증명해 주기를 원함

M: I have an idea. Why not call the chemistry department teaching assistant?
학생의 제안: 화학과 조교에게 전화하기
There's got to be someone that can prove I'm in the class.

W: All right. We still have a little time before everyone leaves for the day.

M: Thanks for taking the time to help me out!

남: 안녕하세요, 화학 실험실을 사용하고 싶은데요, 문이 잠겨있어요. 열쇠를 빌릴 수 있을까요?

여: 어떤 수업을 듣고 있죠?

남: 유기 화학 개론 강의요.

여: 알겠어요, 음 학생 이름은 뭐죠?

남: Darren Robert요.

여: 잠깐만 기다려보세요...음, 명단에 학생 이름이 안 보이는데요. 이 학교 학생 맞아요?

남: 네. 제가 그 수업 대기자 명단에 올라있었는데, 자리가 났거든요. 컴퓨터 시스템에 정보가 업데이트 되려
면 하루 이틀 걸릴 거예요.

여: 네. 가끔 좀 시간이 걸리죠. 그럼 학생증 좀 보여주겠어요?

남: 여기 있습니다.

여: 학생이 그 수업을 듣는다는 것을 증명할만한 무언가가 여전히 필요해요.

남: 이러면 어떨까요. 화학과 조교에게 전화를 해보시죠? 제가 그 강의를 수강하고 있다는 것을 증명할만한
사람이 있을 겁니다.

여: 좋아요. 모두 퇴근하기 전에 아직 시간이 좀 남았네요.

남: 도와주시느라 시간 내주셔서 감사합니다!

어휘 | chemistry 화학 | introduction to ~ 개론 | organic 유기의 | roster 명부 | prove 증명하다 |
waiting list 대기자 명단 | teaching assistant 조교 |

해설 | 스크립트는 화학 실험실을 사용하기를 원하는 학생과 실험실 관리자의 대화로 이루어져 있다. 학생이 바
로 실험실을 사용할 수 없는 이유는 수강 등록을 나중에 해서 명부에 학생의 이름이 없기 때문이다. 관리
자는 학생의 수강 여부를 증명할 수 있는 자료를 원하고 학생은 화학과 조교에게 전화를 해보라고 한다.
대화의 마지막 부분에 문제 해결의 단서가 있다.

W: Well, we still need <u>something to prove you're in the class.</u>

M: I have an idea: <u>why not call the chemistry department teaching assistant?</u>
There's got to be someone that can prove I'm in the class.

>> 화학과 조교에게 전화를 해보라는 학생의 제안에 관리자도 동의하고 있다. 화학과에 전화를 하라는 보기 (D)가
정답이다.

해석 | 실험실 관리자는 학생이 실험실을 사용하는 것을 어떻게 도울 것인가?
(A) 학적과 직원에게 이메일을 보냄으로써
(B) 같은 강의를 듣는 학생의 친구에게 물어봄으로써
(C) 임시로 학생에게 열쇠를 빌려줌으로써
(D) 화학과에 전화를 함으로써

Office Hours

01 

Why does the student want to change her presentation date?

(A) Because of her classmate's request
(B) Because of her mom's online business
(C) Because of her test
(D) Because of her family affair

<table>
<tr><td>Topic:</td></tr>
<tr><td>Details:</td></tr>
</table>

02

What does the professor suggest the student do?

(A) She should buy a dog of her own.
(B) She should carry out an experiment on a dog by herself.
(C) She should make brief mention of her dogs.
(D) She should choose a new topic.

<table>
<tr><td>Topic:</td></tr>
<tr><td>Details:</td></tr>
</table>

Service Encounters

01 

Why can't the student show her cousin around the campus?

(A) She has an art class.
(B) She has to work that day.
(C) She is going out of town.
(D) She is meeting someone for lunch.

> **Topic:**
>
> **Details:**

02

What does the woman suggest the man do?

(A) Commuting to and from his parents' house
(B) Moving out of his current house
(C) Renting a room near campus
(D) Sharing a room with a roommate

> **Topic:**
>
> **Details:**

Lectures

01 

1. Which of the following is true of rattlesnakes?

(A) They attack every hiker they see.
(B) They produce a poisonous substance.
(C) They prefer shady spots.
(D) Their rattle is related to the prey discovery.

2. Which of the following is NOT true of a rattlesnake's rattles?

(A) A new rattle is added when it sheds its skin.
(B) They form at the tip of its tail.
(C) The inside of the rattles is empty.
(D) They tend to stay in their place.

Topic:

Details:

02 🎧

Listen again to part of the lecture. Then answer the question.

1. What does the professor mean when he says this: 🎧

    (A) He thinks penicillin is beneficial to humans.
    (B) He thinks penicillin is not the greatest discovery in the 1900s.
    (C) He thinks penicillin is not different from any other drug.
    (D) He thinks penicillin is of no use in saving lives.

2. Which of the following is true of the discovery of penicillin?

    (A) Penicillin was useful for viral illnesses from the beginning.
    (B) Alexander Fleming deserves to be called the first discoverer.
    (C) Alexander Fleming was the first to extract the active substance.
    (D) A doctor from Costa Rica took over the research of Alexander
        Fleming.

Topic:

Details:

Practice

01 What are the speakers mainly talking about?

Ⓐ The professor is announcing his retirement.
Ⓑ The student is doing great in school.
Ⓒ The professor wants the student to join the search committee.
Ⓓ The department has hired new professors.

Listen again to part of the conversation. Then answer the question.

02 What does the professor mean when he says this:

Ⓐ He has forgotten what he wanted to say.
Ⓑ He is embarrassed because he has given too many compliments.
Ⓒ He is admitting the student was his first choice.
Ⓓ He hopes he has convinced the student by now.

03 Where does the student live?

    Ⓐ With her parents
    Ⓑ Out of town
    Ⓒ In the dormitory
    Ⓓ In an apartment around campus

04 What can be inferred about the student?

    Ⓐ She will not be graduating at the end of the semester.
    Ⓑ She is the representative of the students' association.
    Ⓒ Her parents live in another state.
    Ⓓ She will be traveling during the summer.

05 In the conversation, the professor mentions things the student will need to do in the search committee. Indicate in the table below whether each of the following is mentioned by the professor. Click in the correct box for each phrase.

	Mentioned	Not Mentioned
Ⓐ Interview each candidate one-on-one		
Ⓑ Be present at the committee's final meeting		
Ⓒ Accept the applications of the candidates		
Ⓓ Travel to different cities to observe candidates teaching		
Ⓔ Participate in interviews over the summer		

Questions 6~11] Listen to part of a lecture in an English class.

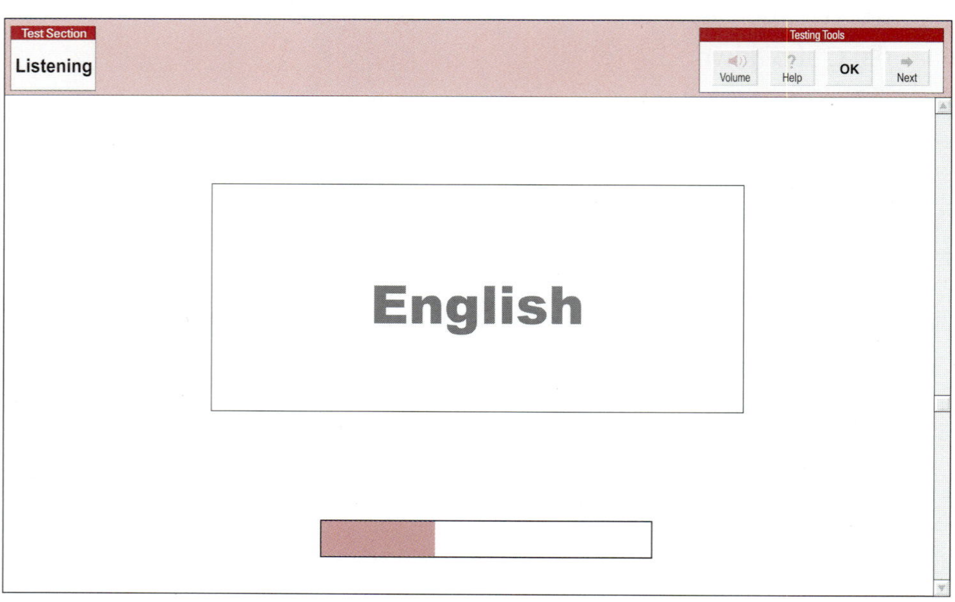
Test Section
Listening
Testing Tools
Volume
Help
OK
Next
English

Test Section
Listening
Testing Tools
Volume
Help
OK
Next

06 What is the lecture mainly about?

    Ⓐ A world famous diamond
    Ⓑ Wilkie Collins' life as a writer
    Ⓒ A comparison between Wilkie Collins and T. S. Eliot
    Ⓓ One of the first English detective novels

07 What can be inferred about Wilkie Collins?

    Ⓐ He had a poverty stricken life.
    Ⓑ He had a bad reputation for his books.
    Ⓒ He was acquainted with Charles Dickens.
    Ⓓ He experienced a life of a detective.

08 According to the professor, what is the Moonstone in Collins' novel
The Moonstone?

    Ⓐ A piece of rock from the moon
    Ⓑ A title of a literary magazine
    Ⓒ A diamond from India
    Ⓓ A nickname of the leading character

Listen again to part of the conversation. Then answer the question.

09 Why does the professor mention this:

    Ⓐ To arouse the students' interest
    Ⓑ To tell the students the end of the story
    Ⓒ To explain the framework of the mystery novel
    Ⓓ To give the students clues about the mystery

10 In the lecture, the professor discusses Wilkie Collins' detective novel. Indicate whether each of the following is mentioned as one of its characteristics. Click in the correct box for each phrase.

	Mentioned	Not Mentioned
Ⓐ Was published less than 200 years ago		
Ⓑ Appeared in a series		
Ⓒ Was translated into many other languages		
Ⓓ Included an amateur detective		
Ⓔ Targeted on readers of the upper classes		

Listen again to part of the conversation. Then answer the question.

11 Why does the professor mention this:

    Ⓐ To explain why the novel was immediate success
    Ⓑ To emphasize the novel's superiority
    Ⓒ To suggest there are other detective novels in other languages
    Ⓓ To contrast Wilkie Collins' writings to those of T. S. Eliot

Review

01 다음 문장들을 듣고, 밑줄에 들어갈 단어를 받아 써보자.

1. Well, my father is a _________ , and he has _____ a major award.

2. That might be a problem, because _____ _________ _________ the other students' schedules.

3. I have a part-time job, so I can't _________ _________ _________ .

4. Well, the semester is _________ to start, but the deadline for getting into the dorms has _________ , so I'm not _________ what to do.

5. Pavlov's famous _________ _________ the bell and the _________ dogs.

02 다음 문장들을 듣고, pause가 들어가는 부분에 사선을 그어보자.

1. I could do it earlier or later if another student will swap with me.

2. You don't want to repeat what others have already said.

3. I doubt that there won't be anybody who wants to reschedule his or her presentation.

4. He's meeting me for lunch at one, and I'll tell him how to get to campus.

5. In the meantime, I think you should try getting a room, at least for a short time.

Part II | Types of Questions

추론
Inference

Chapter
5

Inference

Overview

- Inference(추론) 문제는 대화와 강의에 드러난 직접적인 정보를 답으로 고르는 것이 아니라, 이를 근거로 새롭게 도출할 수 있는 정보를 답으로 고르는 유형이다. Inference 문제는 지문마다 1문항 정도가 출제된다. 들려주는 내용의 정확한 이해에서 한 단계 더 나아가 언급된 내용을 근거로 질문에서 묻고 있는 정보를 유추해 내는 능력을 측정한다.

- 5가지 문제 유형 중 어려운 유형으로 분류되기는 하나, 기본적인 사실 관계를 잘 파악하고 있으면 쉽게 풀 수 있다. 특히, 화자가 다음에 할 일을 묻는 문제는 대화의 마지막 부분만 정확하게 알아들어도 정답을 고를 수 있는 쉬운 문제에 속한다. 반면, 강의에서 어떤 개념을 설명하고 나서 그에 관한 예를 들려준 후, 그와 같은 방식으로 적용되는 예를 고르는 문제 등은 어려운 편에 속한다.

- Inference 문제를 풀 때 주의해야 할 점은 특정 부분만을 듣고 추론해야 하는 문제든, 여러 정황을 종합해서 결론을 내려야 하는 문제든 모두 들려주는 내용만을 근거로 하여 답을 선택해야 한다는 것이다. Detail 문제와 마찬가지로, 지문에서 언급되었던 표현이 그대로 등장하는 보기는 오답일 가능성이 높다는 것을 알아두자.

Sample Questions

- What can be inferred about ~?
- What does the man imply about ~?
- What will the woman probably do next?
- What can be concluded about ~?
- What would be a similar example of ~?
- Which of the following is probably true about ~?

Preview

🎧 Listen to part of a lecture in a contemporary music class.

What can be inferred about Regina Carter?

Ⓐ Paganini's *Il Cannone* passed into her full possession.
Ⓑ She developed her own style taking her instructor's advice.
Ⓒ She was taught to play jazz from the very beginning.
Ⓓ She and Ella Fitzgerald were acquainted with each other.

 Listen to part of a lecture in a contemporary music class.

P(W): I'd like to talk a little bit about Regina Carter in our discussion of great American
강의 주제

musicians. She is still a fairly young woman, born in Detroit in 1966. She started
생존해 있음

out as a classical violinist, but as she grew older, she became interested in jazz.
Carter의 관심 분야

Today, she is considered one of the best jazz violinists in the world.
사람들의 평가

In high school, a friend introduced her to the music of the jazz greats - like Ella
재즈를 접하게 된 계기

Fitzgerald, for example — and that clinched her interest. She went on to attend

the famous New England Conservatory of Music. One of her professors

encouraged her to listen to the play of other musical instruments like trumpet
다른 재즈 바이올리니스트와 차별화된 이유

and horn, rather than other jazz violinists' play. One of the highlights of her career

came in December 2001. She had the honor of playing a concert in Genoa, Italy,

on *Il Cannone*, the famous violin once owned by the violin great Paganini.
제노바에서 바이올린 대가인 Paganini의 바이올린인 *Il Cannone*를 연주하는 영광

It is a rare thing to be granted permission to use the instrument. Carter, however,
Il Cannone(캐논)를 연주한 것의 의의

not only performed with it in concert but used it to record an album titled
Paganini: After a Dream.

P: 미국의 위대한 음악가에 대한 토론 시간의 일부로 Regina Carter에 대해 잠깐 짚고 넘어가겠어요. 그녀는 1966년에 Detroit(디트로이트)에서 태어난 아직 꽤 젊은 여성이에요. 클래식 바이올린 연주자로 활동을 시작했지만, 성장하면서 재즈에 관심을 가지게 되었죠. 오늘날에는 세계 최고의 재즈 바이올리니스트로 불리고 있어요.
고등학생 때, 친구의 영향으로 Ella Fitzgerald(엘라 피츠제럴드)와 같은 재즈 대가들의 음악을 접하게 되었는데, 그 후로 계속 재즈에 관심을 갖게 되었어요. 그녀는 유명한 New England Conservatory of Music(뉴잉글랜드 음악 학교)에 입학했죠. 교수 중 한 명이 다른 재즈 바이올리니스트들의 연주를 듣는 대신, 트럼펫과 호른 같은 다른 악기 연주를 들어보라고 했어요. 음악가로서의 인생에서 가장 빛나던 순간이 2001년 겨울이었어요. 바로 바이올린의 대가인 Paganini가 한 때 소장했던 유명한 바이올린인 *Il Cannone*(캐논)를 들고 이탈리아의 Genoa(제노바)에서 콘서트를 하는 영광을 가지게 된 것이었죠. 그 악기로 연주할 수 있는 허가를 받는 경우는 아주 드물어요. 하지만 Carter는 콘서트에서 그 바이올린으로 연주를 했을 뿐만 아니라 '*Paganini: After a Dream*'이라는 타이틀이 붙은 앨범을 녹음하기도 했어요.

어휘 | clinch 꽉 붙들어매다 | instrument 악기 | grant 주다 | permission 허가

해설 | 스크립트는 미국의 유명한 재즈 바이올리니스트인 Regina Carter에 관한 강의이다. Regina Carter가 처음에는 클래식 바이올린을 배웠으나, 후에 재즈 바이올린 연주자가 되어 성공을 거두면서 제노바에서 Paganini의 바이올린인 *Il Cannone*를 연주하기까지의 이야기를 들려주고 있다. 질문지에서 Regina Carter에 관해 추론할 수 있는 것을 고르라고 하였는데,이는 강의 전체의 토픽이므로 지문 전체의 내용을 주의 깊게 들어야 제대로 풀 수 있는 문제이다. 그럼, 각 보기와 지문의 해당 부분을 비교하여 정답이 무엇인지 확인해보자.

보기(A)에서 Paganini의 바이올린이 등장하는 부분을 보면, Carter가 드물게도 Paganini가 소장했던 바이올린을 연주할 기회를 가졌다고 했다. 허가를 받은 것이기 때문에 Carter가 이 바이올린을 소유했다는 보기 (A)는 오답이다.
보기(B)에서 Carter의 교수와 관련된 이야기가 등장하는 스크립트의 7번째 문장을 보면, 교수가 Carter에게 다른 재즈 바이올리니스트들의 연주 대신, 다른 악기 연주를 들어보도록 조언한 이야기가 나온다. 따라서 Carter가 교수의 조언대로 다양한 악기 연주를 들으며 자신만의 스타일을 창조해냈을 거라 유추할 수 있다.
보기(C)에서 스크립트의 3번째 문장을 보면 Carter가 초기에는 클래식 바이올린을 배웠다는 내용이 나온다. 따라서 오답이다.
보기(D)에서 Ella Fitzgerald가 등장하는 부분을 보면, 그녀와 같은 재즈 대가의 음악을 접했다고 하였지, 개인적인 친분이 있었다고 유추할 만한 내용은 언급된 바가 없다. 따라서 오답이다.

해석 | Regina Carter에 관해 추론할 수 있는 것은 무엇인가?
(A) Paganini의 바이올린인 *Il Cannone*를 완전 소유하게 되었다.
(B) 교수의 조언을 받아 자신만의 스타일을 만들어냈다.
(C) 처음부터 재즈 연주를 배웠다.
(D) Ella Fitzgerald와 친분이 있었다.

Office Hours

01 

What can be inferred about the woman?

(A) She thought her essay was not long.
(B) She wants an extension on her essay.
(C) She won't add anything to her essay.
(D) She will also attend the conference.

> **Topic:**
>
> **Details:**

02

This research project is probably an assignment in which of the student's classes?

(A) English
(B) Linguistics
(C) Psychology
(D) Logic

> **Topic:**
>
> **Details:**

Service Encounters

01 

What can be inferred about the singing club?

(A) It is very confident that all three nights will be a success.
(B) It needs to pay a rental fee to the student center manager.
(C) It has not put the pamphlets into print yet.
(D) It has not planned this out very carefully.

> **Topic:**
>
> **Details:**

02

What can be inferred about the student?

(A) She will be absent from school temporarily.
(B) She will not be able to take the physics class this semester.
(C) She will delete all the spam messages.
(D) She will get a new e-mail account.

> **Topic:**
>
> **Details:**

Lectures

01 

1. Which of the following is NOT a factor that determines market segments?

(A) What kind of work you do
(B) Who you get along with
(C) How much you earn
(D) How old you are

2. A university student is probably going to be interested in which of the following advertisements?

(A) Retirement fund programs
(B) Household commodities
(C) Honeymoon vacation package tours
(D) Laptop computers

> **Topic:**
>
> **Details:**

1. What is the main topic of the lecture?

(A) Nathaniel Hawthorne's writings
(B) James Joyce's teaching career
(C) James Joyce's influence on French philosophers
(D) Novelist James Joyce

2. What can be inferred about James Joyce?

(A) He was a prolific writer.
(B) He lived overseas because of the religious issue.
(C) All of his novels were published in the same company.
(D) All of his stories are autobiographical.

Topic:

Details:

Practice

[Questions 1~5] Listen to part of a conversation at a bookstore.

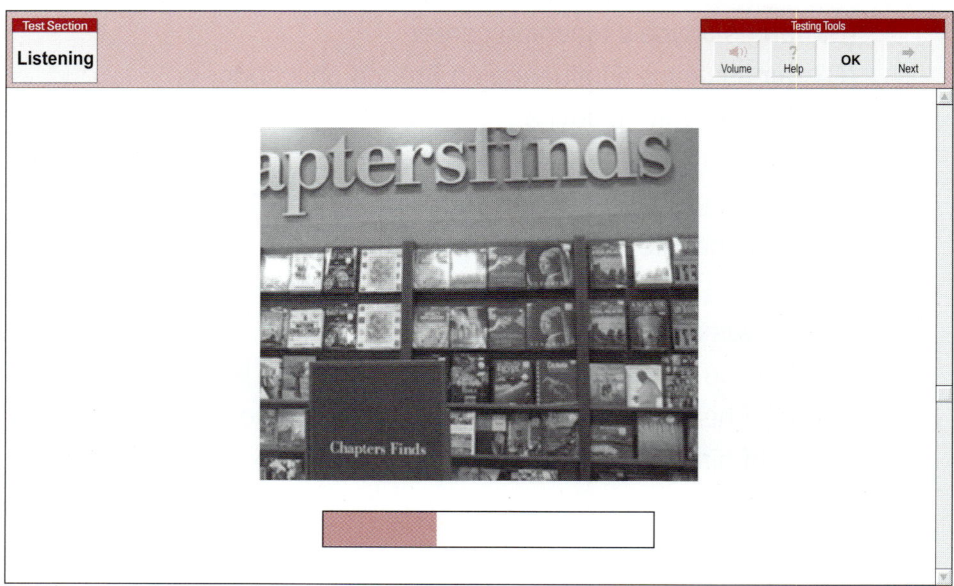

01 What is the nature of the student's problem?

Ⓐ He has not registered for the astronomy class.
Ⓑ He needs to order a new textbook right away.
Ⓒ The bookstore has sold out of a textbook he needs.
Ⓓ The professor didn't have an extra copy of the book for him.

02 The student is looking for a textbook for which course?

Ⓐ Biology
Ⓑ Astronomy
Ⓒ Geography
Ⓓ Astrology

03 What can be inferred about the textbook the student needs?

    Ⓐ It has gone through several editions.
    Ⓑ It is in pretty bad shape.
    Ⓒ It is out of stock because of the bookstore's mistake.
    Ⓓ It is available at the university library.

Listen again to part of the conversation. Then answer the question.

04 What does the woman imply when she says this: 🎧

    Ⓐ Most of the students at this university are very smart.
    Ⓑ Students should register for a course at an appointed time.
    Ⓒ The student should have bought the book a long time ago.
    Ⓓ Some students purchase the book before they are registered in
       the class.

05 In the conversation, the woman suggests possible solutions to the
student's problem. Indicate in the table below whether each of the
following is suggested by the woman. Click in the correct box for
each phrase.

	Suggested	Not Suggested
Ⓐ Trying an online used-textbook supplier		
Ⓑ Borrowing the book from another student		
Ⓒ Visiting the professor to see if he has an extra copy		
Ⓓ Placing an order for a copy of the newer edition		
Ⓔ Copying the textbook		

Test Section
Listening
Testing Tools
Volume
Help
OK
Next
Sociology

Test Section
Listening
Testing Tools
Volume
Help
OK
Next

06 What is the topic of the professor's lecture?

Ⓐ The immigration philosophy of the Canadian government
Ⓑ An overview of the melting pot metaphor in American society
Ⓒ Icons that are symbolic of American society
Ⓓ Early history of the United States

07 Where did the first American settlers mainly come from?

Ⓐ Africa
Ⓑ Latin America
Ⓒ Asia
Ⓓ Europe

08 What can be inferred about the intermarriage in America?

Ⓐ It was illegal before 1967.
Ⓑ It is uncommon these days.
Ⓒ It was only allowed to the white Europeans.
Ⓓ It eliminates one's historical identity.

09 What can be inferred from the current trend in interracial marriages?

Ⓐ New trends usually begin in urban areas.
Ⓑ People in rural areas are more likely to be open-minded about culture differences.
Ⓒ People in large cities tend to stick to their lifestyle.
Ⓓ People in smaller towns have the low marriage rate.

10 What does the professor mean when he says this:

Ⓐ A salad is best if it includes vegetables that go with others.
Ⓑ People of all cultures like to participate in public discussion.
Ⓒ Countries that receive many immigrants tend to have many troubles.
Ⓓ A successful multi-cultural society contains people who have preserved their own ethnic traditions.

11 In the lecture, the professor mentions contemporary metaphors that replace the melting pot. Indicate whether each of the following is mentioned as one of the metaphors. Click in the correct box for each phrase.

	Mentioned	Not Mentioned
Ⓐ Cocktail		
Ⓑ Salad bowl		
Ⓒ Necklace		
Ⓓ Symphony		
Ⓔ Cultural mosaic		

Review

01 다음 문장들을 듣고, 밑줄에 들어갈 단어를 받아 써보자.

1. I'm pretty _________ about how to _________ _________ this research project.

2. Yes, but it needs to be _________ ____ ____ _________ _________.

3. We have _________ _________ from the university but not _________ _________.

4. There's no _________ since you're an _________ club, and it's a medium-sized space.

5. Now we can print the _________ and ____ ____ advertisements.

02 다음 문장들을 듣고, pause가 들어가는 부분에 사선을 그어보자.

1. When you revise it, instead of spending so much time on unnecessary information, you ought to provide more support for the supporting points.

2. Madeleine, I know you need to get to your next class, so I'll keep this brief.

3. I love my daughter but I have to remind myself of this all the time!

4. The system automatically sends out e-mail when that happens.

5. Most of them are smart enough to wait until they're enrolled before buying the books.

Part II | Types of Questions

정보 연결

Connecting Information

Chapter

6

Overview
Preview
Office Hours
Service Encounters
Lectures
Practice
Review

Chapter 6

Connecting Information 정보 연결

Overview

- Connecting Information(정보 연결) 문제는 대화와 강의의 전개 방식을 이해하고, 토픽과 관련하여 언급된 세부 정보들 사이의 연결 관계를 파악하여 질문에서 요구하는 방식대로 분류하는 유형이다. 문제 화면에 분류표가 제시되는데, 분류 항목 아래 빈 칸에 각 보기가 어떤 항목에 해당하는지 클릭하여 답을 표시하면 된다.

- Connecting Information 문제는 보통 지문마다 1 문항 정도가 출제되는데, 간혹 출제되지 않기도 한다. 대화나 강의 전반에 걸쳐 언급된 정보들을 질문에서 모아 분류하는 문제이기 때문에 들려주는 내용의 일부분만 듣고서는 문제를 제대로 풀 수가 없다. 대화와 강의가 어떤 방향으로 흘러가는지를 이해하고 문제를 예측하여 메모를 하며 듣는 것이 문제 해결의 한 방법이다.

☑ **학생이 자신이 가진 문제에 대해 교수의 조언을 구하는 대화 내용**
교수의 조언으로 제시된 것(Suggested)과 제시되지 않은 것(Not Suggested)을 구분하는 문제를 예상할 수 있다. 메모할 때 이를 염두에 두고 제시된 순서대로 간략히 적어두는 것이 좋다.

☑ **교수가 건축가 Frank Lloyd Wright의 건축 양식에 관해 설명하는 강의 내용**
Wright의 건축 양식 특징으로 언급된 것(Mentioned)과 언급되지 않은 것(Not Mentioned)을 구분하는 문제를 예상할 수 있다. 새로운 특징이 언급될 때마다 핵심 내용을 차례대로 적는다.

☑ **교수가 사실주의와 추상주의 미술을 비교하여 설명하는 강의 내용**
각 보기가 어떤 미술 양식의 특징인지를 분류하는 문제를 예상할 수 있다. 두 대상의 특징을 비교(공통점, 차이점) 및 대조(차이점)하여 설명하고 있는 강의에서는 대부분 각 범주 별 특징을 바르게 연결하는 문제가 출제된다. 강의를 들을 때 범주 별로 언급되는 특징을 구분해서 적는다.

☑ **교수가 스테인드글라스를 제작하는 과정을 설명하는 강의 내용**
스테인드글라스를 만드는 순서를 맞추라는 문제를 예상할 수 있다. 사물의 제작 순서나 진행 절차, 사건이 일어난 순서 등에 따라 강의가 전개되면 보기를 순서에 맞게 배열하는 문제가 출제된다. 강의를 들을 때 순서대로 내용을 적고 화살표 등을 이용해 선후 관계를 표시해둔다.

BOOK LIST

"우리는 시대의 변화 속에서도 묵묵히
책의 향기를 담아내고 있습니다."

반석 출판사

·

반석북스

·

탑메이드북

반석출판사　탑메이드북　반석북스

15,000원   15,000원   18,000원

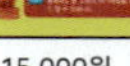

15,000원   15,000원   바로 바로 초등 필수 한자 시리즈 | 각권 12,000원

15,000원   18,000원   18,000원   12,000원

- The speakers discuss the factors leading to the global warming. Indicate on the chart below whether each of the following is mentioned as one of the factors. Click in the correct box for each phrase.

	Mentioned	Not Mentioned
보기 (A)		
보기 (B)		
보기 (C)		

- The professor discusses two types of art forms. Indicate on the chart below to which art form each of the following is attributed. Click in the correct box for each phrase.

	Mentioned	Not Mentioned
보기 (A)		
보기 (B)		
보기 (C)		

- The professor discusses the procedure of recycling. Put the steps in correct order. Drag each sentence to the space where it belongs.

	Procedure of Recycling
1	
2	
3	
4	

보기 (A)

보기 (B)

보기 (C)

보기 (D)

Preview

 Listen to part of a conversation between a student and a professor.

The speakers discuss several benefits of working in Singapore and going to graduate school. Indicate in the table below to which opportunity each of the following is attributed. Click in the correct box for each phrase.

	Singapore	Grad school
Ⓐ A further study of research interests		
Ⓑ Experience in working abroad		
Ⓒ Better career choices		
Ⓓ Learning another language		
Ⓔ Increase in self-esteem		

 Listen to part of a conversation between a student and a professor.

W: Excuse me, Professor Kyle. Am I interrupting you?

M: Oh, Phyllis, come on in. I was waiting for you.

W: Thanks. I wanted to talk to you about... uh, do you mind if I ask some advice?
교수를 찾아온 이유: 조언을 구하려고

M: Of course not. What is it about?

W: Um, I have to decide between graduate school and working overseas next fall.
조언이 필요한 이유: 대학원 진학과 해외 근무 기회 중 선택
I unexpectedly got a job offer in Singapore...

M: Well, the master's degree would look excellent on your resume, of course. It's
대학원의 이점 1
hard to get a good job without grad school nowadays. Besides, you'll have
the chance to dig into what you're really interested in.
대학원의 이점 2

W: True, but international experience is important too, right?
싱가포르 근무의 이점 1

M: Yes, absolutely. Singapore is very multi-cultural, so you'd learn a lot about
diversity by living there. Do you like the job there?

W: Sort of, it's not exactly what I wanted to do, but it seems interesting.

M: Good. You might also be able to study Chinese there, which is a real benefit in
싱가포르 근무의 이점 2
today's world. Um, it's really hard for you to choose one.

W: Yes, it really is.

M: Well, you can't deny that an advanced degree will help your career choices,
though. It will also do a lot for your self-respect. You've been a great student,
대학원의 이점 3
so I think you'll do a great job at graduate school, too.

W: Thanks. Wow, it's such a hard decision! I guess I will have to think more about it.
Thanks for your time!

여: 실례합니다, Kyle 교수님. 제가 방해가 되었나요?
남: 아, Phyllis, 어서 오렴. 기다리고 있었단다.
여: 감사합니다. 교수님과 대화를 하고 싶었던 이유가요... 음, 제가 교수님의 조언을 좀 구할 수 있을까요?
남: 그럼. 무슨 일이지?
여: 다음 가을 학기에 대학원에 갈지 외국에서 일을 할지 결정해야 해요. 뜻밖에 싱가포르에서 일을 해달라
는 제의를 받았거든요...
남: 음, 이력서에 석사 학위를 기재하면 아주 보기 좋겠지. 요즘 대학원을 다니지 않고 괜찮은 직업을 구하기
가 참 어려우니까. 그리고 네가 정말 관심 있는 분야를 파고들어 공부할 기회가 될 거야.

어휘 | interrupt 방해하다 | graduate school 대학원 | overseas 해외의 | unexpectedly 뜻밖에 | master's degree 석사 학위 | resume 이력서 | dig into ~에 파고들다 | benefit 이점 | multi-cultural 다문화의 | diversity 다양성 | advanced degree 고급 학위(석사, 박사) | self-respect 자부심

해설 | 학생은 앞으로의 진로를 정하는데 도움을 받기 위해 교수를 찾아 왔다. 학생은 대학원에 진학해야 할지, 싱가포르에서 받은 일자리 제의를 받아들여 해외로 나가야 할지를 고민하고 있다. 학생과 교수는 각 경우의 이점에 대해 대화를 나누고 있다. 각 보기와 지문의 해당 부분을 확인하여 보자.

연구 관심 분야를 더 연구한다는 보기 (A)의 내용은 스크립트에서 교수가 대학원의 두 번째 이점으로 언급했다.
해외 근무 경험을 얻을 수 있다는 보기 (B)의 내용은 스크립트에서 싱가포르 근무의 첫 번째 이점으로 학생이 언급했다.
더 나은 직업 선택 기회가 있다는 보기 (C)의 내용은 스크립트에서 교수가 대학원의 첫 번째 이점으로 언급했다.
외국어를 배울 수 있다는 보기 (D)의 내용은 스크립트에서 싱가포르 근무의 두 번째 이점으로 교수가 언급했다.
자부심이 높아진다는 보기 (E)의 내용은 스크립트에서 교수가 대학원의 세 번째 이점으로 언급했다.

해석 | 화자들은 싱가포르에서 일하는 것과 대학원에 가는 것의 이점을 논의하고 있다. 아래의 각 보기가 어떤 기회와 관련이 있는지 표시하시오. 각 보기에 맞는 칸에 클릭하시오.

	Singapore	Grad school
(A) 연구 관심 분야를 더 연구함		∨
(B) 해외 근무 경험	∨	
(C) 더 나은 직업 선택		∨
(D) 외국어 배우기	∨	
(E) 자부심이 높아짐		∨

Office Hours

01 

The speakers discuss several benefits of holding the conference on campus and holding it in a nearby hotel. Indicate in the table below to which place each of the following is attributed. Click in the correct box for each phrase.

	Campus	Hotel
Ⓐ Is lower-priced		
Ⓑ Provides comfortable space to stay		
Ⓒ Is better for large number of people		
Ⓓ Has all facilities under one roof		

Topic:

Details:

02 🎧

In the conversation, the professor makes suggestions for improving the student's resume. Indicate in the table below whether each of the following is suggested by the professor. Click in the correct box for each phrase.

	Suggested	Not Suggested
Ⓐ Check misspelled words		
Ⓑ Get more work experience		
Ⓒ Remove junior high school stories		
Ⓓ Print out in a larger font		
Ⓔ Use better-quality paper		

Topic:

Details:

Service Encounters

01 

In the conversation, the man gives the student some advice about leading a tour. Indicate in the table below whether each of the following is suggested by the professor. Click in the correct box for each phrase.

	Suggested	Not Suggested
Ⓐ Guide visitors to the parking lot after tour		
Ⓑ Let visitors introduce themselves		
Ⓒ Speak slowly and clearly during the tour		
Ⓓ Wait a few minutes in case anyone is a little late		
Ⓔ Don't show the visitors too much of the campus		

Topic:

Details:

02

In the conversation, the woman mentions several different meal plans. Indicate in the table below whether each of the following is mentioned by the woman. Click in the correct box for each phrase.

	Yes	No
Ⓐ A card that can be used in other places on campus		
Ⓑ A card with both stored money value and a certain number of meals per week		
Ⓒ A plan with a certain number of meals per day		
Ⓓ A plan that covers all meals on campus, all the time		
Ⓔ A card with stored monetary value		

Topic:

Details:

Lectures

01 

1. What is the main topic of the lecture?

(A) Why do we forget things?
(B) Secrets of phone numbers
(C) Two forms of short-term memory
(D) Everyday exposure to new information

2. The professor discusses two types of short-term memory. Indicate on the chart below to which type each of the following is attributed. Click in the correct box for each phrase.

	Decay	Interference
Ⓐ Retroactive process that new information erases old one		
Ⓑ Normal process of losing memory over time		
Ⓒ Proactive process that old information prevents new information from being retained		

<table>
<tr><td>Topic:

Details:

</td></tr>
</table>

1. Which of the following is true of Frank Gehry?

(A) He is an Englishman.
(B) He is notable for the transportation systems he has designed.
(C) His building facades often use metal.
(D) His buildings meet at right angles.

2. In the lecture, the speakers discuss two contemporary architects. Indicate on the chart below who designed each of the following. Click in the correct box for each phrase.

	Frank Gehry	Norman Foster
Ⓐ Hong Kong International Airport		
Ⓑ A station for the Singapore MRT		
Ⓒ Guggenheim Museum in Bilbao		
Ⓓ 30 St. Mary Axe in London		
Ⓔ Walt Disney Concert Hall in L.A.		

Topic:

Details:

Practice

01 What does the student need at the library?

    Ⓐ He needs to get a library card.
    Ⓑ He needs to check out books.
    Ⓒ He needs to write a report.
    Ⓓ He needs access to journal articles.

Listen again to part of the conversation. Then answer the question.

02 What does the woman imply when she says this: 

    Ⓐ She will explain the process to the student.
    Ⓑ She and the student will walk into another room.
    Ⓒ The student will have to go somewhere else.
    Ⓓ The student will need to come back later.

03 What can be inferred about the student?

    Ⓐ He has been very busy with his papers this semester.
    Ⓑ He has not borrowed any books from the library this semester.
    Ⓒ He does not need the journal articles right away.
    Ⓓ He has lost his library card before he used it the first time

04 What does the library do with more than one-year-old academic journals?

    Ⓐ It turns them into a form that can be read by a computer.
    Ⓑ It saves them all in a separate location.
    Ⓒ It transfers them all to another library.
    Ⓓ It discards them to make room for new books.

05 The woman describes the procedure of getting access to the periodical database. Put the steps in correct order. Drag each sentence to the space where it belongs.

	Use of the periodical database
1	
2	
3	
4	

    Ⓐ Look up the articles in the online database.
    Ⓑ Let the person in charge of periodicals have the list.
    Ⓒ Set up student ID card for use in the library.
    Ⓓ Print a list of the articles.

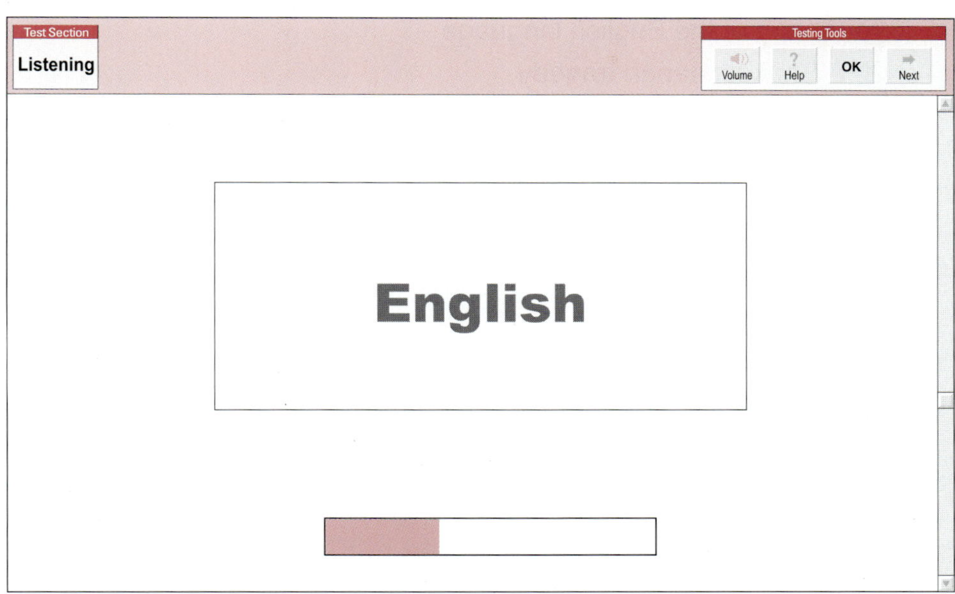

Test Section
Listening
Testing Tools
Volume
Help
OK
Next
English

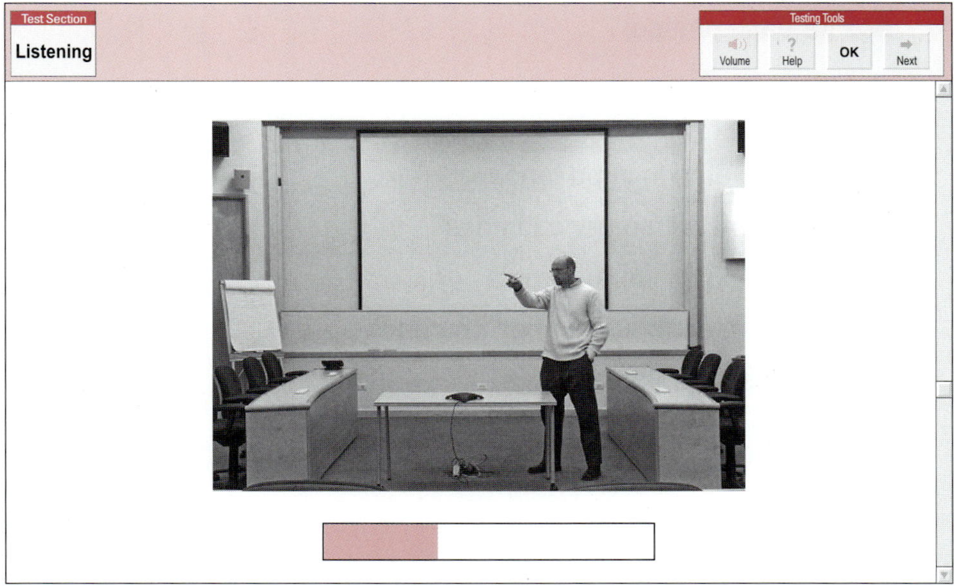

Test Section
Listening
Testing Tools
Volume
Help
OK
Next

06 What is the lecture mainly about?

    Ⓐ History of the English language
    Ⓑ A Shakespearian tragedy
    Ⓒ Shakespeare's effect on the English language
    Ⓓ Extensive English vocabularies

07 Which of the following is true of English before the sixteenth century?

    Ⓐ It was the basic subject of advanced education.
    Ⓑ It was in less use than French and Latin.
    Ⓒ It was not an everyday language.
    Ⓓ Its grammar rules were all established.

08 In the lecture, the professor mentions some events to the rise of English as a major world language. Indicate whether each of the following is mentioned as one of the events. Click in the correct box for each phrase.

	Mentioned	Not Mentioned
Ⓐ Latin's drop in importance		
Ⓑ Relations with other countries		
Ⓒ Popularity of literary works		
Ⓓ Taking a control of foreign countries		
Ⓔ Battles with other nations		

09 What does the professor imply about Shakespeare?

Ⓐ He was from the working classes.
Ⓑ He did not like classical literature.
Ⓒ He knew several other languages
Ⓓ He wanted to be an influential writer.

Listen again to part of the lecture. Then answer the question.

10 What does the professor imply when he says this:

Ⓐ The Oxford English Dictionary includes many words that Shakespeare invented in his plays.
Ⓑ The editors of The Oxford English Dictionary do not believe Shakespeare was the first to use some of the words in their dictionary.
Ⓒ Shakespeare's writings have remained because they were more famous than those of other writers.
Ⓓ Other writers may have used some of the words in The Oxford English Dictionary first.

Listen again to part of the lecture. Then answer the question.

11 What does the professor imply when he says this:

Ⓐ Other writers' contributions should be considered.
Ⓑ Shakespeare's additions to English have been good ones.
Ⓒ Shakespeare's real effect upon English almost ended.
Ⓓ Shakespeare's lines should be in wider use.

Review

01 다음 문장들을 듣고, 밑줄에 들어갈 단어를 받아 써보자.

1. You can usually ________ ________ ________ for conferences.

2. Well, ________ ________ ________ the information about your junior high school.

3. I've just finished registering for my classes, and they ________ ____ ________ here to ________ ____ ________ my meal plan.

4. You ________ ____ use spell check before you ________ ________ ________ again.

5. Can you give me ________ ________ like what to do and ________ ________ ____ do?

02 다음 문장들을 듣고, pause가 들어가는 부분에 사선을 그어보자.

1. Well, I guess you want to decide between using a hotel and using the campus, right?

2. Hotels will sometimes give discounts, though, if you're holding an event during the slow season.

3. I'll be leading a campus tour for visiting parents this afternon, but this is my first time.

4. You also want to wait about five minutes after the official start time, in case anyone is still on their way.

5. And finally, we've got a hybrid card that gives you 10 meals per week, plus stored value.

태도/발화 목적
Stance/Function

Chapter 7

Overview
Preview
Office Hours
Service Encounters
Lectures
Practice
Review

Stance/Function

태도/발화 목적

Overview

- Stance/Function(태도/발화 목적) 문제는 화자의 말이 담고 있는 문맥적 의미, 화자의 말을 통해 미루어 짐작할 수 있는 것, 화자가 어떤 대상에 대해 취하고 있는 입장이나 태도, 화자가 어떤 말을 한 목적이나 의도 등을 파악하여 답을 고르는 유형이다. Stance/Function 문제는 지문마다 1 문항 정도가 출제된다.

- 화자들이 하는 말에는 항상 어떤 특정한 의미가 들어있고 그런 말을 하는 목적이 있다. '배고픈데 밥 먹으러 갈래?' 처럼 문장의 의미나 목적이 겉으로 바로 드러나 있는 말은 별다른 사고의 과정 없이 이해하고 의사소통하기 쉽다. 하지만, 친구와 만나기로 약속을 한 상황에서 친구가 전화를 하여 '나 갑자기 급한 일이 생겼는데, 어쩌지?' 라는 말을 꺼냈다고 가정해보자. 친구가 이 이야기를 하는 의도는 무엇이고, 이 말 속에는 어떤 속뜻이 숨어 있는 것일까? 아마도 이 친구가 진짜로 하고 싶은 말은 급한 일이 생겨서 약속을 지키지 못할 것 같다는 것일 가능성이 높다. 직설적으로 약속을 깨뜨리기가 미안한 상황에서 자신의 상황을 먼저 설명하고 친구의 대답과 양해를 구하는 표현으로 보인다. 이처럼 우리가 하는 말 한마디 한마디에는 그 나름의 목적과 의도, 의미가 함축되어 있다. 따라서 상대방이 하는 말에 드러나는 혹은 숨어있는 감정이나 태도, 의도를 문맥과 정황에 맞게 파악할 줄 아는 것이 원활한 의사소통에 있어 중요한 부분이다.

- Stance/Function 문제는 주로 대화와 강의의 일부분을 다시 들려주는 형태로 출제되는데, 다시 들려주는 부분만을 듣고서는 문제를 제대로 풀기가 어렵다. 단편적인 부분이 아닌 전체적인 흐름 속에서 이 부분이 갖는 의미를 이해하는 것이 중요하다. 주로 화자의 입장과 태도, 감정과 관련된 내용을 묻는 Stance 문제는 화자의 어조가 어떤지를 주의해서 들으면 쉽게 풀 수 있고, 주로 반어, 강조, 의심, 확인, 놀람, 부러움 등과 관련된 문제가 출제된다. Function 문제를 풀 때는 특정 부분을 언급한 이유와 의도, 목적을 빠르게 파악하는 것이 중요하다. 주로 제안을 하거나, 요청을 하거나, 확인 및 재확인을 하거나, 확신 및 불확신을 나타내거나, 예를 들거나, 강조하거나, 불평하는 상황 등에서 문제가 출제된다.

Sample Questions

- Listen again to part of the conversation. Then answer the question.

  What does the woman mean when she says this:

- Listen again to part of the lecture. Then answer the question.

  Why does the professor say this:

- Listen again to part of the lecture. Then answer the question.

  What does the professor imply when she says this:

- Why does the professor mention ~?

- What is the man's stance toward ~?

- How does the student seem to feel about ~?

Preview

 Listen to part of a lecture in a music history class.

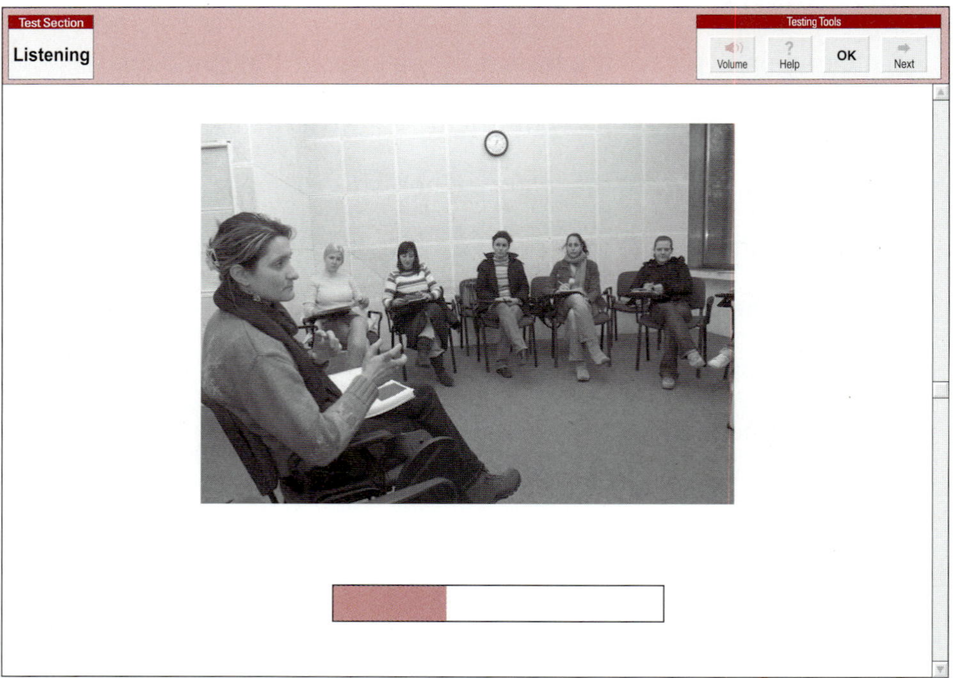

Listen again to part of the lecture. Then answer the question.

What does the professor mean when she says this: 

Ⓐ The opera diva was the prototype for women in all other areas of
   musical performance.
Ⓑ In reality, very few opera divas look like Maria Callas.
Ⓒ Callas influenced on the public image of the opera diva.
Ⓓ Callas wanted to be a model of what an opera diva ought to be.

 Listen to part of a lecture in a music history class.

P(W): To continue our talk about the great performers of the 20th century, we should mention Maria Callas. Maria Callas is a legend, truly one of the greatest opera singers. Despite her relatively short life — she passed away in 1977, at the age of 53 — she had an amazing career, and she has left an enduring mark on the opera world. Although she was born in New York, her ancestry was Greek, and she received her musical education in that country. *In her early career, Callas was exactly what many of us today think of when we imagine the prototypical opera diva: heavyset, full-figured, and temperamental.* Not only that, but she possessed a powerful, versatile, and immediately recognizable voice. One critic claimed that — quite simply — Callas could sing anything that had ever been written for the female voice. Her unparalleled talents earned her the nickname La Divina, and there has been no performer like her since.

P: 20세기의 위대한 가수들에 관한 이야기를 이어가자면, Maria Callas(마리아 칼라스)를 빼놓을 수 없지요. Maria Callas는 최고의 오페라 가수로 꼽히는, 전설적인 인물입니다. Callas는 1977년에 53세의 나이로 생을 마감했는데, 비교적 짧았던 생애에도 불구하고, 눈부신 경력을 가지고 있었고, 오페라 세계에 영원히 남을 영향을 주었어요. Callas는 New York(뉴욕)에서 태어났지만, 선조가 그리스 계였기 때문에 그리스에서 음악 교육을 받았어요. 초창기의 모습은 오늘날 많은 사람들이 오페라 디바의 전형적인 모습을 떠올릴 때 생각하는 모습과 똑같았는데, 몸집과 체격이 크고 개성이 강했죠. 그뿐 아니라, Callas는 힘이 넘치고, 어떤 음악에나 어울리고, 듣자마자 알아볼 수 있는 목소리의 소유자였어요. 한 비평가는 Callas가 여성의 목소리로 불리도록 쓰여진 모든 음악에 맞추어 노래를 부를 수 있다고 말하기도 했죠. 무엇에도 견줄 수 없는 재능으로 그녀는 La Divina(여신)라고 불렸고, 아직 Callas와 같은 가수는 찾아볼 수 없죠.

어휘 | legend 전설, 전설적인 인물 | pass away 죽다 | enduring 영원히 남을 | ancestry 선조, 조상 | prototypical 전형적인 | heavyset 몸집이 큰 | full-figured 체격이 큰 | temperamental 개성이 강한 | possess 소유하다 | versatile 다재다능한, 융통성의 | unparalleled 견줄 바 없는

Listen again to part of the lecture. Then answer the question.

What does the professor mean when she says this: 

In her early career, Callas was exactly what many of us today think of when we imagine the prototypical opera diva: heavyset, full-figured, and temperamental.

해석 | 강의의 일부를 다시 들으시오. 그리고 나서 질문에 답하시오.

교수가 이것을 말할 때 의미하는 것은 무엇인가: 

초창기의 모습은 오늘날 많은 사람들이 오페라 디바의 전형적인 모습을 떠올릴 때 생각하는 모습과 똑같았는데, 몸집과 체격이 크고 개성이 강했죠.

해설 | 스크립트는 미국의 세계적인 오페라 가수인 Maria Callas에 관한 강의이다. 비교적 이른 나이에 세상을 떴음에도 불구하고, 전설로 남아있는 Callas의 생애를 짧게 소개하고 있다. 질문지에서는 교수가 '초창기의 모습은 오늘날 많은 사람들이 오페라 디바의 전형적인 모습을 떠올릴 때 생각하는 모습과 똑같았는데, 몸집과 체격이 크고 개성이 강했죠.'라고 말한 의미가 무엇인지를 묻고 있다. 무엇이 정답인지 보기 하나 하나를 확인해보자.

다른 음악 공연 분야에 관해서는 언급된 적이 없기 때문에 보기 (A)의 내용은 오답이다.
많은 사람들이 생각하는 전형적인 오페라 디바는 Callas의 초창기 모습과 같다고 하였으므로, 현실에서 Callas와 비슷하게 보이는 오페라 디바가 거의 없다는 보기 (B)의 내용은 오답이다.
Callas의 초창기 모습이 많은 사람들이 오페라 디바의 모습을 머리 속에 그릴 때 떠오르는 모습과 같다고 하였다. 이는 Callas가 사람들이 오페라 디바에 관해 갖게 되는 이미지에 영향을 주었다는 것을 의미한다. 따라서 보기 (C)가 정답이다.
Callas가 오페라 디바가 모범으로 삼아야 할 사람이 되기를 원했다는 내용과 관련된 부분은 전혀 언급된 적이 없다. 따라서 보기 (D)는 오답이다.

(A) 오페라 디바는 모든 음악 공연에 등장하는 여성들의 원형이었다.
(B) 실제로는, Maria Callas와 같은 모습의 오페라 디바는 거의 없다.
(C) Callas는 대중들이 오페라 디바에 대해 갖고 있는 이미지에 영향을 주었다.
(D) Callas는 오페라 디바의 모범이 되고 싶어했다.

Office Hours

01

Listen again to part of the conversation. Then answer the question.

What does the professor mean when he says this:

(A) He thinks the student should settle the problem.
(B) He doesn't know about the transportation plans yet.
(C) He wants more information from the student.
(D) He wants to ask the student a question.

> **Topic:**
>
> **Details:**

02

Listen again to part of the conversation. Then answer the question.

What does the woman imply when she says this:

(A) She already knows a lot about the school.
(B) She doesn't feel the orientation is helpful.
(C) She thinks spending time with her brother is more important.
(D) She will not be missing any information from the orientation.

> **Topic:**
>
> **Details:**

Service Encounters

01

Listen again to part of the conversation. Then answer the question.

What does the man mean when he says this:

(A) Good news is usually not true.
(B) He does not believe what the woman said.
(C) He is not interested in winning the award.
(D) Good news is usually accompanied by bad news.

Topic:

Details:

02

Listen again to part of the conversation. Then answer the question.

What does the woman imply when she says this:

(A) Other students have not raised any questions.
(B) The old system is better than the new one.
(C) There have been complaints about the computer errors.
(D) There is an infestation of bugs in the tutoring center.

Topic:

Details:

Lectures

01 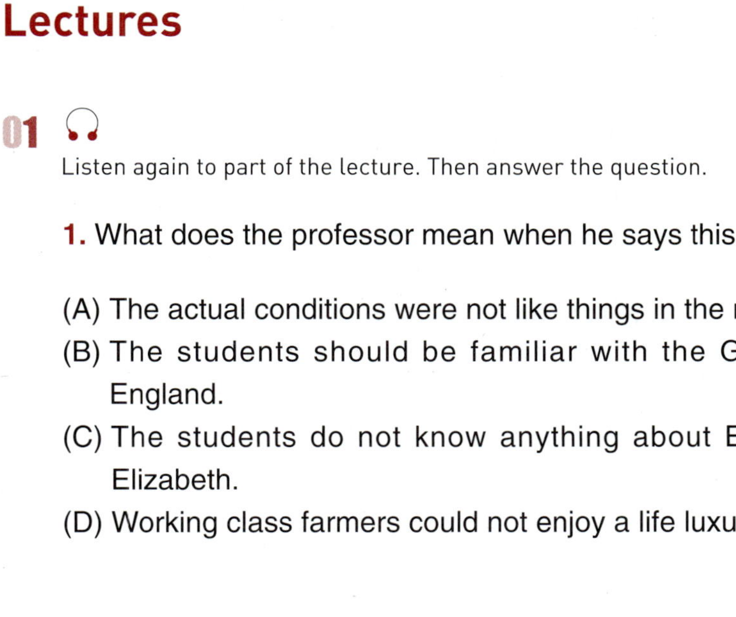

Listen again to part of the lecture. Then answer the question.

1. What does the professor mean when he says this:

(A) The actual conditions were not like things in the movie.
(B) The students should be familiar with the Golden Age of England.
(C) The students do not know anything about England under Elizabeth.
(D) Working class farmers could not enjoy a life luxury.

Listen again to part of the lecture. Then answer the question.

2. What does the professor imply when he says this:

(A) The poor grew their own food.
(B) The poor may have committed crimes.
(C) The poor stayed in the monasteries.
(D) The poor were forced to go into the country.

<table>
<tr><td>Topic:</td></tr>
<tr><td>Details:</td></tr>
</table>

02 

Listen again to part of the lecture. Then answer the question.

1. What does the professor mean when she says this: 

(A) Peary is a very important explorer.
(B) Peary is famous in a slightly negative way.
(C) Peary ought to have more respect.
(D) Peary lied about everything on his expeditions.

Listen again to part of the lecture. Then answer the question.

2. What does the professor mean when she says this:

(A) Peary should be officially named the first to reach the North Pole.
(B) The fact that Peary was decorated with a medal shows he deserves respect.
(C) Because of some reliability issues, Peary should be forgotten by history.
(D) Despite the controversies, Peary should be remembered as an important explorer.

Topic:

Details:

Practice

[Questions 1~5] Listen to part of a conversation between a student and a professor.

01 What is the woman's problem?

    Ⓐ She is unable to find material she needs at the library.
    Ⓑ The professor has treated her unfairly in front of her classmates.
    Ⓒ She is not keeping up with her assigned projects.
    Ⓓ The bookstore is sold out of a textbook that she needs.

02 Why does the bookstore order fewer copies than needed?

    Ⓐ To encourage students to buy and sell used texts
    Ⓑ To avoid getting stuck with too many books
    Ⓒ To make the title stay in high demand
    Ⓓ To sell textbooks in high price

Listen again to part of the conversation. Then answer the question.

03 What does the woman imply when she says this:

Ⓐ Regular bookstores seem to have more stock than campus ones.
Ⓑ Regular bookstores need to be open to campus customers.
Ⓒ The university bookstore should accommodate students' needs.
Ⓓ The university bookstore is able to easily sell off overstock.

Listen again to part of the conversation. Then answer the question.

04 How does the professor seem to feel about the campus bookstore?

Ⓐ The professor is sympathetic to its dilemma.
Ⓑ The professor believes it should order the full amount.
Ⓒ The professor thinks it was more efficient in the past.
Ⓓ The professor is discontented with its current policy.

05 In the conversation, the speakers discuss several options for dealing with the lack of textbooks in the bookstore. Indicate in the table below whether each of the following is suggested by the professor. Click in the correct box for each phrase.

	Suggested	Not Suggested
Ⓐ Lend his own copy to the student to use		
Ⓑ Place a call to the manager of the bookstore		
Ⓒ Allow students to share books during class time		
Ⓓ Shift the focus of the course to individual tasks		
Ⓔ Make photocopies of the essential parts of the book		

🎧 [Questions 6~11] Listen to part of a lecture in a biology class.

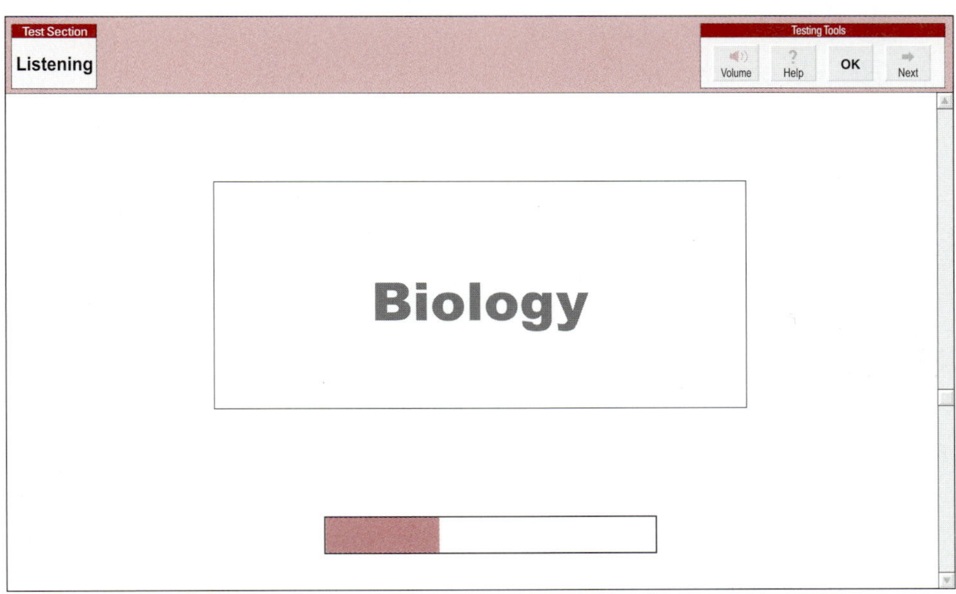

Test Section
Listening
Testing Tools
Volume
Help
OK
Next
Biology

Test Section
Listening
Testing Tools
Volume
Help
OK
Next

06 What is the main topic of the lecture?

Ⓐ Classification of animals
Ⓑ Cold-blooded animals
Ⓒ Body temperature of animals
Ⓓ Warm-blooded animals

Listen again to part of the lecture. Then answer the question.

07 What does the professor mean when he says this:

Ⓐ The term cold-blooded is not perfect.
Ⓑ Most fish are not cold-blooded.
Ⓒ All the fish prefer warm water to cold water.
Ⓓ Technically, cold-blooded organisms are always cold.

08 Which of the following is NOT a type of temperature regulation in cold-blooded animals?

Ⓐ Bradymetabolism
Ⓑ Ectothermy
Ⓒ Poikilothermy
Ⓓ Hypoglycemia

09 When does the metabolic rate of cold-blooded animals slow down?

Ⓐ During the hottest part of the day
Ⓑ During the rainy season
Ⓒ In cold winter
Ⓓ When in a dark place

10 In the lecture, the professor gives examples of temperature regulation mechanisms of cold-blooded animals. Indicate whether each of the following is mentioned as one of the examples. Click in the correct box for each phrase.

	Mentioned	Not Mentioned
Ⓐ Fish changing depth in the water		
Ⓑ Turtles staying at the bottom of ponds during winter		
Ⓒ Snakes basking on warm rocks		
Ⓓ Polar bears hibernating		
Ⓔ Whales beaching themselves		

11 What does the professor imply about mammals?

Ⓐ They have nothing in common with reptiles.
Ⓑ They are not hibernating.
Ⓒ They can't withstand cold weather.
Ⓓ They are not cold-blooded.

Review

01 다음 문장들을 듣고, 밑줄에 들어갈 단어를 받아 써보자.

1. We need to _________ _________ enough _____________ forms.

2. We _________ had _________ _________ to plan this, so we might
   have to do _________ .

3. But the honors program is changing ____ ____ _________ and
   _______________ and you need to know about them.

4. It was the best _________ anyone _________ _________ ____ .

5. It's a new system, and they're still ____ _________ _________
   _________ _________ .

02 다음 문장들을 듣고, pause가 들어가는 부분에 사선을 그어보자.

1. No, we don't have the authority to tell you what to do before the
   semester starts.

2. Well, the hours for one-on-one tutors have been cut back, so it's
   almost impossible to get help from a human being now.

3. You never give the titles of songs when you play them, and your
   listeners want to find those songs again after the show.

4. My family has been planning a trip that week, and it'll be our last
   chance to travel together for a while.

5. It's already ten cents a page and then we still have to buy the books
   when it comes in.

Book List 반석 도서목록

TOEFL

TOEFL myself Reading (Advanced Course)
Steven Oh, Michael Nolan, Richard Owell, Kevin Heiser / 국배판 / 376면 / 22,000원
iBT 시대를 알리는 최초의 iBT Reading 대비 교재. Reading 부분만 20회를 엮고 별권으로 해답과 해설을 실었다. 이 책의 특징은 전체가 영문으로만 되어 있다는 것. advanced reader들에게 필독서가 될 것이다.

TOEFL myself Listening (Advanced Course)
Steven Oh, Michael Nolan, Richard Owell, Kevin Heiser / 국배판 / 440면 / 29,000원 (별권 – Answer Keys, mp3용 CD 포함)
ETS에서 제시된 규정에 따라 편집되어 실제 시험과 같은 조건에서 자기 실력을 평가할 수 있도록 하였다. 본서는 12회분의 iBT Listening 문제를 제시하고 별권인 해설서에는 정답과 영문 해설이 들어 있다. 약간 높은 수준으로 만들어졌기 때문에 실제 시험에서는 더욱 좋은 결과를 얻을 수 있을 것이다.

iBT TOEFL myself Reading (Regular Course)
Steven Oh, Michael Nolan, Richard Owell, Kevin Heiser / 국배판 / 336면 / 22,000원 (별권 – Answer Keys)
iBT 토플을 준비하는 수험생을 위한 Reading 실전문제집. 본서는 ETS에서 제시하는 요구 사항의 형식과 유형에 충실한 최상의 수험서로서, 실제 TOEFL 시험과 똑같은 환경에서 시험을 치르게 된다. 어휘를 넓히고 모든 문제에 대한 이해력을 높여주기 위해 제시문에 대해 정답 및 한글 해설을 꼼꼼히 달았으며 정답부문에 Summary를 첨부했다. 본서는 20회분의 iBT Reading 문제 및 별책인 해설서로 구성되었다.

iBT TOEFL myself Listening (Regular Course)
Jessica Jung / 국배판 / 416면 / 25,000원 (별권 – Answer Keys, mp3용 CD 포함)
iBT 토플을 준비하는 수험생을 위한 Listening 실전문제집. 12회분의 iBT Listening 문제 및 별책인 해설서로 구성되었다. 새로운 iBT TOEFL 형식에 더 익숙해질 수 있도록 실제 미국 대학 강의내용 수준이나 학구적인 내용에 바탕을 두고 있으며 수험생의 어휘를 넓혀주고 모든 문제에 대한 이해력을 높여주기 위해 제시문에 대해 정답 및 한글 해설을 꼼꼼히 달았다. 뿐만 아니라, 지문에 대한 내용 이해를 돕기 위해 정답부문에 Summary(지문요약)를 첨부했다.

iBT TOEFL Reading (Prep–Advanced Course)
Steven Oh, Michael Nolan, Richard Owell, Kevin Heiser / 4×6배판 / 316면 / 21,000원 (별권 – Answer Keys, mp3용 CD 포함)
iBT에 출제되는 지문은 역사적, 과학적, 사회적 사실이 대부분이므로 여러 번 응시하면 내용이 비슷한 것을 만나게 된다. 따라서 영역별로 가장 많이 등장하는 내용을 엄선하였으므로 청취학습을 겯들이면 학습효과가 배가된다. 난이도는 고급자를 목표로 하는 중급자 수준에 맞추었다.

TOEFL Vocabulary & Reading
오규상 / 4×6배판 / 624면 / 19,800원 (mp3 파일 무료제공)
어휘와 독해를 묶은 회심의 역작. 모든 어휘를 테마별로 분류하고 독해지문 100편을 수록했다. 특히 34편에 달하는 미국 역사는 역사 교과서 한 권을 읽는 효과를 준다. 동의어 찾기 문제해설은 英英韓사전 방식으로 되어 많은 동의어를 익히는데 큰 도움이 된다.

Find TOEFL Vocabulary 1 · 2 with Listening & Reading
Steven Oh / 국배판 / 424쪽(1권), 432쪽(2권) / 각권 15,000원 (mp3용 CD 포함)
iBT TOEFL의 어휘, 청취, 독해를 한 권으로 마스터하려는 학습자를 위한 교재. 영역별로 실전에 가장 빈번히 등장하는 중요 어휘와 5천여 개의 어구를 모두 영영한 사전 방식으로 해설하였고 어휘학습 후 청취 문제를 접함으로써 청취 실력을 향상시킬 수 있다. 한 테마에 어휘와 그에 해당하는 다양한 독해를 수록하였으며 독해 지문을 청취와 병행하여 청취 실력을 동시에 올리는 학습효과를 누릴 수 있다.

Essential TOEFL WORDS 5000
임 공 / 신국판 / 432면 / 12,000원 (B + T : 15,900원)
토플 리스닝과 리딩에서 갈수록 비중이 높아져 가는 Lecture 분야를 공략하기 위한 필수어휘서다. 리스닝과 리딩에서 질문하는 토픽이 동일하다는 점에 착안하여 리스닝과 리딩 점수를 동시에 향상시킬 수 있도록 Lecture 빈출지문 40개를 엄선하고, 각 빈출지문을 청취하거나 독해할 때 반드시 알아 두어야 할 핵심문장과 핵심어휘를 정리하였다.

iBT Find TOEFL Reading
Steven Oh / 4×6배판 / 600쪽(별책 156쪽) / 22,000원 (mp3용 CD 포함)
iBT 토플에서 단기간에 고득점을 올릴 수 있도록 테마별 학습이 가능하도록 하였다. 지문별로 중요하거나 어려운 어휘는 영영한 사전식의 설명이 되어 있고, 원어민이 녹음한 mp3 파일이 제공되어 청취를 병행한 입체적 학습이 가능하다. 권말에는 Actual Test를 통해 실전 감각을 키울 수 있도록 하였다.

iBT Find TOEFL Listening
Rebecca Hardy, Naomi Kim / 4*6배판 / 368쪽 / 19,000원 (mp3용 CD 포함)
iBT Listening 출제경향을 분석하고 고득점을 얻을 수 있는 최적의 전략과 학습 방법을 제시하고 있다. 실질적인 청취력 향상을 위하여 Dictation 훈련에 중점을 두고 있다. 긴 지문 중 밑줄로 듣기 능력을 테스트해 나아가 보면 점점 자신감이 높아지는 걸 느낄 수 있다.

iBT Find TOEFL Speaking
Rebecca Hardy, Naomi Kim / 4×6배판 / 379쪽 / 15,000원 (mp3용 CD 포함)
본서는 iBT TOEFL Speaking 섹션의 출제경향을 철저히 분석한 후 고득점을 얻을 수 있는 최적의 전략과 학습 방법을 제시하고 있다. 다양한 출제 예상문제와 대화 상황, 강의 주제를 다루고 있으며, 문제의 이해와 답변 제시 등의 과정을 실제 시험 상황과 동일하게 훈련할 수 있도록 체계적으로 구성되었다. 4주 또는 6주간의 계획에 맞춰 학습하도록 하였고 권말에는 Actual Test를 수록하여 최종 점검이 가능하도록 하였다.

iBT Find TOEFL Writing
Jack Betts, Naomi Kim / 4×6배판 / 332쪽 / 15,000원 (mp3용 CD 포함)
iBT 체제로 바뀐 토플 Writing 섹션의 출제경향을 철저히 분석하고 고득점을 얻을 수 있는 최적의 전략과 학습 방법을 제시하고 있다. 다양한 출제 예상문제와 대화 상황, 강의 주제를 다루고 있으며, 시험을 단계적으로 공략할 수 있도록 난이도를 조정하였다. 자신의 생각을 명확하게 표현할 수 있도록 문제의 이해와 답변 제시 등의 과정을 실제 시험 상황과 동일하게 훈련할 수 있도록 체계적으로 구성하였다.

TOEIC

처음부터 다시 시작하는 토익은 내밥 RC 입문편
Pat Jeon / 4×6배판 / 432면 / 13,800원
본서는 TOEIC Part 5, 6, 7을 위한 입문서로 기획된 책이다. 어휘력과 문법 실력을 동시에 공략할 수 있도록 하였으며 TOEIC 독해를 위한 전략비법 70, 1~2초 안에 정답 고르기 공략법 등으로 구성되었다. 강의용 및 독습자를 위해 강의식 해설이 수록되었고 실전모의고사 10회분 체험하기 프로그램이 포함되어 있다.

처음부터 다시 시작하는 토익은 내밥 LC 입문편
김형주 / 4×6배판 / 456면 / 15,800원 (B+T : 25,000원)
TOEIC Part 1, 2, 3, 4를 위한 입문서로 기획된 책이다. 뉴토익의 경향에 맞춰 각 파트별 문제 유형을 data화하여 분석하였고 각각에 대한 대비책을 제시하여, 수험생들이 실제 시험에 대한 적응력을 높이고 고득점을 얻을 수 있도록 하였다. 각 파트마다 실전 테스트가 수록되었으며 미국인과 영국인 네이티브 발음으로 녹음된 MP3 파일이 제공된다.

뉴토익은 내밥1 LC 실전문제집
Jason Kim, Jay Lee / 국배판 / 256면(별책 146면) / 15,000원(B+T : 25,000원)
뉴토익 수험자의 최종 마무리 테스트용, 네이티브의 말하기 스피드에 적응력을 기르는데 주안점을 두었으며 680점 이상의 중고급자에게 뉴토익 LC의 파트별 공략법을 제시한다. 10회분의 미니테스트인 Pretest가 있고 10회분의 정식 Actual Test가 수록되어 있다.

뉴토익은 내밥2 RC 실전문제집
남재조, 박영광 / 국배판 / 400면(별책 128면) / 16,000원(별책 포함)
최근 토익 RC 문제를 심층 분석하여 적중률 높은 문제를 엄선하여 12회로 구성하였다. 특히 종합적 사고를 기를 수 있도록 출제하였고 혼자서도 공부할 수 있도록 문제의 흐름을 상세히 설명하였다. Part 5, 6에 다채로운 테마의 지문을 수록하였으며, Part 7 장문 독해를 강화하였다.

토익은 내밥 Basic LC
김학용 / 4×6배판 / 446면 / 16,800원(mp3 파일 무료제공)
New TOEIC LC Section, 즉 Part Ⅰ, Ⅱ, Ⅲ, Ⅳ별로 최신 출제유형과 경향을 분석하였고 문제별 핵심을 파악하는 핵심 포인트를 제시했다. 철저한 출제유형 해부에 따른 파트별 공략법이 제시되었으며 실전을 대비한 Model Test와 Actual Test를 통해 실제 시험에 대한 적응력을 키울 수 있다.

토익은 내밥 Basic RC

김학용 / 4×6배판 / 618면(별책 103면) / 16,800원

어휘 문법 독해를 일망타진하는 책! New TOEIC의 출제 유형을 철저히 분석하였으며 그에 따른 내용을 충실히 전달하고자 파트별 출제빈도와 그 유형을 표시해두었다. 어휘편에선 고득점으로 인도하는 토익 어휘 공략법을, 문법편에선 문장을 분석하는 문법 지식을 탄탄하게 쌓을 수 있도록 하였으며, 독해편에선 지문에 관련된 문제의 핵심을 파악하는 훈련이 가능하도록 하였다.

토익은 내밥 Xpeed 700 RC

김영진, 이희연 / 4×6배판 / 624면 / 16,500원

New TOEIC RC 단기 완성용 특강 교재. TOEIC 초급~중급자들이 단기간에 Part 5, 6, 7에서 고득점을 거둘 수 있도록 기획된 책이다. 각 파트별 출제유형과 출제경향에 대한 철저한 분석을 바탕으로, 단순히 문제풀이 요령을 익히는데 그치지 않고 기초 실력 배양까지 가능하도록 12주에 걸쳐 학습하도록 구성되었다.

토익은 내밥 Xpeed 700 LC

이희연, 김영진 / 4×6배판 / 464면 / 16,500원(B+T : 25,000원)

New TOEIC LC 단기 완성용 특강 교재. TOEIC 초급~중급자들이 단기간에 Part 1, 2, 3, 4에서 고득점을 할 수 있도록 기획된 책이다. 각 파트별 출제 유형의 철저한 분석과 더불어, 토익시험이 선호하는 단어와 중요 표현에 대한 반복 청취 훈련과 확인 학습을 할 수 있도록 구성되어 있다.

즉석 토익 VOCA

김학용 / A5 / 432쪽 / 12,000원

파트별로 유용한 어휘를 충분히 연습하도록 구성했고 파트1에서는 사진 문제의 핵심을 파악하는 연습을 시킨다. L/C와 R/C편의 어휘를 종합적으로 공부할 수 있도록 각 Part별로 출제 빈도가 높은 어휘를 실었기 때문에 어휘력 향상에 큰 도움이 될 것이다.

JUNIOR TOEIC RC

도성자 / 4×6배판 / 440쪽 / 15,000원

TOEIC을 처음 치르는 주니어들이 시험 준비 첫걸음을 디딜 수 있도록 구성되었다. 토익의 기본 유형 뿐만 아니라 저자 고유의 〈문장 분석의 해법〉을 통해 영어 독해 전반에 대한 기본실력을 쌓을 수 있도록 하였다. 또 반드시 극복해야 할 문법과 독해 공략법을 꼼꼼한 〈강의식 해설〉로 구성하였다.

독해 · 어휘 · 문법 · 작문

3일만에 끝내는 Super 영문독해 핵심전략

오규상 / 4×6배판 변형 / 312면 / 9,500원

이 책은 영문 독해의 핵심 전략적인 비법을 제공한다. 우선 Reading Skill과 Reading Material에서 독해의 기본구조를 바로 잡고 꼼꼼히 기초를 다진다. 실전문제를 통해 자신감을 배양하며, 학습자에게 부담 없이 꾸며져 있어 읽다보면 독해실력을 검증해볼 수 있다. Part 4에서는 구문과 문법사항을 확인하며 술술 읽을 수 있게 꾸몄다.

3일만에 끝내는 Super 영문법

Ueda Ichizo / 4X6배판 변형 / 339면 / 9,500원

본서는 문법을 처음부터 끝까지 배우는 것이 아니라 문법의 중요사항을 엮어 단기간에 문법 전체의 핵심을 짚을 수 있도록 도와주는 기획서이다. 그리고 영작문 연습과 각종 숙어, 구문별 뉘앙스 설명으로 영어 실력을 특별히 한 단계 업그레이드시킬 수 있다.

3일만에 끝내는 Super 영작문

Hironobu Takeoka / 4×6 변형판 / 272면 / 9,500원

영작을 쉽고 빠르게 마스터할 수 있도록 구성된 영작문 기본서. 영작을 위해 꼭 필요한 58가지 법칙과 빈출패턴 67문형을 제시함으로써 영작의 기본을 다질 수 있으며 자연스럽게 영작 실력을 업그레이드 할 수 있다

영어원론

김건태 / 4×6배판 / 540면 / 25,000원

영어 독해에 어느 정도 자신이 있는 중상급 이상의 영어 학습자를 위한 기획서. 이 책은 친절하고 풍부한 해설을 담고 있으며 문장을 설명하면서 그 문장이 왜 틀렸는지 알기 쉽게 설명해준다. 부자연스러운 문장과 좋은 문장을 나란히 비교하고 차이를 설명한 것을 꾸준히 읽음으로서 조금씩 영어를 보는 안목이 넓어질 수 있도록 도와준다.

반석 영문독해 **1** 사회과학편

편집부 / 4×6배판 / 352면 / 10,000원

TOEFL, 대학원, 국가고시 등에 고정적으로 인용되는 텍스트들을 사회과학 분야(경제학 · 경제사상, 사회학 · 사회사상, 정치학 · 정치사상)별로 엄선, 체계적으로 엮었다.

반석 영문독해 **2** 인문과학편

편집부 / 4×6배판 / 348면 / 10,000원

TOEFL, 대학원, 국가고시 등에 고정적으로 인용되는 텍스트들을 인문과학 분야(문학, 문학 이론, 역사, 역사인식, 철학, 철학인식)별로 엄선하여 체계적으로 엮어놓았다.

반석 영문독해 **3** 자연과학편

편집부 / 4×6배판 / 368면 / 10,000원

TOEFL, 대학원, 국가고시 등에 고정적으로 인용되는 텍스트들을 자연과학 분야(과학기술의 현단계, 과학과 사회, 과학철학)별로 엄선, 체계적으로 구성하였다.

즉석 영단어 3000

오규상 / 국반판 / 496쪽 / 8,900원 (mp3용 CD 포함)

본서는 TOEFL, TOEIC, 공무원 시험 등 각종 시험에 출제되는 많은 어휘들 가운데 시험에 꼭 나오는 핵심어휘들만 모아 동의어, 반의어, 파생어와 함께 예문들을 엮어 놓았다. 이러한 단어만 확실히 익혀둔다면 시험에 나오는 어떤 독해지문이라도 읽어나가는데 어려움이 없을 것이다.

즉석 영숙어 900

편집부 / 국반판 / 464면 / 8,900원 (mp3용 CD 포함)

본서는 영어를 읽고 구사하는데 필요한 900개의 필수 숙어와 2,000개의 각종 시험 대비 기출 숙어로 구성되었다. 필수 숙어는 모두 Q&A의 짧은 대화로 이루어진 상황과 함께 제시되며, 토플, 토익이나 여타 시험에 자주 출제되는 문제를 수록하여 새로운 어휘를 확장할 수 있도록 편집했다.

와신상담 공무원영어 9급 (독해·어휘편)

박기혁 / 4×6배판 / 448면 / 15,000원

각종 공무원 및 공사시험을 위한 강의식 어휘 · 독해 교재. 어휘와 독해를 단번에 정복할 수 있도록 기출 유형을 철저하게 분석하였으며, 셀프체크에서 문제 해결 비법을 제시하여 문제풀이 능력을 업그레이드 할 수 있도록 했다.

와신상담 공무원영어 9급 (문법편)

박기혁 / 4×6배판 / 472면 / 15,000원

독학용 강의식 수험 영문법 교재로서 어떤 유형의 공무원 시험이라도 적용할 수 있는 기초적인 영문법을 총망라하였으며, 각종 수험 영어의 실전에 대비할 수 있도록 문법사항마다 문제풀이 비법과 영문법의 출제 원리를 체계적으로 분석한 기획서이다.

로그인 1318 영문법

윤상범 / 4×6변형판 / 328면 / 12,000원 (Tape 2개 포함)

필요없는 문법은 과감히 생략하고 수능 독해에 꼭 필요한 알짜 문법만을 구어체로 서술하였다. 반복하여 읽다보면 문장과 문법이 자연스럽게 습득되며, 각 장의 끝에 연습문제를 통해 자신의 문법과 독해실력을 평가해 볼 수 있다.

초급 Junior Vocabulary

이홍배·김덕중·서석봉 / 4×6배판 / 300면 / 8,000원

TOEFL · TOEIC을 비롯한 각종 영어시험 빈출 어휘 3,000개와 매 과마다 9가지 이상의 상이한 응용문제를 수록하였다.

중급 College Vocabulary

이홍배, 김덕중 / 4×6배판 / 494면 / 10,000원

TOEFL · TOEIC을 비롯한 각종 영어시험 빈출 어휘 5,000개를 엄선하여 수록하였고 매과 시작전에 어휘력 측정시험(Pretest)을 실시함으로써 자신의 어휘력 수준을 진단할 수 있다.

시험에 잘 나오는 영어문법

선맹수 / 4×6배판 / 508면 / 15,800원

본서는 공무원을 비롯하여 대학원, 편입, 각종 자격시험 따위에 빈출되는 TOEFL 유형을 토대로 기획 및 구성되었으며, 어떤 유형의 시험에서라도 고득점을 올릴 수 있도록 영문법의 기초적인 원리와 개념을 실전적으로 접목

아주 쉽게 배우는 영문법

최희 / 4×6배판 / 431면 / 10,000원

문법을 알기 쉽게 설명했고, 예문을 회화와 실용영어 중심으로 구성하여 '회화 · 작문 · 독해'를 처음부터 끝까지 이 책 하나로 끝낼 수 있다.

처음 시작하는 영작 기술

간series현 / 4×6배판 / 304쪽 / 9,500원

누구나 만들 수 있는 짧고 간단한 문장으로 숨이 찰 만큼 길고 복잡한 문장을 어떻게 수월하게 만들 수 있는가를 보여주고 훈련시켜 준다. 간단한 문장을 확장과 연장의 과정을 통해 자유자재로 원하는 문장을 만들 수 있는 수준까지 끌어올릴 수 있다.

즉석 기초 영작문

장승재 / 4×6배판 / 348면 / 10,000원

어렵게만 느껴졌던 영작문을 초보 학습자들도 쉽게 다가갈 수 있도록 구성한 영작문 교재. 영작을 위한 핵심 문법을 근간으로 하여 쉬운 것부터 점진적이며 반복적인 연습을 통해 영어식 사고 방식을 체득할 수 있다.

ALL ABOUT JUNIOR TOEFL [Reading]

〈ALL ABOUT JUNIOR TOEFL〉시리즈는 4섹션(Reading, Listening, Speaking, Writing), 3스텝(초, 중, 고급)으로 구성되어 있으며, 예비중학생부터 고등학생들을 대상으로 합니다. (전12권)

리딩교재는 학생들의 어휘력과 개별문장의 해석 및 문장 간의 관계와 각 단락의 중심생각을 정확하게 유추할 수 있게 구성했습니다. 학생들이 반드시 알아야 할 각 섹션별 기초스킬들에 대한 충분한 예제와 연습문제를 제공하고 있으며, 강의준비에 바쁜 강사들을 위해 모든 예제와 문제(Mini Test, Actual Test, Vocabulary Review 등)를 자세하게 설명(해석, 해설 포함)하고 있습니다.

ALL ABOUT JUNIOR TOEFL Reading [R1 : Pre-intermediate Course]
대상 : 예비중학생 ~ 중 1, 2학년
판형 : 4×6배판 / 12,000원

ALL ABOUT JUNIOR TOEFL Reading [R2 : Intermediate Course]
대상 : 중 1, 2학년 ~ 중 2, 3학년
판형 : 4×6배판 / 12,000원

ALL ABOUT JUNIOR TOEFL Reading [R3 : Advanced Course]
대상 : 중 2, 3학년 ~ 고 1, 2학년
판형 : 4×6배판 / 12,000원

〉〉〉〉〉 목 차

JUNIOR iBT TOEFL®

Answer / Script / Explanation

L₁

Bansok Junior

ALL ABOUT JUNIOR TOEFL [LISTENING]

Pre-intermediate Course

Answer / Script / Explanation

Bansok Junior

Chapter 1 Pronunciation

---

1. L / R 발음

2. (1) rim (2) rot (3) lead (4) right (5) flee (6) berry (7) jelly (8) law (9) boring (10) climb (11) walk (12) frame (13) lime (14) lift (15) rock

3. (1) Carrie was very upset when she realized that she had lost the <u>race</u>. (2) The class was surprised to learn that Ronald comes from a <u>royal</u> family. (3) The lawyer was very proud that he was able to complete the <u>crime</u>. (4) Dr. Richard Karras was <u>elected</u> during the last federal election. (5) No one really liked Larry because he always thought he was <u>right</u>.

4. When Larry <u>lived</u> in Alberta, he loved to <u>ride</u> the range. He <u>regularly</u> left early in the morning and rode until he saw the lovely <u>lake</u> on his <u>land</u>. Larry then <u>required</u> his horse, Lady, to wait while he <u>ran</u> into the lake and did several <u>laps</u>. Luckily, the weather is <u>rarely</u> rainy in <u>Alberta</u>. So Larry could ride and swim every morning. <u>Lucky</u> Larry!

2. F / P 발음

2. (1) fine (2) peel (3) open (4) fork (5) depend (6) supper (7) few (8) cheap (9) cuffs (10) pry (11) copy (12) ferry (13) past (14) fare (15) fair

3. (1) Perry had a <u>file</u> of papers on his purple desk. (2) The bus <u>fare</u> has been raised again. (3) Frank told his father that he didn't want him to <u>pry</u>. (4) The children went to the washroom to wash their hands before going to <u>supper</u>. (5) Pam was upset because the <u>coffee</u> machine was out of order again.

4. Last Friday, Fiona <u>felt</u> like going to a poppy <u>field</u> for a change of <u>pace</u>. The wind felt wonderful on her <u>face</u>, and birds <u>flew</u> by, fluffing their <u>feathers</u>. She felt like she was <u>floating</u> out on a blanket of soft clouds, but she was soon <u>pelted</u> by hailstones and her <u>frolicking</u> ended.

3. B / V 발음

2. (1) biking (2) van (3) banish (4) bet (5) vent (6) vow (7) bail (8) vest (9) base (10) balance (11) ballet (12) volley (13) buy (14) voice (15) bury

3. (1) Sally put the flower in a <u>vase</u> that her boyfriend brought for her. (2) It is difficult to keep the family and work in <u>balance</u>. (3) Dinosaurs <u>vanished</u> from the geological record about 65 million years ago. (4) I <u>bet</u> she hasn't finished her final project yet. (5) Ally invited all of

her classmates to her <u>ballet</u>.

4. Ugly Betty is my <u>favorite</u> television show <u>broadcast</u> on ABC. Betty works at a <u>publishing</u> company as an assistant to her boss Daniel. Everyone <u>believes</u> Betty is not <u>beautiful</u> and can never <u>survive</u> in the fashion industry. However, Betty is the only one <u>brilliant</u> and <u>brave</u> in the building.

4. TH 발음

2. (1) thing (2) sin (3) father (4) dare (5) doze (6) breathe (7) breeding (8) bath (9) thick (10) saw (11) moss (12) sink (13) path (14) myth (15) sigh

3. (1) The weeds in the garden were <u>breeding</u> like rabbits. (2) Roy G. Mathers is often <u>sued</u> by his clients. (3) I <u>thought</u> you'd come to my birthday party. (4) Professor Smith did not believe Thomas' essay to be <u>worthy</u>. (5) <u>Moth</u> is considered a harmful pest in many areas in the world.

4. Three <u>thieves</u> were sleeping under a tree when <u>they</u> woke to the sound of <u>thunder</u>. One of the thugs said that he <u>thought</u> the weather was changing and it would soon rain. The other two were <u>lethargic</u> and didn't want to move. Rather than wait for his companions, the first thief left the other two <u>thugs</u>. He decided it was not <u>worth</u> getting wet in the <u>weather</u>. And off he went.

5. [æ]와 [e] 발음

2. (1) than (2) bat (3) mat (4) blend (5) guess (6) ladder (7) pet (8) peck (9) past (10) dad (11) mad (12) pen (13) mess (14) last (15) den

3. (1) The girls <u>set</u> their purses down on the table. (2) Rachel bought a <u>pet</u> from the store for her grandmother. (3) When Max saw the woman, he <u>left</u>. (4) I was <u>sending</u> an email when my dad arrived. (5) Many farmers have used agrochemicals to control <u>pest</u> populations.

4. Pat was so <u>fat</u> that she made a <u>bet</u> with Lenny the <u>vet</u>. She bet him that she could get a fat <u>cat</u> and a wet <u>rat</u> under her hat. Unfortunately, the fat cat was not Fat Pat's <u>pet</u>, and it sat on the rat. The rat naturally ran away. Poor Fat Pat. She lost her <u>bet</u>.

Chapter 2 Rhythm

1. Contraction 단축

1. (1) <u>Isn't</u> it on sale? (2) I <u>haven't</u> seen you in ages. (3) I <u>can't</u> find my jacket in the closet. (4) <u>You'd</u> better get going now. (5) <u>Weren't</u> you there at the party last night? (6) <u>I've</u> had it with her. (7) <u>Won't</u> it be necessary to bring an umbrella?

2. (1) I'll <u>have</u> <u>him</u> <u>take</u> <u>it</u> back to the garage. (2) <u>Don't</u> <u>you</u> like the spaghetti? (3) <u>I'd</u> <u>like</u> <u>to</u> charge that to my credit card. (4) I <u>could've</u> <u>won</u> the competition. (5) That's <u>out</u> <u>of</u> <u>my</u> price range. (6) We'll give you a full refund <u>if</u> <u>you</u> <u>have</u> <u>a</u> receipt. (7) I <u>should've</u> <u>kept</u> <u>him</u> here all day.

2. Liaison 연음

1. (1) The light is <u>out</u>. (2) Look <u>at</u> you! (3) I'll pick it <u>up</u> at a flower shop. (4) I'll catch <u>up</u> with you later! (5) Seth ignored my request to send <u>in</u> his report. (6) Serena was called <u>upon</u> to make a speech. (7) You need to know how to put <u>out</u> a fire.

2. (1) <u>One</u> <u>of</u> <u>her</u> sons is a lawyer. (2) The pen is <u>right</u> <u>in</u> <u>front</u> <u>of</u> you. (3) What <u>kind</u> <u>of</u> salad would you like with your soup? (4) She made <u>a</u> <u>lot</u> <u>of</u> money last year. (5) I <u>made</u> <u>up</u> <u>with</u> her. (6) You can <u>ask</u> <u>him</u> about our project. (7) I can't <u>put</u> <u>up</u> <u>with</u> him anymore.

3. Word Stress 단어 강세

1. (1) <u>key</u>board (2) per<u>mit</u> (3) <u>black</u>board (4) take <u>out</u> (5) <u>water</u> tank (6) <u>per</u>mit (7) <u>tax</u> return (8) <u>pre</u>sent (9) <u>application</u> form (10) <u>sports</u> car (11) <u>sales</u> promotion (12) pre<u>sent</u> (13) <u>re</u>ference (14) <u>complicated</u> (15) <u>telecommunications</u> industry

2. (1) <u>body</u> language (2) <u>solar</u> system (3) <u>information</u> desk (4) <u>application</u> form (5) greenhouse <u>effect</u> (6) heart <u>attack</u> (7) daughter in <u>law</u> (8) <u>death</u> penalty (9) <u>profit</u> margin (10) <u>identification</u> card (11) food <u>poisoning</u> (12) generation <u>gap</u> (13) <u>fairy</u> tale (14) <u>junk</u> food (15) mineral <u>water</u>

4. Sentence Stress 문장 강세

1. (1) <u>Freedom</u> is a <u>system</u> based on <u>courage</u>. (2) The <u>sad</u> <u>dog</u> <u>walks</u> <u>slowly</u> to his <u>house</u>. (3) <u>Body</u> <u>functioning</u> can be <u>affected</u> by an <u>imbalance</u> of <u>nutrients</u> in the <u>diet</u>. (4) (4) I'm <u>taking</u> a <u>Spanish</u> <u>class</u> for my <u>business</u> <u>trip</u> to <u>Spain</u>. (5) I have a <u>craving</u> for <u>chocolate</u> <u>cake</u>. (6) <u>Poor</u> <u>school</u> <u>attendance</u> is <u>linked</u> to <u>low</u> <u>academic</u> <u>standing</u>. (7) <u>Youth</u> <u>clubs</u> <u>provide</u> <u>teenagers</u> with <u>opportunities</u> for <u>social</u> <u>interaction</u>.

2. (1) Many people don't listen to <u>politics</u> and <u>law-making</u>. (2) <u>Talking</u> and <u>forgiveness</u> end <u>conflicts</u> between friends. (3) Shopping at a <u>department</u> <u>store</u> is <u>convenient</u> and <u>efficient</u>. (4) Many of the <u>students</u> didn't <u>show</u> <u>up</u> yesterday. (5) <u>Right</u> <u>after</u> I graduated, I got a job at a law firm. (6) A fierce <u>debate</u> has been sparked over the issue of human <u>reproductive</u> <u>cloning</u>. (7) Korea has a rich artistic <u>tradition</u> that goes back <u>thousands</u> of years.

5. Pause 끊어 읽기

1. (1) I'll go and check / what's wrong. (2) I don't know / whether it will rain or not. (3) I stayed up all night / studying / so that I could get good results. (4) There are neither books / nor magazines / in the library. (5) Heaven helps those / who help themselves. (6) All of my classmates / like Ms. Claire / who is kind and generous. (7) Because of the heavy snow, / many people / couldn't get to the work.

2. (1) I'll tell you <u>how</u> <u>I</u> <u>met</u> your mother. (2) <u>If</u> <u>I</u> <u>were</u> <u>you</u>, I would not believe what he says. (3) Mikaela needed a friend <u>to</u> <u>whom</u> she could talk. (4) Do you know <u>how</u> <u>much</u> I love you? (5) <u>Making</u> <u>a</u> <u>budget</u> is not something you can learn at school. (6) <u>Be</u> <u>sure</u> <u>to</u> <u>hire</u> <u>one</u> that is prepared when hiring a lawyer. (7) Professor Kim wants to know <u>why</u> <u>you</u> <u>were</u> <u>absent</u> last week.

Chapter 3 Main Idea

Office Hours

1. (D) **2.** (B)

---

1. 남자는 왜 교수를 만나러 가는가?
  (A) 그는 일본어 공부를 고려중이다.
  (B) 그는 전공에 관해 조언을 받길 원한다.
  (C) 그는 외국으로 유학을 갈 계획이다.
  (D) 그는 어떤 언어를 공부해야 할지 정하지 못했다.

W: Come on in. What can I help you with?
M: Well, you're the head of the foreign language department, and I need some advice. I'm not sure which language to take for my elective.
W: Which ones are you most interested in?
M: I'm thinking about the big three — French, Spanish, and Chinese. I think they would be the most useful.
W: Don't let the Japanese professor hear you say that! I understand your point, though. What's your major?
M: Economics, and I want to get an MBA.
W: If you're interested in business, then you ought to consider Chinese. China has become an economic superpower, and the language will give you a big advantage.
M: I hadn't thought of it that way — thanks!

여: 어서 오렴. 무엇을 도와줄까?
남: 음, 교수님이 외국어학부 학장님이시잖아요. 그래서 조언 좀 구하려고요. 선택 과목으로 어떤 외국어 강의를 들어야 할지 잘 모르겠어요.
여: 어떤 언어에 가장 관심이 있니?
남: 가장 많이 배우는 프랑스어와 스페인어, 중국어 중에서 하나를 배울까 생각 중이에요. 이 3가지가 가장 유용할 것 같아요.
여: 일본어 교수님이 들으시면 서운해 하시겠구나! 하지만, 무슨 말을 하는지 잘 알겠다. 전공은 무엇이니?
남: 경제학인데요, MBA 학위도 따고 싶어요.
여: 네가 비즈니스에 관심이 있다면, 중국어를 한 번 고려해보도록 하렴. 중국이 경제대국으로 부상하고 있어서, 중국어를 배워두면 이점이 많을 거야.
남: 그런 식으로는 생각해본 적이 없었어요. 감사합니다!

어휘 | head 장 | advice 조언 | elective 선택 과목 | major 전공 | superpower 초강대국 |
advantage 이점

2. 여자는 왜 남자와 이야기하고 있는가?

   (A) 남자의 성적이 너무 낮다.

   (B) 남자가 항상 수업에 지각한다.

   (C) 남자가 Catherine 교수의 수업에 관해 불평하고 있다.

   (D) 다른 강의로 옮기고 싶어 한다.

W: We need to talk about why you're always late for class. What's the problem?

M: I'm so sorry. I work at the hospital in the afternoon, and I come straight to school afterward. Sometimes traffic is terrible ...

W: I understand, but I can't let you come to class late every day. You know it will affect your grade?

M: I know that, but ....

W: Well, it seems that you need to either change your work hours or take another class. Dr. Catherine's class starts an hour later than mine. We're using the same textbook, and we've covered the same topics, so maybe you could transfer.

M: But your class is so much more interesting!

W: Thanks, but it won't help your grade. If you arrive on time for Dr. Catherine's class for the rest of the semester, you might get a better grade.

M: I see. I guess I should take her class, then.

여: 네가 항상 수업에 늦는 이유에 관해 이야기 좀 해보자. 대체 무슨 문제니?

남: 정말 죄송해요. 제가 오후에 병원에서 일하고, 바로 학교로 오거든요. 가끔 길이 너무 막혀서요.....

여: 이해는 하지만, 매일 수업에 지각하도록 내버려 둘 수는 없단다. 성적에 영향을 준다는 것은 알고 있지?

남: 알고는 있지만요.......

여: 음, 네가 일하는 시간을 바꾸거나 다른 수업을 들어야 할 것 같구나. Catherine 교수의 수업이 내 수업보다 한 시간 늦게 시작해. 수업 교재도 같고 똑같은 주제를 다루었으니까, 아마 그 쪽으로 옮길 수 있을 거야.

남: 하지만 교수님 수업이 훨씬 더 재미있는 걸요!

여: 고맙구나, 하지만 네 점수에는 별 도움이 되지 않을 거야. 남은 학기 동안 Catherine 교수의 수업에 지각하지 않으면, 더 나은 점수를 받을 수 있을 거란다.

남: 알겠습니다. 그 분 수업을 들어야겠네요.

어휘ㅣ traffic 교통 ㅣ affect 영향을 끼치다 ㅣ cover 다루다 ㅣ transfer 옮기다 ㅣ semester 학기

Service Encounters

1. (A)   **2.** (D)

---

1. 남자는 왜 여자와 이야기하고 있는가?

   (A) 그는 신입생 오리엔테이션에 참석하지 못했다.

   (B) 그는 도서관에 가는 방법을 알기를 원한다.

(C) 그는 캠퍼스에 늦게 도착했다.
(D) 그는 여자에게 컴퓨터 설치를 요청한다.

W: Hi, can I help you?
M: Yes, I wanted to ask about freshman orientation. I couldn't make it that day. In fact, I only arrived on campus yesterday afternoon. I still have a few boxes to unpack.
W: It's all right. Don't worry about it.
M: I thought orientation was required for all freshmen?
W: No, it's not. Many students live far away, and it's not convenient to come to campus a few days early.
M: Then, can I find the information somewhere else?
W: Well, the student handbook is available online. If you don't have your own computer, or it's not set up yet, why not stop by the computer lab in the library?
M: That's a great idea, thanks!
W: You're welcome, and if you have more questions, you can come ask me.

여: 안녕하세요, 무엇을 도와드릴까요?
남: 네, 신입생 오리엔테이션에 대해 여쭤보려고요. 그 날 참석하지 못했어요. 사실 어제 오후에나 캠퍼스에 도착했거든요. 아직 풀어야 할 짐도 더 있고요.
여: 괜찮아요. 걱정 말아요.
남: 전 모든 신입생이 오리엔테이션에 꼭 참석해야 하는 줄 알았는데요?
여: 아니에요. 많은 학생들이 멀리 떨어진 곳에 살고, 며칠 앞당겨 학교에 오는 것이 좀 불편한 일이죠.
남: 그럼 다른 곳에서 정보를 얻을 수 있을까요?
여: 음, 온라인으로 학생 편람을 볼 수 있어요. 개인 컴퓨터가 없거나 아직 설치가 안 되어 있으면, 도서관에 있는 컴퓨터실에 가보는 것이 어때요?
남: 정말 좋은 생각이네요, 감사합니다!
여: 네, 질문이 더 생각나면, 다시 와서 물어보세요.

어휘 I freshman 신입생 I unpack 짐을 풀다 I convenient 편리한 I handbook 편람 I set up 설치하다

2. 여자는 무슨 문제를 가지고 있는가?
(A) 여자는 직접 다른 대학 도서관에 갈 수 없다.
(B) 여자가 찾고 있는 책을 월요일에 예약해 둘 수 없다.
(C) 여자는 리포트 주제를 아직 정하지 못했다.
(D) 여자가 필요로 하는 책이 도서관에 없다.

W: Excuse me. Can you help me find a book?
M: Sure, what are you looking for?
W: It is called *History of Serbia*. The online catalog says it's checked out.
M: Just one moment, let me double-check... that's right, and it's due in two weeks. Another student checked it out yesterday.
W: Oh, no! I have a paper due on Monday. What should I do?
M: Well, it's available at two other universities nearby. I can get a copy from one of them.

어휘 | check out 대출하다 | reserve 예약해두다

Lectures

1. 1) (C)   2) (B)   **2.** 1) (A)   2) (D)

---

1. 1. 교수는 주로 무엇에 관해 이야기 하고 있는가?
  (A) 현대 사회에서는 한 사람이 많은 다른 역할을 가지고 있다.
  (B) 역할 갈등에 대한 꼭 맞는 해결책을 찾는 것이 쉽지 않다.
  (C) 한 사람이 가지고 있는 다양한 역할이 갈등을 일으킨다.
  (D) 역할 갈등은 높은 사고율과 관련이 있다.

2. 다음 중 어느 것이 사회적 역할의 예가 아닌가?
  (A) 개인의 직업
  (B) 개인의 거주지
  (C) 개인의 성
  (D) 개인의 가족 관계

understand our roles clearly. We know what to do in different situations. Besides, we know what to expect from other people. Sometimes, though, roles come into conflict with each other. This is natural when you think about how many roles each person might have. For example, imagine you are a police officer. People expect you to be very strict and honest about upholding the law. And you expect that of yourself. However, what if your son or daughter breaks the law? Like drinking under age? Will you arrest him or her? In cases of role conflict, three solutions have been identified: choosing among roles, finding a compromise, or removing yourself from the situation altogether.

P: 오늘은 역할 갈등에 관해 강의를 할 건데, 시작하기 전에 역할이라는 개념을 다시 한 번 짚어보고 넘어가죠. 모든 사회에서, 사람들은 역할들을 가지고 있어요. 여러분의 역할은 인생에서 여러분이 차지하는 위치나 직분과 같은 것이죠. 직업이 될 수도 있고, 가족과의 관계일 수도 있고, 학생이라는 신분일 수도 있죠. 개인이 갖게 되는 가능한 역할은 아주 많아요. 각 역할에는 그만의 권리와 의무, 기대와 행동 양식이 뒤따르죠. 대개, 우리는 우리의 역할을 잘 이해하고 있어요. 다른 상황에서 무엇을 해야 하는지 알고 있죠. 그리고 다른 사람들에게서 무엇을 기대해야 하는지도 알고 있고요. 하지만, 때로 다양한 역할들은 서로 갈등을 일으키게 됩니다. 한 사람이 얼마나 많은 역할을 가지고 있는가를 생각하면 이는 당연한 일이죠. 예를 들어, 여러분이 경찰관이라고 생각해보세요. 사람들은 여러분이 법을 지키는데 있어 매우 엄격하고 정직하기를 기대하죠. 물론 여러분 스스로도 그러한 점을 기대하고요. 하지만, 여러분의 자녀가 법을 위반한다면 어떨까요? 가령 미성년 음주 같은 것? 여러분은 여러분의 자녀를 체포하겠어요? 역할 갈등이 일어나는 경우에, 세 가지 해결방법이 있어요. 역할 중에 하나를 선택하든가, 절충점을 찾거나, 아니면 그 상황에서 완전히 빠지는 것이죠.

어휘 | assign 할당하다 | status 신분, 상태 | right 권리 | responsibility 책임 | expectation 기대 | uphold 지키다 | under age 미성년의 | arrest 체포하다 | compromise 타협, 절충점

2. 1. 강의의 주제는 무엇인가?
(A) 북부 지역에서 많이 찾아볼 수 있는 호수 지형
(B) 열카르스트가 어떻게 그러한 이름을 갖게 되었는가.
(C) 해빙 호수가 형성되는 원인
(D) 영구 동토층이 녹고 있는 현재의 추세

2. 다음 중 어느 것이 해빙 호수에 관해 맞지 않는가?
(A) 히말라야 산맥과 알프스 산맥에서 발견된다.
(B) 보통 수심이 깊지 않다.
(C) 지구 온도 상승이 호수 형성의 원인이다.
(D) 염분이 많이 함유되어 있는 편이다.

P: The landscape of northern Alaska is dominated by a feature known as thermokarst, which refers to marshy areas of melted permafrost. This type of land somewhat resembles the limestone formations known as karst, which is where the name comes from. When the ice in permafrost melts, the runoff water forms lakes, which are more commonly known as thaw lakes. These lakes are usually shallow. The water in them is fresh, not salty.

But, Alaska is not the only place in the world where thaw lakes are found, although they are quite prevalent there. In fact, some 75% of the northern Barrow Peninsula is covered with thermokarsitic lakes. They can also be found in Siberia, the Arctic regions of Canada, and in high mountain areas like the Himalayas and the Swiss Alps. Obviously these including their drainage basins are an important feature in northern biomes.

Well, many of you might wonder why these thaw lakes form. Apparently, global warming is one of the major causes for them and the ecosystems they are a part of. In recent years, as temperatures in the Arctic have been rising, more of these lakes form. Permafrost has been melting, so less water exists as ice in these regions. These areas will become more arid as the frozen water is lost to runoff and evaporation.

P: 알래스카(Alaska) 북부에서는 열카르스트라는 지형이 광범위하게 존재하는데, 이는 영구 동토층이 녹아서 형성된 습지에요. 이런 지형은 카르스트라고 불리는 석회암 대지와 약간 비슷해요. 그래서 그런 이름이 붙은 것이죠. 영구 동토층의 얼음이 녹을 때, 배수되는 물이 호수를 만드는데, 이런 호수는 흔히 해빙 호수라고 알려져 있어요. 이 해빙 호수는 대개 물이 깊지 않아요. 호수 물은 염분이 없는 담수죠.

하지만, 알래스카에 이런 해빙 호수가 많이 있기는 해도, 알래스카에서만 발견되는 것은 아닙니다. 사실, Barrow 반도 북부의 75% 정도가 열카르스트 호수로 덮여 있어요. 또한 시베리아와 캐나다 북극 지역, 히말라야와 알프스 같은 높은 산악 지대에서도 발견되죠. 배수지를 포함한 이 열카르스트 지형은 북부 생물 군계에서 중요한 지형임에 틀림없습니다.

여러분 중 상당수가 왜 이런 해빙 호수가 만들어지는지 궁금해 할 겁니다. 지구 온난화가 해빙 호수와 이러한 호수가 속해 있는 생태계를 형성시킨 주요 원인 중 하나라는 것은 분명해요. 최근 북극의 온도가 계속 오르면서, 해빙 호수가 더 많이 만들어지고 있어요. 영구 동토층이 녹아서 이 지역에는 얼음의 형태로 존재하는 물이 적어지는 것이죠. 이 지역들은 얼어있던 물이 녹아서 흐르고 증발되어 사라지기 때문에 점점 더 건조해지겠죠.

어휘 | feature 지형 | marshy 늪의, 습지의 | permafrost 영구 동토층 | resemble 닮다 | limestone 석회석 | runoff 흐르는 물 | shallow 얕은 | salty 염분이 있는 | prevalent 우세한 | drainage basin 배수지 | ecosystem 생태계 | arid 건조한 | evaporation 증발

Practice

1. (D)   **2.** (B)   **3.** (A)   **4.** Suggested - (A), (D) Not Suggested - (B), (C), (E)   **5.** (C)   **6.** (C)
7. (C)   **8.** (D)   **9.** Yes - (A), (B), (D) NO - (C), (E)   **10.** (D)   **11.** (A)

[문제 1~5] 학생과 학적과 직원 사이의 대화의 일부를 들으시오.

1. 학생은 왜 학적과 직원을 찾아가는가?

(A) 남자는 등록금을 내는데 재정적인 문제가 있다.
(B) 남자는 이 학교로 편입하기를 원한다.
(C) 남자는 수강 과목을 철회하기를 원한다.
(D) 남자는 예전 학교에서 서류를 받지 못했다.

해설ㅣ 학생은 다른 학교에서 편입한 학생인데, 전에 다니던 학교 직원이 학적부 송부 요청서를 잃어버려서 현재 학교에서 신분 확인도 제대로 이루어지지 않고 있으며, 수강 신청도 못하고, 등록금 납부도 원활하지 못한 상황이다. 학생이 학적과 직원을 찾아간 이유는 예전 학교에서 서류를 받지 못했다는 것을 알리고 도움을 받기 위해서이다. 정답은 보기 (D).

2. 학생의 예전 학교에 관해 추론할 수 있는 것은 무엇인가?
(A) 남자의 집에서 멀다.
(B) 학교 크기 때문에 효율적이지 못하다.
(C) 매우 비싸다.
(D) 어려운 과목이 많다.

해설ㅣ 학생의 말에 따르면, 학생이 전에 다니던 학교는 규모가 너무 커서 일 처리가 상당히 느리다고 하였다. 이를 통해 학교 크기 때문에 효율적이지 못할 것임을 추론할 수 있다. 따라서 정답은 보기 (B).

3. 학생은 왜 상급 과목을 수강할 수 없는가?
(A) 남자의 교수가 그가 전에 기초 과목을 들었는지 확인하고 싶어한다.
(B) 남자는 이 과목들이 공부하기가 상당히 어렵다고 생각한다.
(C) 이 과목들의 수강 신청 기한이 지났다.
(D) 이 과목들은 아침에 너무 일찍 시작한다.

해설ㅣ 학생은 이미 필수 기본 과목을 들었는데, 학적부가 없어서 교수가 그 과목을 들었는지 확인을 못하고 있다. 교수가 확인하기 전까지는 상급 과목을 수강할 수가 없다. 정답은 보기 (A).

4. 대화에서, 여자는 남자의 문제를 해결하는데 도움이 될 여러 아이디어를 제시하고 있다. 아래 표의 각 보기가 여자가 제시한 아이디어에 속하는지 표시하시오. 각 보기에 맞는 칸에 클릭하시오.

	Suggested	Not Suggested
(A) 학생의 예전 학교의 학적과 직원에게 전화를 하기	∨	
(B) 학생의 예전 학교의 학적과 직원에게 이메일 보내기		∨
(C) 학생이 상급 강의를 들을 수 있도록 허용하기		∨
(D) 학생의 예전 학교에 학적부를 팩스로 보내달라고 요청하기	∨	
(E) 학생이 등록금을 내지 않고 강의를 들을 수 있도록 허락하기		∨

해설ㅣ 직원은 학생의 상황을 듣고, 우선 학생이 전에 다니던 학교의 학적과에 전화를 걸어보겠다고 했다. 그리고 학생 기록을 팩스나 이메일로 보내달라고 요청할 것이라 했다. 정답은 보기 (A), (D).

대화의 일부를 다시 들으시오. 그러고 나서 질문에 답하시오.
  여: 전에도 다른 학생들에게 이런 일이 있었어요. 학적과 직원에게 학생의 기록을 팩스나 이메일로 바로 보내달라고 할게요. 제가 그 기록을 받으면, 학생의 학과장님께 보내줄게요.

남: 그럼 등록금 납부 마감일 이전에 모든 일이 처리되는 거겠죠?

5. 여자가 이것을 말할 때 암시하는 것은 무엇인가 :
여: 전에도 다른 학생들에게 이런 일이 있었어요.

(A) 남자는 스스로 문제를 해결해야 한다.
(B) 남자의 문제는 정말 짜증나는 일이다.
(C) 어렵지만, 남자의 문제는 해결될 수 있다.
(D) 남자는 다른 학생들과 이야기 해봐야 한다.

해설 | 전에도 다른 학생들에게 이런 일이 있었다는 말은 학생을 안심시키기 위해 하는 말이며, 문제가 해결될 수 있음을 암시한다. 정답은 보기 (C).

[Questions 1~5] Listen to part of a conversation between a student and a registrar.

W: Good afternoon. Can I help you?
M: Well, Hi, I'm a transfer student, and this is my first semester here. I just arrived on Monday. I'm a little worried, because the registrar at my old university lost the request to transfer my records. This university doesn't know who I am. Classes start next week, and I'm not sure I'll be able to get the ones I want. Paying tuition on time also might be a problem.
W: I see. How can I help you?
M: Well, I guess it will take a long time to resolve this problem. My old university is very large, and sometimes things there happen very slowly. If my class schedule here is messed up this semester, I will need time to sort it out. But tuition is due next week...
W: So you need time to get your records from your old university?
M: Right, and I need time to set up my class schedule here. Once all that is done, then I can pay the tuition. The head of my major department wants me to take some required basic courses. I've already taken them, but he can't let me register for more advanced courses without seeing those records.
W: That is a messy situation, isn't it?
M: Yes, it is. I'm very frustrated.
W: All right. I think I can help. This is what we need to do. First, I will call the registrar at your old university. Let's do that now.
M: That's great!
W: Well, this has happened to other students before, too. I will ask the registrar to fax me your records, or e-mail them, right away. Once I have them, I will forward them to the head of your department.
M: So I should have everything before the tuition is due?
W: Yes, I think so. If your old university is too slow, then we'll find another solution next week.
M: That's so helpful. Thank you!

Now get ready to answer the questions. You may use your notes to help you answer.

Q. 5 Listen again to part of the conversation. Then answer the question.

W: Well, this has happened to other students before, too. I will ask the registrar to fax me your records, or e-mail them, right away. Once I have them, I will forward them to the head of your department.
M: So I should have everything before the tuition is due?

What does the woman imply when she says this :
W: Well, this has happened to other students before, too.

여: 안녕하세요. 무엇을 도와 드릴까요?
남: 아, 안녕하세요. 저는 편입생인데요, 이번이 제 첫 학기입니다. 월요일에 막 도착했어요. 제가 전에 다니던 학교의 학적과 직원이 제 학적부를 보내달라는 요청서를 잃어버려서 좀 걱정이 되네요. 이 학교에서 제가 누군지도 모르게 됐거든요. 다음 주에 수업이 시작되는데, 제가 원하던 수업을 들을 수 있을지 모르겠어요. 등록금을 제때 내는 것도 문제가 될 것 같고요.
여: 그렇군요. 그럼 제가 어떻게 도와드릴까요?
남: 제 생각엔 이 문제를 해결하는데 시간이 좀 걸릴 것 같아요. 이전 학교는 너무 커서 가끔 일 처리 가 매우 느리거든요. 이번 학기에 강의 스케줄이 엉망이 되면, 그걸 정리하는데 시간이 필요할 것 같아요. 그런데 등록금 납부 마감도 다음 주라....
여: 그럼 학생의 이전 학교에서 학적부를 전해 받을 시간이 필요하다는 것이죠?
남: 네, 그리고 이 학교의 강의 스케줄을 짜는데도 시간이 필요합니다. 그런 것들이 다 해결되면, 그 때 등록금을 납부할 수 있을 것 같군요. 전공 학과장님께서 저에게 필수 기본 과목을 수강하라고 하셨 어요. 벌써 그 과목들을 들었지만, 학과장님이 제 학적부를 보시기 전에는 제가 상급 과목을 수강 하도록 해주시지 않을 거예요.
여: 일이 참 복잡하게 되었군요.
남: 네. 정말 힘들어요.
여: 알겠어요. 도움을 줄 수 있을 것 같아요. 이렇게 하도록 하죠. 먼저, 학생의 예전 학교의 학적과 직 원에게 전화를 해볼게요. 지금 바로 하도록 하죠.
남: 좋습니다.
여: 전에도 다른 학생들에게 이런 일이 있었어요. 학적과 직원에게 학생의 기록을 팩스나 이메일로 바 로 보내달라고 할게요. 제가 그 기록을 받으면, 학생의 학과장님께 보내줄게요.
남: 그럼 등록금 납부 마감일 이전에 모든 일이 처리되는 거겠죠?
여: 네, 그렇게 될 거예요. 예전 학교에서 일 처리가 늦어지면, 다음 주에 다른 방법을 강구해보도록 하죠.
남: 정말 큰 도움이 되었네요. 감사합니다!

어휘 | registrar 학적 담당 사무원 | request 요청(서) | resolve 해결하다 | mess up 망쳐 놓다 | required 필수 교과목의

[문제 6~11] 심리학 강의의 일부를 들으시오.

6. 강의는 주로 무엇에 관한 내용인가?
 (A) 즐거운 감정을 유발하는 방법
 (B) 누군가의 도움을 고맙게 여기는 행위
 (C) 긍정적인 보상
 (D) 부정적 강화

해설 Ⅰ 오늘 강의의 주제는 원하는 행동을 증대시키는 방법인 적극적 강화 또는 긍정적 강화이다. 강의 첫 머리에 주제가 언급되어 있다. 정답은 보기 (C).

강의의 일부를 다시 들으시오. 그러고 나서 질문에 답하시오.
누군가 당신에게 호의를 베풀어주면, 여러분은 나중에 그들에게 그 호의를 다시 갚아주어야 하는데, 이 이야기는 오늘 강의 내용과는 약간 벗어나는 내용이네요.

7. 교수가 이것을 말할 때 의미하는 것은 무엇인가 : 🎧
이 이야기는 오늘 강의 내용과는 약간 벗어나는 내용이네요.

 (A) 교수는 수업 마지막에 다시 그것에 대해 언급할 것이다.
 (B) 교수는 그것이 전혀 논의할 가치가 없다고 생각한다.
 (C) 교수는 그것에 관해 말하지 않을 것이다.
 (D) 교수는 다음번에 그것에 대해 언급할 것이다.

해설 Ⅰ 오늘 강의 내용과는 벗어난다는 얘기는 주제와 상관 없기 때문에 더 이상 그것에 대해 얘기하지 않을 것임을 나타낸다. 정답은 보기 (C).

강의의 일부를 다시 들으시오. 그러고 나서 질문에 답하시오.
누군가 여러분에게 호의를 베풀면, 여러분은 어떻게 하나요? 고마워하죠. '고맙습니다'라고 단순히 말하는 것도 적극적 강화의 한 형태입니다. 매우 작고, 간단한 강화의 형태이지만, 매우 강력하죠.

8. 교수가 이것을 말할 때 의미하는 것은 무엇인가 : 🎧
매우 작고, 간단한 강화의 형태이지만, 매우 강력하죠.

 (A) 사람들은 가족으로부터 칭찬 받고 싶어한다.
 (B) 모든 사회에는 고마움을 표시하는 방식이 있다.
 (C) 사람들은 다른 사람들에게 도움을 주는 것을 좋아한다.
 (D) 단순한 보상이 매우 효과적일 수 있다.

해설 Ⅰ 단순히 '고맙습니다'라고 말하는 것도 적극적 강화의 한 형태라고 하였는데, 상대방에게 고마움을 표시하는 단순한 보상 행위가 매우 큰 효과를 낼 수 있다는 것을 의미한다. 정답은 보기 (D).

9. 강의에서, 교수는 긍정적인 보상에 관해 이야기 하고 있다. 아래 표의 각 보기가 이런 보상에 포함되는지 표시하시오. 각 보기에 맞는 칸에 클릭하시오.

	Yes	No
(A) 참 잘했어요!	V	
(B) 고맙습니다.	V	
(C) 그래서 뭐요?		V
(D) 정말 친절하시네요.	V	
(E) 당신 일이나 잘하세요.		V

해설 l 고마움을 표시하는 행위, 잘했다고 칭찬해주는 행위 등이 긍정적 보상에 해당한다. 이에 해당하는 보기는 (A), (B), (D).

10. 다음 중 어느 것이 1차 보상의 예가 아닌가?
    (A) 물
    (B) 주거
    (C) 음식
    (D) 웃음

해설 l 미소를 지어 보이는 것, 즉 웃는 행위는 2차 보상에 해당한다. 정답은 보기 (D).

강의의 일부를 다시 들으시오. 그러고 나서 질문에 답하시오.
무언가를 보상과 교환할 때, 가장 먼저 생각나는 것은 무엇인가요? 그렇죠, 바로 돈이죠. .

11. 교수가 이것을 말할 때 암시하는 것은 무엇인가 :
그렇죠, 바로 돈이죠.

    (A) 돈은 가장 강력한 2차 보상일지도 모른다.
    (B) 돈은 더 고상하게 사용되어야 한다.
    (C) 돈은 1차 보상에 대해서만 유익하기 때문에 가치가 적다.
    (D) 돈은 전세계 모든 사회에 존재한다.

해설 l 무언가를 보상과 교환할 때 가장 먼저 떠오르는 것이 무엇이냐고 묻고 나서 답을 두 번 생각할 것도 없이 돈이라는 듯한 말투로 이야기 하고 있다. 그만큼 돈이 강력하고 효과적이라는 의미다. 따라서 정답은 보기 (A).

[Questions 6~11] Listen to part of a lecture in a psychology class.

P(M): All right, students, today we're going to be talking about reinforcement. First, we'll focus on ways to increase a desired behavior. Tomorrow, we'll talk about ways to decrease negative behavior.
When someone does a favor for you, what do you do? You thank them. Just saying 'thank you' is a form of positive reinforcement. It's a very small, simple reinforcement, but it's also very powerful. Do you know why? Because our society has put a certain positive value on the act of thanking someone. When someone thanks us, we know we have done a good job. We have done something well, or helped the other person, or

whatever. If someone has done you a favor, you may also owe them a favor sometime later, but that's a little off the point of today's lecture. The important thing to remember is that desired behavior may be repeated or increased by giving these positive rewards.

When we talk about rewards, we need to think of them in several categories. A reward may be that positive value I was just discussing. Standard phrases like 'thank you' and 'good job' are very common rewards when people interact with each other. There are other categories of reward, though. Primary rewards are the ones that are important to life and bodily functions: things like food and water. Some psychologists believe shelter is also a primary reward. Does that mean you give someone a house for doing you a favor? Maybe, if you're very rich! Secondary rewards get their value from the primary reward — which is another way of saying they may be exchanged for primary rewards. When you exchange something for a reward, what's the first thing you think of? Money, of course. But there are more subtle secondary rewards, as well. Pleasant touch can be a secondary reward, and so can a smile.

The purpose of a reward is to modify behavior, to cause positive emotions, and to cause learning to happen. In other words, when we receive a reward, we learn that if we like it, we should continue whatever we were doing. This can happen on both the conscious and the subconscious levels. We meet a positive stimulus — which is the reward — and we want more of it. In time, we may continue the desired behavior without even consciously thinking about it.

Now get ready to answer the questions. You may use your notes to help you answer.

Q. 7 Listen again to part of the conversation. Then answer the question.

If someone has done you a favor, you may also owe them a favor sometime later, but that's a little off the point of today's lecture.

What does the professor mean when he says this :
but that's a little off the point of today's lecture.

Q. 8 Listen again to part of the conversation. Then answer the question.

When someone does a favor for you, what do you do? You thank them. Just saying 'thank you' is a form of positive reinforcement. It's a very small, simple reinforcement, but it's also very powerful.

What does the professor mean when he says this :
It's a very small, simple reinforcement, but it's also very powerful.

Q. 11 Listen again to part of the conversation. Then answer the question.
When you exchange something for a reward, what's the first thing you think of? Money, of course.

What does the professor imply when he says this :
Money, of course.

P: 좋아요, 여러분, 오늘은 강화에 관해 이야기 해보겠어요. 먼저, 원하는 행동을 증대 시키는 방법에 관해 이야기 해보겠어요. 내일은 부정적인 행동을 감소시키는 방법에 관해 이야기 하도록 하죠. 누군가 여러분에게 호의를 베풀면, 여러분은 어떻게 하나요? 고마워하죠. '고맙습니다' 라고 단순히 말하는 것도 적극적 강화의 한 형태입니다. 매우 작고, 간단한 강화의 형태이지만, 매우 강력하죠. 그 이유를 아나요? 바로 우리 사회가 누군가에게 고마움을 표시하는 행위에 긍정적인 가치를 부여 하기 때문이죠. 누군가 우리에게 고맙다고 하면, 우리는 우리가 좋은 일을 했다는 것을 알게 됩니다. 일을 잘 했거나, 다른 사람을 도왔거나, 그러한 것들 말이죠. 누군가 여러분에게 호의를 베풀어 주면, 여러분은 나중에 그들에게 그 호의를 다시 갚아주어야 하는데, 이 이야기는 오늘 강의 내용과는 약간 벗어나는 내용이네요. 여기서 기억해야 할 것은 이렇게 긍정적인 보상을 제공함으로써 원하는 결과가 반복되거나 증대된다는 것이에요.

우리가 보상에 관해 이야기 할 때는 몇 가지 범주 안에서 생각해보아야 합니다. 보상은 조금 전에 이야기 했던 그런 긍정적 가치가 될 수도 있어요. '고맙습니다' 와 '잘했어요' 와 같은 관례적인 말들은 사람들이 상호 작용을 할 때 발견할 수 있는 매우 일반적인 보상이에요. 하지만 보상에는 다른 범주도 있죠. 1차 보상은 생명과 신체 기능에 중요한 보상으로, 음식과 물 같은 것입니다. 일부 심리학자들은 주거 역시 1차 보상에 속한다고 생각해요. 이 말이 여러분이 은혜를 받은 대가로 누군가에게 집을 사주는 것을 의미하는 걸까요? 여러분이 아주 부자라면, 그럴 수도 있죠! 2차 보상은 1차 보상을 통해 그 가치를 얻게 되는데, 즉 1차 보상과 교환할 수 있다는 말이에요. 무언가를 보상과 교환할 때, 가장 먼저 생각나는 것은 무엇인가요? 그렇죠, 바로 돈이죠. 그 외에도 좀 더 미묘한 2차 보상도 있어요. 부드럽게 어루만져 주는 것도 2차 보상이 될 수 있고, 미소를 지어보이는 것 역시 2차 보상이 될 수 있습니다.

보상의 목적은 행동을 바꾸고, 긍정적인 감정을 유발하고, 학습이 이루어지도록 하는 것입니다. 즉, 우리가 보상을 받을 때, 우리가 그 보상을 좋아한다면, 무엇을 하든 그것을 계속해야 한다는 것을 알게 됩니다. 이는 의식적으로도, 잠재적으로도 일어날 수 있는 일이에요. 우리가 긍정적인 자극을 받으면, 즉 보상을 받으면, 우리는 더 많이 원하게 되죠. 곧 그에 관해서 의식적으로 생각하지 않고도 보상을 받을 수 있는 행동을 계속하게 되는 겁니다.

어휘 | reinforcement 강화 | owe 빚지다 | standard 표준적인 | interact with ~와 상호작용을 하다 | primary 1차의 | psychologist 심리학자 | exchange 교환하다 | subtle 미묘한 | modify 바꾸다 | conscious 의식적인 | subconscious 잠재적인 | stimulus 자극

Review

1. (1) If you're <u>interested in</u> business, then you <u>ought to</u> consider Chinese.
   (2) Well, it <u>seems</u> that you need to <u>either</u> change your work hours <u>or</u> take another class.
   (3) China has become an <u>economic superpower,</u> and the language will give you a <u>big advantage</u>.
   (4) Well, you could also go to <u>one of those</u> libraries yourself, and borrow the book.
   (5) I <u>work at</u> the hospital in the afternoon, and I <u>come straight to</u> school afterward.

2. (1) I'm not sure / which language to take / for my elective.

(2) We need to talk about / why you're always late for class.

(3) If you arrive / on time/ for Dr. Catherine's class / for the rest of the semester, / you might get a better grade.

(4) If you don't have your own computer, / or it's not set up yet, / why not stop by the computer lab / in the library?

(5) The online catalog says / it's checked out.

Chapter 4 Detail

Office Hours

1. (D)   **2.** (C)

---

1. 왜 학생은 자신의 프리젠테이션 날짜를 바꾸기를 원하는가?

(A) 같은 반 친구의 부탁 때문에

(B) 엄마의 온라인 사업 때문에

(C) 시험 때문에

(D) 가족 일 때문에

M: How can I help you?

W: Well, it's about my presentation on Friday. I need to reschedule it, if that's possible?

M: That might be a problem, because it would affect the other students' schedules. Why do you want to do this?

W: Well, my father is a photographer, and he has won a major award. The ceremony is on Friday. If you don't believe me, we can look online. My mom really wants me there for my father.

M: Wow, you must be very proud.

W: I am. And I'm totally ready to do the presentation now. I could do it earlier or later, if another student will swap with me. Is that okay?

M: Sure. This is a special occasion. We can ask in class tomorrow. I doubt that there won't be anybody who wants to reschedule his or her presentation.

W: Thanks!

남: 무슨 일이니?

여: 금요일에 있을 제 프리젠테이션에 관한 건데요. 가능하다면, 스케줄을 조정할 수 있을까요?

남: 글쎄, 다른 학생들의 스케줄에도 영향을 주기 때문에 좀 어려울 것 같구나. 왜 날짜를 바꾸려고 하니?

여: 음, 저희 아버지가 사진가이신데요, 이번에 큰 상을 받게 되었어요. 금요일에 시상식이 있거든요. 못 믿으시면, 온라인으로 찾아보셔도 좋아요. 어머니가 아버지를 위해 제가 꼭 참석하기를 바라세요.

남: 아버지가 정말 자랑스럽겠구나.

여: 네. 그리고 전 지금이라도 프리젠테이션을 할 준비가 완전히 되어 있어요. 다른 학생이 바꾸어주면
　　금요일보다 더 빨리 아니면 더 늦게 할 수도 있고요. 괜찮을까요?
남: 그럼. 특별한 경우니까. 내일 수업 시간에 다른 학생들에게 물어보도록 하자. 프리젠테이션 일정을
　　바꾸어줄 학생이 아무도 없을 것 같지는 않구나.
여: 감사합니다!

어휘 | reschedule 일정을 변경하다 | award 상 | ceremony 의식, 식 | swap 바꾸다, 교환하다 |
occasion 경우, 행사

2. 교수가 학생에게 하라고 제안하는 것은 무엇인가?
　　(A) 학생은 직접 개를 사야 한다.
　　(B) 학생은 개에 대한 실험을 직접 해보아야 한다.
　　(C) 학생의 개에 관해 짧게 언급한다.
　　(D) 학생은 새로운 토픽을 선택해야 한다.

M: Shannon, do you have a question?
W: Yes, professor. I need some help. I'm having some trouble with my paper. I think I
　　have writer's block.
M: I see. What topic did you choose?
W: Pavlov's famous experiment with the bell and the salivating dogs. I don't know what to
　　say.
M: You mean you don't understand the experiment?
W: No, it's simple. But there are so many books and papers about it. It's hard to say
　　something new.
M: Ah, now I understand. You don't want to repeat what others have already said. Do you
　　have a dog?
W: Yes! I have two, but they're not here at school. My parents are keeping them at home.
M: Well, then, why don't you start with a brief story about your own dogs? From there, it
　　should be easy to talk about Pavlov's dogs.
W: That's a great idea!

남: Shannon, 질문이 있니?
여: 네, 교수님. 교수님 도움이 좀 필요해요. 리포트를 작성하는데 문제가 좀 있어요. 아무래도 작가들
　　이 겪게 되는 슬럼프에 빠진 것 같아요.
남: 그렇구나. 어떤 토픽으로 정했니?
여: 벨 소리와 침 흘리는 개의 관계를 보여주는 Pavlov(파블로프)의 유명한 실험이요. 무슨 이야기를
　　써야 할지 모르겠어요.
남: 실험이 이해가 안 된다는 말이니?
여: 아뇨, 실험은 간단해요. 그런데 그 실험에 관한 책과 논문이 너무 많아요. 새로운 무언가를 쓰는 것
　　이 어려워요.
남: 아, 이제 무슨 말인지 알겠구나. 다른 사람들이 말한 것을 반복하고 싶지 않다는 거구나. 너 개를
　　기르니?

여: 네! 두 마리가 있는데요, 지금 학교에 있지는 않아요. 부모님이 집에서 키우고 계세요.

남: 그럼, 네가 기르는 개들에 관한 짧은 이야기로 시작하는 것이 어떻겠니? 거기서부터 시작하면, Pavlov(파블로프)의 개 실험에 관해 이야기하는 것이 쉬울 거야.

여: 좋은 생각이에요!

어휘 | writer's block 작가의 슬럼프 | experiment 실험 | salivate 침을 흘리다

Service Encounters

1. (B)   **2.** (C)

---

1. 왜 학생은 사촌에게 캠퍼스 구경을 시켜줄 수 없는가?
 (A) 학생은 미술 강의가 있다.
 (B) 학생은 그 날 일을 해야 한다.
 (C) 학생은 다른 지역에 갈 것이다.
 (D) 학생은 점심시간에 다른 사람과 약속이 있다.

M: Hi, how can I help you?

W: Hi, I'd like to ask about a campus tour?

M: Sure. Can you tell me when, and for how many people?

W: Actually, It's just my cousin. He's interested in the art department here, and he'll be visiting on Saturday. I have a part-time job, so I can't show him around...

M: Sure, I understand. That's no problem. We have two tours already scheduled for Saturday: one at eleven, and another at three. He could join either one. Which time do you think is better?

W: Three, definitely. He's meeting me for lunch at one, and I'll tell him how to get to campus.

M: That's good. I'm glad I could help!

남: 안녕하세요, 어떻게 오셨죠?

여: 안녕하세요, 캠퍼스 투어에 관해 여쭤보고 싶은데요?

남: 네. 언제, 얼마나 많은 인원이 참여하는지 알려주겠어요?

여: 실은, 제 사촌 한 명이에요. 제 사촌이 우리 학교 미대에 관심이 있는데요, 이번 토요일에 학교에 올 거예요. 제가 아르바이트를 해야 해서 학교 구경을 못 시켜줄 것 같아요...

남: 이해해요. 그런 일이라면 아무 문제없어요. 벌써 토요일에 두 번의 투어가 잡혀있는 걸요. 하나는 11시고, 또 하나는 3시에요. 둘 중 아무거나 참가할 수 있어요. 언제가 더 좋겠어요?

여: 3시가 좋겠네요. 1시에 저랑 점심을 하기로 했으니까 캠퍼스에 가는 길을 알려주도록 할게요.

남: 잘됐네요. 도움이 되었다니 다행이네요!

어휘 | cousin 사촌 | definitely 물론, 그럼

2. 여자가 남자에게 하라고 제안하는 것은 무엇인가?

(A) 부모님 집에서 통학하기
(B) 현재 살고 있는 집에서 이사하기
(C) 캠퍼스 근처에 방 구하기
(D) 룸메이트와 방 같이 쓰기

M: Hi, I need to ask a couple of questions about my housing situation.
W: Sure, go right ahead.
M: Well, the semester is about to start, but the deadline for getting into the dorms has passed, so I'm not sure what to do. I'm a full-time student, and I work on campus, too.
W: I see. It sounds like you'll need to spend a lot of time here.
M: That's right. My parents live two hours away. Commuting is expensive, and it wastes time.
W: True, you'll waste much of your time on the road. Well, most students in your situation rent an apartment off-campus.
M: But that costs a lot of money, too. Isn't there any other option?
W: Well, I can put your name on the waiting list for a dorm room. In the meantime, I think you should try getting a room, at least for a short time.
M: Thanks. I'll try that.

남: 안녕하세요, 숙소 문제에 관해 몇 가지 질문이 있는데요.
여: 네, 말씀해 보세요.
남: 음, 이제 곧 학기가 시작할 텐데요, 기숙사 신청 마감일이 지났잖아요. 그래서 어떡해야 할지 모르겠어요. 저는 풀타임 학생이고요, 학교에서 일도 해요.
여: 알겠어요. 학교에서 시간을 많이 보낼 것 같군요.
남: 네. 부모님은 학교에서 2시간 걸리는 곳에 살고 계세요. 통학은 돈이 많이 드는데다, 시간 낭비에요.
여: 그렇죠, 길 위에서 시간을 많이 버리게 될 거예요. 음, 학생과 같은 경우에는 주로 캠퍼스 외부의 아파트를 빌리죠.
남: 하지만 그것도 돈이 많이 들잖아요. 다른 방법은 없을까요?
여: 음, 기숙사 대기자 명단에 학생 이름을 올려놓을게요. 그 동안에 잠깐이라도 묵을 방을 알아보는 게 좋을 것 같네요.
남: 감사합니다. 그러도록 하죠.

어휘 | commuting 통학 | waste 낭비하다 | off-campus 캠퍼스 외부의

Lectures

1. 1. (B) 2. (D) **2.** 1. (A) 2. (C)

---

1. 1. 다음 중 어느 것이 방울뱀에 관해 맞는가?
    (A) 방울뱀은 마주치는 모든 하이커를 공격한다.
    (B) 방울뱀은 유독한 물질을 만들어낸다.
    (C) 방울뱀은 그늘진 곳을 선호한다.

(D) 방울뱀이 만들어 내는 소리는 먹이 발견과 관련이 있다.

2. 다음 중 어느 것이 방울뱀의 각질 마디에 관해 맞지 않는가?
   (A) 방울뱀이 탈피할 때 새로운 마디가 생겨난다.
   (B) 방울뱀의 꼬리에 생겨난다.
   (C) 속이 비어있다.
   (D) 원래 자리에 붙어 있는 편이다.

P: Now, I'd like to talk a little about rattlesnakes and their rattles. If you've ever gone for a hike, you've probably been cautioned about rattlesnakes. These are among the most common venomous snakes of North America, and they're certainly the most distinctive. The rattle of these species — and there are about 50 species — is widely understood to be a warning. Rattlesnakes aren't likely to attack humans unless they feel threatened... and since they like to sun themselves in the middle of places like hiking trails, you can see where this would be a problem. Being familiar with the sound of the rattle is one way to protect yourself in the wild. After my talk, I'll play a recording for you. The rattle is made of a series of modified scales that grow from the end of the snake's tail. These scales are like hollow beads, and they make a sound when the snake moves a certain way. Each time a snake molts — sheds its skin — it gains a new bead. It's a common myth that you can tell the age of a snake by the number of beads on its tail, because rattles can break. However, it's generally true that older snakes may have longer rattles, and newborn snakes none at all.

P: 자, 이제 방울뱀과 방울뱀의 향음기관(響音器官)에 대해 이야기를 해볼까 해요. 하이킹을 해본 적이 있는 사람이라면, 방울뱀을 조심해야 한다는 주의를 받은 적이 있을 거예요. 방울뱀은 북미에 서식하는 가장 일반적인 독사로, 뚜렷한 특색을 가지고 있기도 해요. 50여 종의 방울뱀이 있는데, 이 방울뱀들이 만들어내는 소리는 경계용으로 이해되고 있어요. 방울뱀은 위협 받고 있다고 느끼지 않는 이상 인간을 공격하지는 않는 편이에요. 하이킹 코스와 같은 길 한가운데서 햇볕을 쬐는 것을 좋아하기 때문에, 어떤 곳에서 방울뱀을 조심해야 하는지 알 수 있죠. 방울뱀의 방울 소리를 귀에 익혀두는 것이 야생에서 여러분 스스로를 보호하는 한 가지 방법이에요. 설명이 끝난 후에 방울뱀 소리를 녹음한 것을 들려주도록 하죠. 방울뱀의 각질(角質) 마디는 꼬리 끝에서부터 자라나는 몇 개의 변형된 비늘이에요. 이 각질 마디는 속이 비어 있는 구슬 같아서, 방울뱀이 움직일 때 소리를 내요. 뱀이 탈피할 때마다 새로운 각질 마디가 하나씩 늘게 됩니다. 방울뱀의 꼬리에 있는 각질 마디 수를 보고 뱀의 나이를 알 수 있다고 잘못 알고 있는 사람이 많은데, 마디가 떨어져 나갈 수도 있기 때문이에요. 하지만, 일반적으로 더 나이가 많은 뱀의 각질 마디가 더 길고, 새끼에게는 마디가 하나도 없을 수 있다는 것은 사실이에요.

어휘 ┃ rattlesnake 방울뱀 ┃ rattle 덜거덕거리는 소리 ┃ caution 경고하다, 주의시키다 ┃ venomous 독이 있는 ┃ threaten 위협하다 ┃ modify 변형하다 ┃ scale 비늘 ┃ tail 꼬리 ┃ hollow 속이 빈 ┃ bead 구슬 ┃ molt 탈피하다, 허물 벗다 ┃ shed 벗기다 ┃ gain 얻다 ┃ myth 근거 없는 이야기, 사회적 미신 ┃ newborn 갓 태어난

2. 강의의 일부를 다시 들으시오. 그러고 나서 질문에 답하시오.

페니실린이 20세기의 가장 위대한 발견이라고 말하는 사람들도 있어요. 그게 사실인지는 잘 모르겠군요.
하지만 페니실린이 우리 삶에 좋은 영향을 끼쳤다고 말하는 것이 더 쉽겠네요.

1. 교수가 이것을 말할 때 의미하는 것은 무엇인가 :

   하지만 페니실린이 우리 삶에 좋은 영향을 끼쳤다고 말하는 것이 더 쉽겠네요.

   (A) 교수는 페니실린이 인간에게 유익하다고 생각한다.
   (B) 교수는 페니실린이 1900년대의 가장 위대한 발견이 아니라고 생각한다.
   (C) 교수는 페니실린이 여느 약과 다를 바 없다고 생각한다.
   (D) 교수는 페니실린이 생명을 구하는데 소용이 없다고 생각한다.

2. 다음 중 어느 것이 페니실린 발견에 관해 맞는가?
   (A) 페니실린은 처음부터 바이러스 질병 치료에 쓰였다.
   (B) Alexander Fleming은 최초의 발견자라고 불릴 자격이 있다.
   (C) Alexander Fleming은 최초로 활성 물질을 추출해냈다.
   (D) 코스타리카 출신의 의사가 Alexander Fleming의 연구를 계승했다.

P(M): Well, here we are in late fall, and the weather's turning cold... I can hear several sniffles in the audience, and a few of you are coughing, too. I bet at least one of you is taking an antibiotic right now. You don't have to raise your hand, but I do want you to think for a moment. Where would we be without antibiotics? Some people say that penicillin was one of the greatest discoveries of the 20th century. I don't know whether that's true or not. But it's easy to make out a case for it, though. Penicillin, a drug used in the treatment of bacterial infections, has saved a lot of lives!

Most of us were taught that a Scottish scientist, Sir Alexander Fleming, discovered it in 1928. That's not quite true, though. Although he was the first to isolate the active substance, a doctor from Costa Rica, in fact, had experimented on penicillin mold and documented its effects years before Fleming did. He didn't patent his process, though. Not only that, but a third scientist — an Australian this time — was responsible for developing penicillin as a medicine.

Early experiments on penicillin were not promising. At first it was thought to be useful as a general-purpose disinfectant, rather than a form of medication. Scientists were uncertain it would be powerful enough to work inside the body. Several years of experiments were needed before the medicinal properties of penicillin were purified and concentrated enough for use on human infections.

Q Listen again to part of the lecture. Then answer the question.

Some people say that penicillin was one of the greatest discoveries of the 20th century. I don't know whether that's true or not. But it's easy to make out a case for it, though.

Why does the professor mention this:
But it's easy to make out a case for it, though.

P: 자, 이제 늦가을에 접어들었고, 날씨도 쌀쌀해지고 있군요... 여러분 중에 코를 훌쩍거리는 사람도 있고, 기침을 하는 사람도 있네요. 적어도 여러분 중 한 명 정도는 항생제를 복용하고 있을 거예요. 손을 들어 보일 필요는 없지만, 잠깐 한 번 생각해봐요. 항생제가 없었다면 우리는 지금 어떤 상황에 처해 있을까요? 페니실린이 20세기의 가장 위대한 발견이라고 말하는 사람들도 있어요. 그게 사실인지는 잘 모르겠군요. 하지만 페니실린이 우리 삶에 좋은 영향을 끼쳤다고 말하는 것이 더 쉽겠네요. 박테리아 감염 치료에 사용되는 약인 페니실린은 많은 생명을 구해냈어요!
우리는 대개 스코틀랜드 과학자인 Alexander Fleming(알렉산더 플레밍) 경이 1928년에 페니실린을 발견했다고 배웠어요. 하지만 그건 사실이라고는 할 수 없어요. Fleming 경이 활성 물질을 최초로 분리해내기는 했지만, 실은 코스타리카 출신의 의사가 이미 페니실린 균을 가지고 실험을 했었고 Fleming 경보다 몇 년 앞서 그 효능을 기록해두었어요. 하지만 그런 과정에 대해 특허를 내지는 않았죠. 뿐만 아니라, 호주 출신의 제 3의 과학자도 약으로 쓰일 수 있는 페니실린을 개발했죠.
초기의 페니실린 실험 결과는 그다지 앞날이 밝지 않았어요. 처음에는 약물이라기보다는 다용도 살균제로 쓸모 있을 거라 생각되었어요. 과학자들은 페니실린이 몸 안에서 큰 효능을 발휘할 만큼 강력한 물질인지 확신할 수 없었죠. 수년간의 실험 결과 페니실린의 의학적 특성을 살릴 수 있도록 정제되었고 인간의 감염 치료에 쓰일 수 있도록 농축되었어요.

어휘 | sniffle 코를 훌쩍거림 | audience 청중 | cough 기침하다 | antibiotic 항생제 | make out a case for ~의 옹호론을 펴다 | isolate 분리하다 | mold 곰팡이, 균 | patent 특허를 내다 | promising 전도유망한 | general-purpose 다용도의, 만능의 | disinfectant 살균제 | uncertain 확신하지 못하는 | property 특성, 특질 | purify 정제하다 | concentrate 농축시키다

Practice

1. (C) **2.** (D) **3.** (D) **4.** (A) **5.** Mentioned - (B), (E) Not Mentioned - (A), (C), (D) **6.** (D)
7. (C) **8.** (C) **9.** (A) **10.** Mentioned - (A), (B), (D) Not Mentioned - (C), (E) **11.** (B)

[문제 1~5] 학생과 교수 사이의 대화의 일부를 들으시오.

1. 화자들은 주로 무엇에 관해 이야기 하고 있는가?
 (A) 교수가 자신의 은퇴 소식을 알리고 있다.
 (B) 학생이 학교에서 잘 하고 있다.
 (C) 교수가 학생이 추천위원회에 합류하기를 원한다.
 (D) 학과에서 교수들을 신규 채용했다.

 해설 | 교수는 학생이 후임 학과장 선출을 위한 추천위원회에 참여하기를 바라고 있다. 정답은 보기 (C).

대화의 일부를 다시 들으시오. 그리고 나서 질문에 답하시오.
남:그 동안 줄곧 아주 잘해왔고, 연구에도 전념하여 열심히 해왔고, 신중하게 생각하고... 그 밖에 또 뭘 말해

야겠니? 참여할 마음이 있니?

2. 교수가 이것을 말할 때 의미하는 것은 무엇인가 : 🎧
  남: 그 밖에 또 뭘 말해야겠니?

  (A) 하고 싶은 말을 잊어버렸다.
  (B) 칭찬을 너무 많이 했기 때문에 당황하고 있다.
  (C) 다른 학생들 가운데 학생을 가장 먼저 선택했다는 것을 인정하고 있다.
  (D) 지금쯤이면 학생을 설득했기를 바란다.

  해설 | 교수는 학생이 위원회에 참여할 자격이 충분하다고 생각하고 있다. 학생의 장점을 열거한 뒤 '그 밖에 또 뭘 말해야겠니?' 라고 묻는 건 더 이상 얘기하지 않아도 학생이 교수의 마음을 알아주기를 원하는 것이다. 따라서 정답은 보기 (D).

3. 학생은 어디에 살고 있는가?
  (A) 부모님과 함께
  (B) 다른 도시에
  (C) 기숙사에
  (D) 캠퍼스 근처 아파트에

  해설 | 7월에 인터뷰가 예정되어 있기 때문에, 교수는 학생에게 여름에 학교에 남아있을 건지를 묻고 있다. 학생은 여름에 다른 곳에 가지 않을 것이고, 캠퍼스 근처에 아파트가 있다고 말하고 있다. 정답은 보기 (D).

4. 학생에 관해 추론할 수 있는 것은 무엇인가?
  (A) 이번 학기 말에 졸업하지 않을 것이다.
  (B) 학생회 대표이다.
  (C) 부모님께서 다른 주에 살고 계신다.
  (D) 여름에 여행을 할 예정이다.

  해설 | 여름에 계속 학교에 나올 수 있다는 것을 통해 이번 학기 말에 졸업을 하지 않는다고 미루어 짐작할 수 있다. 정답은 보기 (A).

5. 대화에서, 교수는 추천위원회에서 학생이 해야 할 일을 언급하고 있다. 아래 표의 각 보기가 교수가 언급한 내용인지 표시하시오. 각 보기에 맞는 칸에 클릭하시오.

	Mentioned	Not Mentioned
(A) 일대일로 각 후보자를 인터뷰하기		V
(B) 위원회의 최종 모임에 참석하기	V	
(C) 지원자의 지원서를 접수하기		V
(D) 지원자들이 가르치는 모습을 관찰하기 위해 다른 도시로 여행하기		V
(E) 여름에 인터뷰에 참여하기	V	

  해설 | 7월 중하순에 시작되는 인터뷰에 최소 한 차례 이상 참석해야 하고, 후임자를 결정하여 선출하는 모임에도 참석해야 한다. 정답은 보기 (B), (E).

M: Come on in, Felicity. I'm glad you had some free time this afternoon, because I'd like to ask a favor of you.

W: A favor?

M: Well, something like that. I'm on the search committee to replace the department head, who's retiring this fall. The committee includes members of the faculty, the administration, and the student body.

W: Are you asking if I'd like to serve on the committee?

M: Yes, I am. I can see you're excited. I've mentioned you to a couple of other instructors, and they agreed you'd make a great addition to the committee. Your work is consistently excellent, and it's clear you're committed to your studies. You think about things carefully, and... what else can I say? Would you like to be involved?

W: Absolutely! I'm really flattered. Can you tell me what I'd have to do?

M: Well, we've just begun to advertise for the position, and we'll be accepting applications until the end of June. That's several months away. The only issue is that we expect to hold interviews in the second half of July. Will you be in town over the summer?

W: Yes, I have an apartment near campus. Even if I go visit my parents, they're only one hour away. Distance isn't a problem.

M: You'd need to attend at least one stage of each interview, which would be a mock class and a question-and-answer session afterward. That would be about an hour per candidate, maybe a little more. Also, you'd need to attend the meetings where we'll actually make the selection. Does that sound like something you could do?

W: Sure, I'll have plenty of time this summer. Thanks for this opportunity!

M: I'm glad to hear you'll be part of the process.

Now get ready to answer the questions. You may use your notes to help you answer.

Q. 2 Listen again to part of the conversation. Then answer the question.

M: *Your work is consistently excellent, and it's clear you're committed to your studies. You think about things carefully, and... what else can I say? Would you like to be involved?*

What does the professor mean when he says this: 🎧
M: *what else can I say?*

남: 어서 오렴, Felicity. 너에게 부탁하고 싶은 것이 있었는데 오늘 오후에 시간이 좀 있다니 다행이구나.

여: 부탁이요?

남: 부탁이라고 할 수 있지. 내가 올 가을에 은퇴하시는 학과장님의 뒤를 이을 후임 학과장을 선출할 추천위원회에 있어. 위원회에는 교수, 행정본부 대표, 학생회 임원들이 참여해.

여: 저보고 위원회 활동을 하라고 말씀하시는 건가요?

남: 그래. 흥미가 있는 것 같구나. 몇몇 교수님들에게 네 이야기를 했는데, 모두 네가 참여하는 것이 좋

어휘 | replace 대신하다, ~의 후임자가 되다 | retire 은퇴하다 | faculty 교수진 | consistently 줄곧 | be committed to ~에 헌신하다 | flatter 칭찬을 하다, 추켜세우다 | mock class 모의 수업 | afterward 후에

[문제 6~11] 영문학 강의의 일부를 들으시오.

6. 강의는 주로 무엇에 관한 것인가?
(A) 세계적으로 유명한 다이아몬드
(B) Wilkie Collins의 작가로서의 생애
(C) Wilkie Collins와 T. S. Eliot의 비교
(D) 최초의 영어 탐정 소설

해설 | 탐정 소설이라는 새로운 장르를 탄생시킨 영국 작가 Wilkie Collins와 그의 작품 '월장석'에 관해 이야기를 들려주고 있다. 정답은 보기 (D). 주로 그의 작품을 중심으로 강의가 진행되고 있으므로 보기 (B)의 'Wilkie Collins의 작가로서의 생애'는 오답이다.

7. 다음 중 Wilkie Collins에 관해 추론할 수 있는 것은 무엇인가?
(A) 가난한 생활을 했다.
(B) 책으로 평판이 나빴다.
(C) Charles Dickens와 친분이 있었다.
(D) 탐정 생활을 체험했다.

해설 | 그의 새로운 소설 '월장석'을 찰스 디킨스가 발행하던 문학 잡지 "All the Year Round"에 발표했다는 것으로 보아 둘 사이에 친분이 있었을 것임을 짐작할 수 있다. 정답은 보기 (C). '월장석' 이전의 작품들이 많이 팔려 돈을 많이 벌어들였다고 했으므로 가난한 생활을 했다는 보기 (A)는 오답이다. 또한 작가로서 상당한 성공을 거두고 인기가 많았다고 했으므로 책으로 평판이 나빴다는 보기 (B) 역시 오답이다. Collins가 직접 탐정 생활을 체험했다는 내용은 언급된 바가 없으므로 보기 (D) 역시 오답이다.

8. 교수에 따르면, Collins의 소설 '월장석'에서 월장석(문스톤)은 무엇인가?

   (A) 달에 있던 암석 덩어리
   (B) 문학잡지 이름
   (C) 인도산 다이아몬드
   (D) 주인공의 애칭

해설 | 작품 속 주인공인 Rachel Verinder가 삼촌으로부터 유산으로 물려받은 다이아몬드의 이름이 월장석(문스톤)이다. 정답은 보기 (C).

강의의 일부를 다시 들으시오. 그러고 나서 질문에 답하시오.
이 미스터리는 어떻게 풀리게 될까요?

9. 교수는 왜 이것을 언급하는가 :
이 미스터리는 어떻게 풀리게 될까요?

   (A) 학생들의 흥미를 불러일으키기 위해
   (B) 학생들에게 이야기의 결말을 알려주기 위해
   (C) 탐정 소설의 구성을 설명하기 위해
   (D) 학생들에게 미스터리에 관한 단서를 주기 위해

해설 | 작품의 기본 줄거리인 미스터리 사건의 개요를 들려준 후, '이 미스터리는 어떻게 풀리게 될까요?' 라고 물음으로써 학생들의 호기심과 흥미를 자극하고 있다. 정답은 보기 (A).

10. 강의에서, 교수는 Wilkie Collins의 탐정 소설에 관해 이야기 하고 있다. 아래 표의 각 보기가 이 소설의 특징에 해당되는지 표시하시오. 각 보기에 맞는 칸에 클릭하시오.

	Mentioned	Not Mentioned
(A) 출간된 지 200년도 안되었음	V	
(B) 연재되었음	V	
(C) 여러 다른 언어로 번역되었음		V
(D) 아마추어 탐정이 등장함	V	
(E) 상류층 독자들을 독자층으로 설정했음		V

해설 | 소설이 1868년에 발표되었다고 했으므로 보기 (A)와 같이 출간된 지 200년이 안되었다고 말할 수 있다. 오늘날의 출판 방식과는 달리 문학 잡지에 한 챕터씩 연재했다고 하였으므로 보기 (B)도 맞는 내용이다. 작품 속에서 문스톤이라는 다이아몬드가 도난을 당해서 유능한 아마추어 탐정이 사건 해결을 위해 등장하므로 보기 (D)도 맞는 내용이다. 정답은 보기 (A), (B), (D).

강의의 일부를 다시 들으시오. 그러고 나서 질문에 답하시오.
하지만, 이 소설로 Collins는 새로운 장르를 개척했다고 할 수 있어요. T. S. Eliot(엘리엇)은 '월장석'을 격찬했으며, 작품을 가리켜 "영국의 최초이자 최대의 추리소설"이라고 평했어요.

11. 교수는 왜 이것을 언급하는가 :
   T. S. Eliot(엘리엇)은 '월장석'을 격찬했으며, 작품을 가리켜 '영국의 최초이자 최대의 추리소설' 이라고

평했어요.

(A) '월장석'이 왜 즉각적인 성공을 거두었는지 설명하기 위해
(B) '월장석'의 탁월함을 강조하기 위해
(C) 다른 언어로 쓰여진 탐정 소설들도 있다는 것을 보여주기 위해
(D) Wilkie Collins의 작품과 T. S. Eliot의 작품을 대조하기 위해

해설 | 저명한 시인이자 극작가로 많은 사람들에게 알려져 있는 엘리엇의 비평을 인용하여 들려줌으로써 이 '월장석'이라는 작품의 가치가 얼마나 뛰어난지를 강조하고 있다. 정답은 보기 (B).

[Questions 6~11] Listen to part of a lecture in an English class.

P: The novel is a fairly young literary form, only a few centuries old. The English writer Wilkie Collins is credited with writing the first English-language detective novel... as recently as 1868! That's barely 150 years ago, not long compared to other art or literary forms.

The title of this groundbreaking novel was *The Moonstone*, and it was published in Charles Dickens's literary magazine *All the Year Round*. Rather than being published all at once, which is how most books are produced today, it was published serially: one chapter at a time. Collins had published a number of other novels already. As a matter of fact, he was a very successful author. He often combined social commentary with a great deal of suspense, and as a result there were few other writers who could match his level of popularity.

Now, let's go further into the novel. *The Moonstone* concerns Rachel Verinder, a young woman who inherits a diamond from her uncle. The fabulous yellow diamond is named the Moonstone. It was originally in the forehead of the idol of an Indian moon-god, was taken from its rightful place, and was passed on through generations. Three mysterious Indian Brahmins have sworn their lives to protect it and followed it. Then Rachel's uncle, a British officer, takes it to England. Rachel receives the stone on her birthday, which is stolen the same night. A detective from London is summoned to solve the crime. How will the mystery be finally solved?

The Moonstone contains many elements that later became standard detective novel fare: incompetent police, talented amateurs who were present when the crime happened, red herrings in the plot, and a large number of suspects. Considering the importance of *The Moonstone*, it is ironic that it was not seen as a success for Collins when it was published. Many of his earlier books sold well and earned more money. However, with this novel he more or less created a genre. T. S. Eliot praised *The Moonstone* highly and called it "The first and greatest of English detective novels."

Now get ready to answer the questions. You may use your notes to help you answer.

Q. 9 Listen again to part of the conversation. Then answer the question.

Why does the professor mention this : 🎧
How will the mystery be finally solved?

Q. 11 Listen again to part of the conversation. Then answer the question.

However, with this novel he more or less created a genre. T. S. Eliot praised The Moonstone highly and called it "The first and greatest of English detective novels."

Why does the professor mention this : 🎧
T. S. Eliot praised The Moonstone highly and called it "The first and greatest of English detective novels."

P: 이 소설은 세상의 빛을 본지 아직 몇 세기 밖에 안 된 문학작품이에요. 영국 작가 Wilkie Collins(윌키 콜린스)는 영어탐정 소설의 선구자로 작품은 1868년에 발표되었어요! 다른 예술 형태나 문학 장르와 비교해서 오래되지 않은, 겨우 150여 년 전에 출간되었죠.
이 새로운 소설의 제목은 '월장석'(*The Moonstone*)으로 Charles Dickens의 문학잡지인 'All the Year Round'에 발표되었어요. 한꺼번에 모두 발표되는 오늘날의 출판 방식과는 달리, 이 작품은 한 번에 한 챕터씩 잡지에 연재되었죠. Collins는 이미 여러 편의 소설을 출간한 상태였어요. 사실, 상당한 성공을 거둔 작가였죠. 그는 사회적 현실에 대한 논평과 서스펜스를 결합시킨 작품을 써 냈기 때문에, 그의 인기를 필적할 작가는 거의 없었어요.
자, 작품에 대해 더 깊이 알아보도록 하죠. '월장석'에는 삼촌으로부터 다이아몬드를 유산으로 물려받은 젊은 여성인 Rachel Verinder가 등장해요. 이 눈부신 다이아몬드는 문스톤(월장석)이라고 불려요. 이 문스톤은 원래 인도의 월신상의 이마에 장식되어 있었는데, 원래 자리에서 누가 가져가서 수세대가 흘러가죠. 베일에 가려진 3명의 인도 브라흐마나(승려 계급)들이 다이아몬드를 지키기로 목숨을 걸고 맹세하고 뒤를 쫓아요. 그러다 영국 장교였던 Rachel의 삼촌이 다이아몬드를 영국으로 가져가요. Rachel은 생일날 이 다이아몬드를 선물로 받는데, 그 날 밤 도난을 당하죠. 런던에서 온 탐정이 이 사건을 해결하기 위해 불려와요. 이 미스터리는 어떻게 풀리게 될까요?
'월장석'에는 후에 탐정 소설의 전형적 형식이 된 많은 요소가 들어있어요. 바로 무능한 경찰과 사건이 일어날 당시 현장에 있었던 재능 있는 아마추어 탐정, 사건 해결을 어렵게 하는 다양한 장치들, 그리고 많은 용의자가 등장하죠. '월장석'의 문학적 의의를 고려할 때, 출간 당시 대성공을 거두지 않은 것으로 인식된 것은 아이러니해요. 이보다 앞서 출간된 그의 작품은 상당히 많이 팔렸고, 돈도 많이 벌어들였죠. 하지만, 이 소설로 Collins는 새로운 장르를 개척했다고 할 수 있어요. T. S. Eliot(엘리엇)은 '월장석'을 격찬했으며, 작품을 가리켜 "영국의 최초이자 최대의 추리소설"이라고 평했어요.

어휘 | fairly 꽤 | detective novel 탐정 소설 | barely 겨우 | groundbreaking 혁신적인 | all at once 한꺼번에 | serially 연재로 | suspense 서스펜스, 지속적 긴장감 | match ~에 필적하다 | inherit 상속하다 | fabulous 멋진, 눈부신 | forehead 이마 | idol 우상 | pass on 전해 내려지다 | swear 맹세하다 | summon 소환하다 | element 요소, 장치 | fare 상태, 추세 | incompetent 무능한 | present 존재하는 | suspect 용의자 | red herring 사람을 헷갈리게 하는 정보 | more or less 다소

1. 1. Well, my father is a <u>photographer</u>, and he has <u>won</u> a major award.

2. That might be a problem, because <u>it would affect</u> the other students' schedules.

3. I have a part-time job, so I can't <u>show him around</u>.

4. Well, the semester is <u>about</u> to start, but the deadline for getting into the dorms has <u>passed</u>, so I'm not <u>sure</u> what to do.

5. Pavlov's famous <u>experiment with</u> the bell and the <u>salivating</u> dogs.

2. 1. I could do it / earlier or later / if another student will swap with me.

2. You don't want to repeat / what others have already said.

3. I doubt / that there won't be anybody / who wants to reschedule his or her presentation.

4. He's meeting me / for lunch / at one, / and I'll tell him / how to get to campus.

5. In the meantime, / I think / you should try getting a room, / at least / for a short time

Chapter 5 Inference

Office Hours

1. (B)   **2.** (C)

1. 여자에 관해 추론할 수 있는 것은 무엇인가?

(A) 여자는 에세이가 길지 않다고 생각했다.

(B) 여자는 에세이 제출을 연기하기를 원한다.

(C) 여자는 에세이에 아무것도 덧붙이지 않을 것이다.

(D) 여자도 컨퍼런스에 참석할 것이다.

M: Madeleine, I know you need to get to your next class, so I'll keep this brief. You did a pretty good job with your essay, but it still needs some work.

W: Really? What's the matter with it?

M: Several sections are too long. You need to trim it by about 500 words.

W: Hmm, I thought it might be. I guess I was right.

M: When you revise it, instead of spending so much time on unnecessary information, you ought to provide more support for the supporting points.

W: Do you mean I should add more detail?

M: Yes, but it needs to be related to the supporting points. Can you do this before 4 p.m. tomorrow? I have a conference after that.

W: Hmm, I have two papers due for other classes...

남: Madeleine, 네가 다음 수업에 가야 하니까 짧게 얘기하도록 하마. 에세이를 아주 잘 써냈는데, 좀 고쳐야 할 부분이 있단다.

여: 정말이요? 무슨 문제가 있나요?

남: 몇 부분이 너무 길더구나. 500자 정도로 다듬으면 좋겠어.

여: 음, 저도 그럴지도 모른다고 생각했었어요. 제 생각이 맞았네요.

남: 수정할 때, 별로 필요치 않은 내용에 시간을 많이 들이는 것보다는 하위 주제를 뒷받침 할 내용을 더 첨가하는 편이 좋단다.

여: 더 상세하게 설명해야 한다는 말씀이세요?

남: 그래, 하지만 하위 주제와 꼭 관련이 있는 내용이어야 해. 내일 오후 4시까지 할 수 있겠니? 4시 이후에 컨퍼런스가 있어.

여: 그런데 제가 다른 수업에 제출해야 할 리포트가 2개나 있어요...

| 어휘 | revise 수정하다 | due 예정인, ~하기로 되어 있는

2. 이 리서치 프로젝트는 학생의 어떤 강의에서 수행하는 프로젝트겠는가?

(A) 영문학

(B) 언어학

(C) 심리학

(D) 논리학

M: Thanks for meeting with me. I'm pretty confused about how to proceed with this research project.

W: Children aren't the easiest subjects in the world!

M: That's true. Plus, the rules about research on children are very strict.

W: It sounds like you've already done some reading?

M: Yes. Next, I need to do some observations. My concern is about making predictions. That part doesn't make sense to me.

W: Adults usually think with logic. Children don't. You're trying to use logic on illogical creatures. I love my daughter but I have to remind myself of this all the time!

M: So I should focus on age-related behaviors, but I should remember that children won't do things the way I would do them?

W: Right!

남: 시간을 내주셔서 감사합니다. 이 리서치 프로젝트를 어떻게 계속 진행시켜 나가야 할지 잘 모르겠어요.

여: 아이들이 쉬운 연구 대상은 아니지!

남: 맞아요. 그리고 아이들을 대상으로 하는 연구 방식도 너무 까다로워요.

여: 들어보니 이미 읽기 자료는 읽은 것 같은데?

남: 네. 이제 관찰을 해야 하는데요. 제가 걱정하는 부분은 예측을 하는 거예요. 그 부분이 잘 이해가 가지 않아요.

여: 어른들은 대개 논리적으로 생각해. 아이들은 그렇지 않지. 너는 비논리적인 대상에 논리를 적용하려 하고 있어. 난 내 딸을 사랑하지만, 항상 이 사실을 명심하고 있어야 해!

남: 그럼, 나이와 관련된 행동에 초점을 맞추되, 아이들이 저와 같은 방식으로는 행동하지 않을 거라는 것을 기억해야겠네요?

여: 그렇지!

어휘 I proceed 계속해서 나아가다 I strict 엄격한, 세밀한 I observation 관찰 I prediction 예측 I logic 논리 I remind A of B A에게 B를 상기시키다

Service Encounters

1. (C)   **2.** (B)

---

1. 노래 동아리에 관해 추론할 수 있는 것은 무엇인가?
(A) 3일 간의 공연 모두 성황을 이룰 거라 자신하고 있다.
(B) 학생회관 매니저에게 사용료를 지불해야 한다.
(C) 아직 팸플릿을 인쇄하지 않았다.
(D) 공연을 자세히 기획하지 않았다.

W: Hi, um, I'm here as a representative of the new singing club. We need a space for our first performance.
M: Are you with the chorus? Don't you already use the concert hall?
W: No, we're different. The chorus does more traditional music, and we wanted to be more experimental. More modern?
M: I see. Well, that sounds like fun. So you want to perform on campus - where?
W: Hmm, that's a good question. Ah, is there a charge? We have official status from the university but not much funding.
M: Why don't we book you in at the student center? There's no charge since you're an official club, and it's a medium-sized space. You can have up to three nights.
W: That's great! We wanted to do three.
M: Then, you need to fill out the form and talk to the student center manager.
W: Great, thanks! Now we can print the brochures and put up advertisements.

여: 안녕하세요, 새로 생긴 노래 동아리 대표로 왔는데요. 첫 공연을 할 장소가 필요해요.
남: 합창단 소속인가요? 이미 콘서트홀에서 공연을 하지 않았어요?
여: 아뇨, 저희는 다른 동아리에요. 합창단은 좀 더 전통적인 음악을 하는데, 저희는 좀 더 실험성이 강한 음악을 하고 싶었어요. 더 현대적이라고 할까요?
남: 그렇군요. 재미있겠네요. 캠퍼스에서 공연을 하고 싶다는 거죠? 어디에서 할 거죠?
여: 음, 잘 물어봐 주셨어요. 저희가 사용료를 내야 하나요? 저희 동아리가 학교에서 허가를 받긴 했지만, 보조금은 별로 못 받아서요.
남: 그럼 학생회관을 예약해줄까요? 공식 동아리이라 사용료는 안 내도 되고, 중간 규모의 공간이에요. 최대 3일간 사용할 수 있어요.
여: 잘됐네요! 3일간 공연하고 싶었거든요.
남: 자, 사용 신청 양식을 작성하고 학생회관 매니저와 이야기를 해보도록 해요.
여: 네, 감사합니다! 이제 팸플릿을 인쇄하고 광고 전단지를 붙일 수 있겠어요.

어휘 I experimental 실험적인 I charge 요금, 사용료 I fill out ~를 작성하다 I put up 세우다, 붙이다

2. 학생에 관해 추론할 수 있는 것은 무엇인가?

(A) 당분간 휴학할 것이다.

(B) 이번 학기에 물리학 수업을 들을 수 없을 것이다.

(C) 스팸 메일을 모두 지울 것이다.

(D) 이메일 계정을 새로 만들 것이다.

W: What happened to the two o'clock physics class? Here's the course number. I went, but the room was empty.

M: One second, let me look that up... OK, that class was cancelled.

W: Really? What happened?

M: The usual. Not enough students registered for it, so it was cut.

W: But no one notified me?

M: Really? The system automatically sends out e-mail when that happens. Is this your e-mail address?

W: Um, let me see it... yes, it is, but I never got it.

M: It's just some e-mail services treat these messages as spam. That happens sometimes.

W: Oh, so I might have gotten it, but it was never in my inbox. Oh, well, it's too late to check now. So what should I do?

M: You probably ought to take it next semester.

여: 2시에 시작하는 물리학 수업이 어떻게 된 거죠? 여기 강좌번호가 있어요. 강의실에 갔는데, 아무도 없었어요.

남: 잠깐만요, 찾아볼게요... 아, 그 수업은 취소되었네요.

여: 네? 무슨 일이죠?

남: 흔한 일이에요. 수강 신청을 한 학생들이 많지 않아서 폐강되었어요.

여: 그런데 저한테는 아무도 알려주지 않았고요?

남: 그래요? 강의가 취소되면 시스템에서 자동적으로 이메일을 보내는데요. 이것이 학생의 이메일 주소인가요?

여: 음, 좀 볼게요... 맞아요, 그런데 메일을 못 받았어요.

남: 일부 이메일 시스템에서는 이런 메시지를 스팸으로 인식해서 그래요. 가끔 그런 일이 일어나요.

여: 그럼 제가 받았을 수도 있지만, 수신함에는 없었어요. 이제 와서 확인해보기에는 너무 늦었죠. 그럼 이제 전 어떡하죠?

남: 다음 학기에 그 강의를 들어야 할 것 같군요.

어휘 | empty 텅 빈 | automatically 자동으로 | inbox 수신함

Lectures

1. 1. (B) 2. (D)   **2.** 1. (D) 2) (B)

---

1. 1. 다음 중 수요자층을 정하는 요인이 아닌 것은?

(A) 무슨 일을 하는가
(B) 누구와 어울리는가
(C) 얼마를 버는가
(D) 나이가 몇인가

2. 대학생은 다음 중 어느 광고에 관심을 갖게 될 것 같은가?
  (A) 은퇴 펀드 프로그램
  (B) 가정용품
  (C) 신혼여행 패키지 투어
  (D) 노트북

P: Whenever you watch TV or read a magazine, you experience target marketing. I don't need to tell you that commercials and ads exist to sell things, right? Their job is to make a sports car look like your guarantee to an exciting future. If you buy one, according to the ads and commercials, you'll have a great boyfriend or girlfriend in about 30 seconds. You'll be glamorous and rich. You'll have a gleaming white smile and perfect skin. Of course, no car can deliver all those things, but depending on your age, your income level, and a great many other factors, the people responsible for those ads are going to do their best to make you believe otherwise. Products are marketed to groups of people called market segments. A market segment takes into account a great many things. I just mentioned age and income. But what else could a market segment include? Geography, gender, education level, occupation, family size, sexual orientation... everything that makes you who you are. Are 80-year-old grandmothers in northern Canada likely to want to buy fast sports cars? No, probably not. Is a university student in Los Angeles going to be interested in vitamin supplements aimed at senior citizens? No to that one too. So advertisers look at all these things, because the companies that produce these things obviously want to be able to sell them. Companies spend a lot on research in order to understand who their customers are. The practice of breaking the population down into market segments is not a new science, not at all. So how many different market segments do you think you belong to?

P: 여러분이 텔레비전을 볼 때나, 잡지를 읽을 때마다, 여러분은 타깃 마케팅을 경험하고 있어요. 광고가 물건을 팔 목적으로 만들어진다는 것은 굳이 말 안 해도 되겠죠? 광고의 목적은 스포츠카가 여러분을 멋진 미래로 데려다준다고 믿도록 만드는 것이죠. 광고 내용대로라면, 여러분이 스포츠카를 한 대 사면, 30초 후에 멋진 남자 친구나 여자 친구가 생기죠. 매력적으로 보이고 부자가 될 거예요. 반짝반짝 빛나는 미소와 결점 없는 완벽한 피부를 갖게 되겠죠. 물론 이런 것들을 가져다 줄 수 있는 차는 어디에도 없지만, 여러분의 나이와 수입 레벨, 그 외 많은 요인들에 따라 이런 광고를 만드는 사람들은 여러분이 이런 것을 믿게 만들려고 할 거예요. 상품은 수요자층(market segments)이라고 불리는 집단에게 팔려요. 수요자층에는 많은 요인들이 고려되죠. 방금 전에 나이와 수입을 언급했었죠. 그리고 또 뭐가 있을까요? 지역과 성, 교육 수준, 직업, 가족 규모, 성적 성향 등등 여러분의 정체성을 만들어주는 것들이죠. 캐나다 북부에 살고 있는 80세 할머니가 빠른 스포츠카를 사고 싶어 할까요? 아마도 아니겠죠. LA에 사는 대학생이 노령자를 겨냥해 만들어진 비타민 보충

어휘 | commercial 광고 | glamorous 매력적인 | gleaming 빛나는 | income 수입 | take A into account A를 고려하다 | gender 성 | occupation 직업 | orientation 성향 | supplement 보충물 | senior citizen 노령자

2. 1. 강의의 주제는 무엇인가?
   (A) Nathaniel Hawthorne의 작품
   (B) James Joyce의 교사 경력
   (C) 프랑스 철학자들에게 준 James Joyce의 영향
   (D) 소설가 James Joyce

2. James Joyce에 관해 추론할 수 있는 것은 무엇인가?
   (A) 작품을 많이 쓴 작가였다.
   (B) 종교 문제 때문에 외국에 살았다.
   (C) 모든 작품이 같은 출판사에서 출판되었다.
   (D) 모든 작품이 자전적 이야기이다.

P: So, we talked a little about Nathaniel Hawthorne and his writings last week, and I guess you've all done your reading material for today's class. Well, the Irish author James Joyce published very few novels, but let's say very few writers have enjoyed anything like Joyce's impact upon literature in the English language. Joyce was born in Dublin in the late 19th century but, um, spent most of his life outside of Ireland. For a time he taught English at the Berlitz language schools in Pula and Trieste, which now belong to Croatia and Italy. He remained in Trieste for years, and moved on to Rome later, with his wife.

He was a hard drinker with a deeply troubled past that included conflict with and alienation from the Catholic Church and, uh... Irish society in general. His semi-autobiographical novel *A Portrait of the Artist as a Young Man* was published in 1916, and it followed his short story collection *Dubliners* but preceded his major novel *Ulysses*. Um, Joyce had tried writing a fictional account of his life story earlier, under the title *Stephen Hero*, but he met with no success getting it published. He later reused significant parts of this early book in *A Portrait of the Artist as a Young Man*, although he made changes in order to fit them in. Joyce's experimental style and his use of language have influenced many important contemporary writers, including Salman Rushdie, Samuel Beckett, and many others. The French philosophers Jacques Derrida and Jacques Lacan even owe him a literary debt. Joyce's writing is difficult, just as his life was, but he is among the most important writers in English.

P: 자, 지난 주 Nathaniel Hawthorne(나다니엘 호손)과 그의 작품에 관해 수업을 했는데, 여러분 모두 오늘 수업 주제에 관한 읽기 자료를 다 읽어왔겠죠. 아일랜드 작가인 James Joyce(제임스 조이스)는 몇 편 밖에 안 되는 소설을 출간했지만, Joyce만큼 영문학에 큰 영향을 끼친 작가는 많지 않다고 말해두죠. Joyce는 19세기 후반에 Dublin(더블린)에서 태어났는데, 아일랜드가 아닌 곳에서 주로 살았어요. 한 때는 Pula(풀라)와 Trieste(트리에스테)에 있는 Berlitz 언어 학교에서 영어를 가르쳤는데, 현재는 크로아티아와 이탈리아에 속하는 곳이죠. Trieste에서 몇 년간 살다가 아내와 함께 로마로 옮겨갔어요.

Joyce는 대주가로 고통으로 가득 찬 과거의 기억을 갖고 있었는데, 예전에 가톨릭교회 및 아일랜드 사회와 갈등을 겪고 단절되어 있었어요. 반자전적인 소설인 '젊은 예술가의 초상(*A Portrait of the Artist as a Young Man*)'은 1916년에 출간되었는데, 이보다 앞서 단편모음집인 '더블린 사람들(*Dubliners*)'이 출간되었었고, 후에는 역작인 '율리시스(*Ulysses*)'가 출간되었죠. Joyce는 이 작품이 세상에 나오기 이전에 '스티븐 히어로(*Stephen Hero*)'라는 제목으로 자신의 이야기를 담은 소설을 썼었는데, 출간되지 못했어요. 후에 '젊은 예술가의 초상'이 책의 상당 부분을 삽입했죠, 물론 내용에 맞게 변형하기는 했지만요. Joyce의 실험적인 문체와 언어 사용은 Salman Rushdie(살만 루시디)와 Samuel Beckett(사무엘 베케트) 등과 같은 많은 현대 작가들에게 영향을 주었어요. 프랑스 철학가 Jacques Derrida(자크 데리다)와 Jacques Lacan(자크 라캉) 역시 Joyce에게서 문학적 영향을 받았죠. Joyce의 작품은 그의 인생이 그러했던 것처럼 어렵지만, 영문학에서 빼놓을 수 없는 뛰어난 작가죠.

어휘 | impact 영향 | conflict 갈등 | alienation 소원, 단절 | semi-autobiographical 반자전적인 | contemporary 동시대의 | debt 빚

Practice

1. (C) **2.** (B) **3.** (A) **4.** (D) **5.** Suggested - (A), (C), (D) Not Suggested - (B), (E) **6.** (B)
7. (D) **8.** (A) **9.** (A) **10.** (D) **11.** Mentioned - (B), (D), (E) Not Mentioned - (A), (C)

[문제 1~5] 서점에서 일어난 대화의 일부를 들으시오.

1. 학생이 가진 문제는 무엇인가?
(A) 천문학 강의에 등록하지 못했다.
(B) 지금 당장 새 책을 주문해야 한다.
(C) 서점에 그가 필요로 하는 책의 재고가 없다.
(D) 교수님이 그가 사용할 수 있는 여분의 책을 갖고 있지 않았다.
해설 | 학생이 강의 교재를 구입하려고 서점에 들렀는데, 찾는 책의 재고가 없는 상황이다. 정답은 보기 (C).

2. 학생은 어떤 강의에 사용할 책을 찾고 있는가?
(A) 생물학
(B) 천문학
(C) 지리학
(D) 점성학

해설 ┃ 학생이 추가 신청한 과목은 천문학 개론으로 지금 이 강의의 교재를 구입하려 하고 있다. 정답은 보기 (B).

3. 학생이 필요로 하는 책에 관해 추론할 수 있는 것은 무엇인가?
 (A) 여러 개정판이 있다.
 (B) 상태가 안 좋다.
 (C) 서점의 실수로 재고가 없다.
 (D) 대학 도서관에도 있다.

해설 ┃ 서점 직원이 책을 구할 방법으로 언급한 내용 중 하나가 새 책을 주문하는 것인데, 강의 시간에 교수가 사용하는 책은 이미 절판된 예전 판이라고 하였다. 이 부분을 통해 학생이 찾고 있는 책에는 여러 개정판이 있다는 것을 알 수 있다. 정답은 보기 (A).

대화의 일부를 다시 들으시오. 그러고 나서 질문에 답하시오.
여: 이해해요. 그런 일이 항상 일어나죠. 대부분은 현명해서 등록하기 전까지는 책을 사지 않고 기다리죠.

4. 여자가 이것을 말할 때 암시하는 것은 무엇인가: 🎧
 여: 대부분은 현명해서 등록하기 전까지는 책을 사지 않고 기다리죠.

 (A) 이 학교 학생들은 대부분 매우 똑똑하다.
 (B) 학생들은 제 때에 수강 신청을 해야 한다.
 (C) 학생은 오래 전에 책을 구입했어야 한다.
 (D) 일부 학생들은 강의에 등록하기 전에 책을 구입한다.

해설 ┃ 학생이 대기자 명단에 올라 있는 상태에서는 강의 수강 여부를 확신할 수 없기 때문에 교재를 구입하고 싶지 않았다고 말하자, 직원이 대부분의 학생들이 그 학생처럼 수강 등록을 하기 전까지는 책을 구입하지 않고 기다린다고 하였다. 대부분이 그렇다는 것은 그렇지 않은 학생들도 있다는 뜻이다. 따라서 직원은 보기 (D)와 같이 강의 등록 전에 책을 구입하는 학생들도 있다는 것을 드러내고 있다. 정답은 보기 (D).

5. 대화에서, 여자는 남자의 문제에 대한 해결책을 제시하고 있다. 아래 표의 각 보기가 여자가 제시한 내용인지 표시하시오. 각 보기에 맞는 칸에 클릭하시오.

	Suggested	Not Suggested
(A) 온라인 헌책 사이트를 찾아보기	√	
(B) 다른 학생에게 책을 빌리기		√
(C) 교수님이 여분을 가지고 있는지 알아보기 위해 찾아가기	√	
(D) 개정판 한 부를 주문하기	√	
(E) 책을 복사하기		√

해설 ┃ 직원은 학생에게 4가지 옵션을 제시하고 있다. 서점 측에서 책 구입 후 아직 컴퓨터에 등록하지 않은 책이 있는지 확인하기, 개정판을 한 권 주문하기, 인터넷 헌책 판매 사이트를 알아보기, 교수가 여분의 책을 가지고 있는지 알아보기 등이다. 이 중 보기에 언급된 것은 보기 (A), (C), (D).

🎧 [Questions 1~5] Listen to part of a conversation at a bookstore.

M: Hi, can you help me locate a textbook?

W: Sure, can you tell me either the title or the course number?

M: Here you are... it's on the course guidelines. I've just added the class, intro to astronomy. I was on the waiting list, and I didn't want to buy the book if I couldn't take the class.

W: I understand. That happens to students all the time. Most of them are smart enough to wait until they're enrolled before buying the books... hmm, this is not good...

M: What is it? That doesn't sound good.

W: Well, we're out of stock.

M: I thought it might be. Isn't there anywhere else I can get it?

W: Well, you've got a few options. I can check to see if we've just bought one and haven't logged it yet, but that's unlikely. Don't get your hopes up.

M: That would be the best-case scenario. What are the other options, if you don't have a copy here?

W: We can order a new one for you, but according to your course guideline, the professor is using an older edition that's gone out of print. So it would be a bit different from everyone else's books.

M: Hmm, let's do that as a last resort. Is there anything else you can think of?

W: Anything else... um... ah, you should also check the Internet. The sites that sell secondhand textbooks are great in situations like this. You might be able to find the book and have it shipped to you faster than we could get a new one... more cheaply, too.

M: That's a good idea!

W: But, in the meantime, talk to your professor as soon as you can. He might have an extra copy or two in his office.

M: I'll do that. Thanks for all the great suggestions!

Now get ready to answer the questions. You may use your notes to help you answer.

Q. 4 Listen again to part of the conversation. Then answer the question.
> W: I understand. That happens to students all the time. Most of them are smart enough to wait until they're enrolled before buying the books...

What does the woman imply when she says this : 🎧
> W: Most of them are smart enough to wait until they're enrolled before buying the books...

남: 안녕하세요, 책 찾는 걸 좀 도와주시겠어요?

여: 네, 책 제목이나 강의 번호를 알려줄래요?

남: 여기 있어요... 강의 가이드라인에 나와 있어요. 천문학 개론 과목을 방금 추가 신청했어요. 대기자

목록에 올라 있었는데요, 강의를 듣지 못하게 될 까봐 책을 구입하고 싶지 않았어요.

여: 이해해요. 그런 일이 항상 일어나죠. 대부분은 현명해서 등록하기 전까지는 책을 사지 않고 기다리죠. 음, 이거 안 좋은데요...

남: 무슨 일이죠? 안 좋은 일 같은데요.

여: 재고가 없네요.

남: 그럴지도 모른다고 생각했었어요. 책을 구할 수 있는 곳이 없을까요?

여: 음, 몇 가지 옵션이 있어요. 먼저 우리가 책을 구입하고 나서 아직 등록하지 않은 책이 있는지 알아볼게요. 그럴 가능성은 거의 없지만요. 너무 기대하지는 마세요.

남: 그렇게 되면 정말 좋겠어요. 책이 서점에 없으면, 다른 옵션은 무엇인가요?

여: 새로 한 권 주문해 줄 수도 있지만, 강의 가이드라인을 보니, 교수님이 이미 절판된 예전 판을 쓰고 계시네요. 그렇게 되면, 다른 학생들이 쓰는 책과는 조금 다를 거예요.

남: 그렇다면 그 옵션은 최후의 방법으로 남겨둬야겠네요. 또 다른 방법은 없을까요?

여: 다른 방법이라... 아, 인터넷을 알아봐요. 헌책을 파는 웹사이트가 이런 경우에 큰 도움이 되죠. 원하는 책을 발견해서 여기서 새 책을 주문해 받아보는 것보다 더 빨리 배송 받을 수 있을지도 몰라요... 더 저렴하기도 하고요.

남: 좋은 생각이네요!

여: 그 동안에 빨리 교수님과 이야기를 해봐요. 연구실에 여분의 책이 몇 권 있을 수도 있으니까.

남: 그렇게 할게요. 유용한 방법들을 알려주셔서 감사합니다!

어휘 | astronomy 천문학 | out of stock 재고가 없는 | unlikely 가망 없는 | out of print 절판된 | resort 수단 | secondhand 중고의 | ship 운송하다 | in the meantime 그 사이에

[문제 6~11] 사회학 강의의 일부를 들으시오.

6. 교수의 강의 주제는 무엇인가?

(A) 캐나다 정부의 이민 정책

(B) 미국 사회를 표현하는 멜팅팟이란 비유에 대한 개관

(C) 미국 사회를 상징하는 아이콘

(D) 미국의 초기 역사

해설 | 미국의 다문화 사회를 표현하는 '멜팅팟'이라는 비유의 유래와 이 표현이 현대 미국 사회를 얼마나 잘 대변해주는지를 주로 다루고 있다. 정답은 보기 (B).

7. 초기 미국 정착자들은 주로 어디에서 왔는가?

(A) 아프리카

(B) 남아메리카

(C) 아시아

(D) 유럽

해설 | 전세계 이주민 가운데, 특히 유럽인들이 미국 대륙으로 많이 건너왔다. 정답은 보기 (D).

8. 미국의 인종간 결혼에 관해 추론할 수 있는 것은 무엇인가?

(A) 1967년 이전에는 불법이었다.

(B) 요즘에는 찾아보기 어렵다.
(C) 백인 유럽인에게만 허용되었다.
(D) 개인의 역사적 정체성을 없애버린다.

해설 l 백인 유럽인들끼리 결혼하는 일은 잦았지만, 1967년 이전에는 다른 인종 간의 결혼을 막는 법이 있었다고 하였다. 이는 이 시기에 인종간 결혼이 불법이었다는 것을 뜻한다. 정답은 보기 (A). 최근에 미국 대도시에서 인종간 결혼이 증가하고 있다고 하였으므로 보기 (B)는 오답이다. 백인과 아시아인의 결혼이 허용되던 때도 있었으므로 보기 (C) 역시 오답이다.

9. 현재 인종간 결혼 추세로부터 추론할 수 있는 것은 무엇인가?
  (A) 새로운 경향은 도시 지역에서 보통 시작된다.
  (B) 시골 지역 사람들이 문화 차이에 대해 더 포용력이 있는 편이다.
  (C) 대도시에 거주하는 사람들은 자신들의 생활방식을 고집하는 경향이 있다.
  (D) 소도시에 거주하는 사람들은 결혼율이 낮다.

해설 l 최근에 미국 대도시에서 인종간 결혼이 증가하고 있다는 것으로 보아 보통 새로운 경향은 도시 지역에서부터 생겨난다고 결론 내릴 수 있다. 정답은 보기 (A).

강의의 일부를 다시 들으시오. 그러고 나서 질문에 답하시오.
현재 많은 새로운 개념들이 공개적으로 논의되고 있으며, 멜팅팟이란 비유는 시대에 뒤떨어진 표현으로 간주되고 있어요. 이런 새로운 개념들 중에 가장 사람들 입에 자주 오르내리는 것이 바로 샐러드 그릇(salad bowl)이란 용어에요, 즉 각각의 재료가 한 그릇에 담기지만, 각 재료는 본래의 향과 모양, 신선함을 간직하잖아요. 이 샐러드 그릇에서 만들어지는 최상의 결과는 모든 맛과 느낌이 조화를 이루는 거죠.

10. 교수가 이것을 말할 때 암시하는 것은 무엇인가 :
  이 샐러드 그릇에서 만들어지는 최상의 결과는 모든 맛과 느낌이 조화를 이루는 거죠.

  (A) 다른 재료와 잘 어울리는 채소가 들어있는 샐러드가 최고다.
  (B) 다양한 문화를 받아들이는 사람은 공개 토론에 참여하는 것을 좋아한다.
  (C) 이민자를 많이 받아들이는 국가는 여러 문제가 생겨나는 편이다.
  (D) 성공적인 다문화 사회는 사람들이 자신의 민족적 전통을 간직한 사회이다.

해설 l 최근 미국의 다문화 사회를 비유하는 표현으로 멜팅팟이란 용어 대신 샐러드 그릇이란 용어가 더 적합하다는 의견들이 제시되고 있다. 교수는 우리가 샐러드를 만들 때 다양한 채소를 샐러드 그릇 안에 넣고 버무리지만 각 채소의 고유한 맛이 서로 조화를 이루어 더 좋은 맛을 내는 것처럼, 다양한 문화적 배경을 가진 사람들이 모여 사는 미국 사회에서도 각 구성원에게 하나의 문화를 강요하는 대신 각자가 자신의 문화적, 민족적 전통을 지키며 남들과 조화를 이루며 살아가는 것이 바람직하다고 말하고 싶어한다. 따라서 정답은 보기 (D).

11. 강의에서, 교수는 멜팅팟을 대체할 현대적인 비유 표현을 언급하고 있다. 아래 표의 각 보기가 이런 비유 표현에 포함되는지 표시하시오. 각 보기에 맞는 칸에 클릭하시오.

	Mentioned	Not Mentioned
(A) 칵테일		V
(B) 샐러드 그릇	V	
(C) 목걸이		V
(D) 심포니	V	
(E) 문화 모자이크	V	

해설 l 멜팅팟을 대체할 새로운 표현으로 언급된 것은 보기 (B)의 샐러드 그릇과 보기 (D)의 심포니, 보기 (E)의 문화 모자이크이다. 정답은 (B), (D), (E).

[Questions 6~11] Listen to part of a lecture in a sociology class.

P(W): One of the best-known and most enduring metaphors for the American way of life is the melting pot. When you think of the American ideal, it's probably the first thought that comes to your mind, along with democracy and the Statue of Liberty. But what is the melting pot? What exactly are we melting down, and what is the finished product?

In the first two centuries of America's existence, immigrants were pouring in from all over the world. The initial settlers were Europeans. Of course we are all aware of the horrors of slavery, and the arrival of African people in the U.S. Yet many of us aren't so familiar with American's early immigrants from Asia and Latin America. Despite the often racist and exclusionary practices against darker-skinned people, many Americans of that time had high hopes for what could be achieved. They imagined all the old animosities and prejudices could disappear, and a truly new person, the American, came into being.

The result, however, has been rather different from what many early proponents of the melting pot ideal might have imagined. The idea carries with it notions of assimilation into the new culture — meaning that one's historical identity is lost. The idea also suggests intermarriage. However, that is not quite how American history has played out. The white European ethnic groups have over time increasingly intermarried, so that any given person might have — for example — German, English, French, Italian, and Scottish ancestors. However, until 1967 there were laws against marriage between people of different races. Blacks and whites could not marry; at first, whites and Asians could, but in some states, laws were changed to prohibit that. Only in recent years, in the largest American cities, have we truly seen sharp increases in the number of interracial marriages.

Now a number of new concepts are entering public discussion, and the melting pot metaphor is considered outdated. One of the most common new ones is the salad bowl: individual ingredient vegetables come together, but they retain their taste, their shape, and — hopefully — their freshness. The successful result is a combination of all the flavors and textures. This philosophy has been adopted by the Canadian government, which has been aggressive in recruiting new immigrants. Other metaphors include the symphony and the cultural mosaic. It is likely that different countries that receive large numbers of immigrants will choose metaphors appropriate for their culture. I predict this will be a truly fascinating subject to watch, as years go by.

Now get ready to answer the questions. You may use your notes to help you answer.

Q. 10 Listen again to part of the lecture. Then answer the question.

Now a number of new concepts are entering public discussion, and the melting pot metaphor is considered outdated. One of the most common new ones is the salad bowl: individual ingredient vegetables come together, but they retain their taste, their shape, and — hopefully — their freshness. The successful result is a combination of all the flavors and textures.

What does the professor mean when he says this: 🎧
The successful result is a combination of all the flavors and textures.

P: 미국을 표현하는 말들 중에 가장 잘 알려지고 가장 오래된 은유가 바로 멜팅팟(인종이나 문화 등 여러 요소가 융합된 곳)이죠. 미국의 이상적인 모습에 관해 생각할 때 민주주의와 자유의 여신상과 더불어 아마 가장 먼저 떠오르는 생각일겁니다. 그런데 이 멜팅팟이란 무엇일까요? 대체 우리가 녹이고 있는 것은 무엇이고, 마지막에 완성되는 것은 무엇일까요?
미국이라는 나라가 세워지고 나서 처음 2백여 년간 전세계에서 이주민들이 몰려 왔어요. 처음 발을 디딘 개척자들은 유럽인들이었죠. 물론 노예 관습과 미국에 건너온 아프리카 인들에 관해서는 우리 모두 알고 있어요. 그런데 아시아와 남아메리카에서 건너온 초기 이주민들에 관해서는 잘 모르고 있죠. 어두운 피부색을 가진 사람들에 가해진 인종차별적이고 배제적인 관습에도 불구하고, 당시의 많은 미국인들은 그들이 이룰 수 있는 것에 관해 큰 희망을 가지고 있었어요. 그들은 과거의 모든 원한과 편견이 사라지고 완전히 새로운 인간, 즉 미국인이 등장할 것이라 생각했죠.
하지만 결과는 멜팅팟이란 이상 사회를 꿈꾸던 많은 초기 지지자들이 바라던 것과는 다르게 나타났어요. 멜팅팟이란 아이디어에는 새로운 문화 속으로 동화된다는 개념이 수반되죠, 즉 개인의 역사적 정체성이 사라지는 것이죠. 멜팅팟은 다른 인종 간의 결혼도 포함해요. 하지만, 미국 역사가 이런 식으로 전개되지는 않았어요. 백인 유럽인들은 시간이 지나면서 인종 간의 결혼이 증가했는데, 그 결과 독일인이나 영국인, 프랑스인, 이탈리아인, 그리고 스코틀랜드인 조상을 가진 사람들이 생겨나게 되었어요. 하지만, 1967년까지 다른 인종 간의 결혼을 막는 법이 있었어요. 흑인과 백인은 결혼할 수 없었죠. 처음에는 백인과 아시아인이 결혼할 수 있었지만, 일부 주에서 이런 관습조차 금지하도록 법이 바뀌었어요. 최근에서야 미국 대도시에서 인종간 결혼을 하는 수가 크게 증가하고 있지요.
현재 많은 새로운 개념들이 공개적으로 논의되고 있으며, 멜팅팟이란 비유는 시대에 뒤떨어진 표현으로 간주되고 있어요. 이런 새로운 개념들 중에 가장 사람들 입에 자주 오르내리는 것이 바로 샐러드 그릇(salad bowl)이란 용어에요, 즉 각각의 재료가 한 그릇에 담기지만, 각 재료는 본래의 향과 모양, 신선함을 간직하잖아요. 이 샐러드 그릇에서 만들어지는 최상의 결과는 모든 맛과 느낌이 조화를 이루는 거죠. 새로운 이민자를 받아들이는데 적극적으로 나서고 있는 캐나다 정부에서 이런 개념을 채택하였어요. 멜팅팟을 대신할 또 다른 비유로 심포니와 문화 모자이크가 있어요. 대규모의 이민자를 받아들이는 여러 다른 나라에 각국의 문화에 알맞은 비유 표현을 선택하겠죠. 내 생각에는 시간이 흐르면서 이를 지켜보는 것이 아주 재미있는 연구 주제가 될 것 같군요.

 ALL ABOUT JUNIOR TOEFL

어휘 | enduring 영속하는 | metaphor 은유 | democracy 민주주의 | melt down 녹이다 | immigrant 이주민 | initial 초기의 | settler 개척자 | horror 공포 | slavery 노예제 | racist 인종차별적인 | exclusionary 배제적인 | achieve 달성하다 | animosity 악의, 원한 | prejudice 편견 | proponent 지지자 | notion 개념 | assimilation 동화 | intermarriage 인종 간의 결혼 | ethnic 인종의 | prohibit 금지하다 | sharp 급격한 | outdated 낡은, 진부한 | ingredient 재료 | retain 간직하다 | flavor 맛, 향 | texture 느낌, 질감 | adopt 채택하다 | recruit 모집하다 | appropriate 적절한 | fascinating 매우 재미있는

Review

1. 1. I'm pretty <u>confused</u> about how to <u>proceed</u> <u>with</u> this research project.
2. Yes, but it needs to be <u>related</u> <u>to</u> <u>the</u> <u>supporting</u> points.
3. We have <u>official</u> <u>status</u> from the university but not <u>much</u> <u>funding</u>.
4. There's no <u>charge</u> since you're an <u>official</u> club, and it's a medium-sized space.
5. Now we can print the <u>brochures</u> and <u>put</u> <u>up</u> advertisements.

2. 1. When you revise it, / instead of spending so much time / on unnecessary information, / you ought to provide more support / for the supporting points.
2. Madeleine,/ I know / you need to get to your next class, / so I'll keep this brief.
3. I love my daughter / but I have to remind myself of this / all the time!
4. The system automatically sends out e-mail / when that happens.
5. Most of them are smart enough to wait / until they're enrolled / before buying the books...

Chapter 6 Connecting Information

Office Hours

1. Campus - (A), (C) Hotel - (B), (D)   **2.** Suggested - (A), (C), (D) Not Suggested - (B), (E)

1. 대화에서, 여자는 남자의 문제를 해결하는데 도움이 될 여러 아이디어를 제시하고 있다. 아래 표의 각 보기가 여자가 제시한 아이디어에 속하는지 표시하시오. 각 보기에 맞는 칸에 클릭하시오.

	Campus	Hotel
(A) 더 저렴함	V	
(B) 묵기에 더 편안한 공간을 제공함		V
(C) 더 많은 인원을 수용할 수 있음	V	
(D) 같은 건물 안에 모든 시설이 있음		V

W: Hi, I'm on the committee to organize this year's student marketing conference. We're trying to decide the place. Could you help?
M: Sure. Well, I guess you want to decide between using a hotel and using the campus, right?

W: How did you know?
M: I've been to lots of conferences. Well, if your money's limited, you ought to think about the campus. Also, the school can accommodate more people.
W: If we hold the conference on campus, where will people stay?
M: Well, they can stay in dorms, if you hold the conference between semesters.
W: It might require red tape formalities.
M: Or you can consider hotels nearby. You can usually negotiate reasonable rates for conferences.
W: But won't that be expensive?
M: Perhaps. Hotels will sometimes give discounts, though, if you're holding an event during the slow season. They are also very convenient: everything is in one place. And they're more comfortable than the dorms.

여: 안녕하세요, 저는 올해 학생 마케팅 컨퍼런스 조직위원회 소속입니다. 컨퍼런스 장소를 결정하려고 하는데요. 도와주시겠어요?
남: 그럼. 내가 보기엔 호텔과 캠퍼스 둘 중에서 결정하고 싶은 것 같은데, 그렇지?
여: 어떻게 아셨어요?
남: 난 많은 컨퍼런스에 참석했단다. 한정된 재원을 생각한다면, 캠퍼스를 더 염두에 두어야겠지. 그리고 더 많은 인원을 수용할 수 있고.
여: 캠퍼스에서 컨퍼런스를 개최한다면, 참석자들이 어디에 묵죠?
남: 음, 학기 사이(방학)에 연다면, 기숙사를 이용할 수 있단다.
여: 절차가 복잡하겠네요.
남: 아니면 근처 호텔을 고려해보렴. 컨퍼런스를 열 때는 적절한 가격 협상을 할 수 있어.
여: 그렇지만 비싸지 않을까요?
남: 그럴지도 모르지. 하지만 비성수기에 행사를 열면 할인을 해주기도 한단다. 호텔은 편리한 것도 장점이지. 모든 것이 한 곳에서 해결되니까. 기숙사보다 더 편안하기도 하고.

어휘 | organize 조직하다 | accommodate 수용하다 | red tape 형식주의 | formality 절차 | nearby 근처의 | negotiate 협상하다 | reasonable 비싸지 않은 | discount 할인 | convenient 편리한 | comfortable 편안한

2. 대화에서, 교수는 학생의 이력서의 개선점을 제시하고 있다. 아래 표의 각 보기가 교수가 제시한 내용인지 표시하시오. 각 보기에 맞는 칸에 클릭하시오.

	Suggested	Not Suggested
(A) 철자가 틀린 단어를 확인하기	∨	
(B) 직장 경력을 늘리기		∨
(C) 중학교 이야기를 빼기	∨	
(D) 더 큰 폰트로 바꾸어 인쇄하기	∨	
(E) 질이 더 좋은 종이를 사용하기		∨

M: Would you mind taking a look at my resume? I'm applying for a summer internship, and I want to make sure my resume looks as good as possible.

ALL ABOUT JUNIOR TOEFL

W: Sure, let me see... hmm, at first glance, it looks good, but I think you ought to use a larger font. It's difficult to read.

M: Really? OK, that's easy to change. What else can you suggest?

W: Well, I'd leave out the information about your junior high school. It's usually fine to leave your high school in, but junior high was a long time ago.

M: All right, I know what you mean.

W: Oh... and there are a number of spelling errors. You ought to use spell check before you print this out again. Aside from those things, I think it looks fine.

M: OK, thank you... I guess I should go back to the computer lab now!

남: 제 이력서 좀 봐주시겠어요? 하계 인턴에 지원하려고 하는데요, 이력서를 최대한 괜찮게 쓰고 싶어요.

여: 그래, 한 번 보자... 음, 얼핏 보기에는 아주 좋아 보이는데, 폰트(글자체)를 좀 더 크게 하는 것이 좋겠구나. 읽기가 힘들어.

남: 그런가요? 네, 그건 바꾸기가 쉽네요. 다른 건 뭐가 있을까요?

여: 나라면 너의 중학교 시절 이야기는 뺄 것 같구나. 보통 고등학교 시절 이야기는 쓰는 것이 좋지만, 중학교는 너무 오래 전 일이잖니.

남: 네, 무슨 말씀이신지 알겠어요.

여: 아, 그리고 철자가 틀린 곳이 몇 군데 있구나. 이력서를 인쇄하기 전에 맞춤법 검사를 하도록 해. 그런 것들 말고는 잘 쓴 것 같구나.

남: 네, 감사합니다. 컴퓨터 실습실에 바로 가서 고쳐야겠어요!

어휘 | at first glance 얼핏 보기에 | leave out 빼다 | junior high school 중학교

Service Encounters

1. Suggested - (C), (D), (E) Not Suggested - (A), (B) **2.** Yes - (B), (C), (E) No - (A), (D)

---

1. 대화에서, 남자는 학생에게 투어 진행에 대한 조언을 하고 있다. 아래 표의 각 보기가 남자가 제시한 조언에 속하는지 표시하시오. 각 보기에 맞는 칸에 클릭하시오.

	Suggested	Not Suggested
(A) 투어가 끝난 후 방문객들을 주차장으로 안내하기		V
(B) 방문객들이 자기 소개를 하도록 하기		V
(C) 투어를 하는 동안 천천히 그리고 명료히 말하기	V	
(D) 늦는 사람이 있는 경우를 대비하여 몇 분 정도 기다리기	V	
(E) 캠퍼스의 너무 많은 곳을 보여주지 않기	V	

W: Hi, I'll be leading a campus tour for visiting parents this afternoon, but this is my first time. Can you give me any suggestions like what to do and what not to do?

M: Sure. First, remember to introduce yourself. Make sure you tell the visitors you're a senior, where you're from, what your major is, and so on.

W: That sounds good. What else should I do?

M: You also want to wait about five minutes after the official start time, in case anyone is still on their way. It can be hard to find parking.

W: Oh, good point. Is there anything else?

M: Um, remember not to talk too fast. Some of the visitors may not speak English well.

W: I had forgotten about that!

M: And finally, don't try to show them everything on campus. You don't want to give them too much information.

W: All right, I'll remember your advice. Thanks!

여: 안녕하세요, 제가 오늘 오후에 학교에 방문하는 학부모들을 위한 캠퍼스 투어를 맡았어요, 그런데 이번이 처음이거든요. 해야 할 일과 하지 말아야 할 일과 같은 조언 좀 해주실 수 있으세요?

남: 좋아요. 먼저, 본인 소개를 꼭 하도록 해요. 학생이 4학년생이고, 어디 출신이며, 전공이 무엇인지 등등을 이야기 해주도록 해요.

여: 알겠어요. 또 무엇이 있나요?

남: 투어가 공식적으로 시작한 후 5분 정도는 이동하지 말고 기다리도록 해요, 아직 오고 있는 중인 사람도 있을 수 있으니까. 주차 공간을 찾기가 힘들 수 있잖아요.

여: 아, 그렇군요. 다른 건요?

남: 말을 너무 빨리 하지 않도록 주의해요. 방문객들 중 일부는 영어를 잘 못할 수도 있으니까요.

여: 그 부분을 잊고 있었네요!

남: 마지막으로, 캠퍼스에 있는 모든 곳을 보여주려고 하지는 말아요. 한꺼번에 너무 많은 정보를 주면 곤란하니까요.

여: 네, 조언 해 주신 것들을 기억하도록 할게요. 감사합니다!

어휘 | senior 4학년 in case ~인 경우를 대비하여 | on one's way ~하는 도중인

2. 대화에서, 여자는 여러 다른 밀플랜을 언급하고 있다. 아래 표의 각 보기가 여자가 언급한 것에 속하는지 표시하시오. 각 보기에 맞는 칸에 클릭하시오.

	Yes	No
(A) 캠퍼스에 있는 다른 곳에서도 사용할 수 있는 카드		V
(B) 금전적 가치도 저장되어 있고, 일주일에 정해진 횟수의 식사를 할 수 있는 복합 카드	V	
(C) 하루에 정해진 횟수의 식사를 하는 것	V	
(D) 캠퍼스에서 아무 때나 사용할 수 있는 것		V
(E) 금전적 가치가 저장되어 있는 카드	V	

M: I've just finished registering for my classes, and they sent me over here to sign up for my meal plan. How do I do that?

W: Sure, you can do that online. Let's go into my office. What kind of meal plan do you need?

M: What are the choices?

W: The most popular lets you choose either 2 or 3 meals a day. This is a use-it-or-lose-it

  ALL ABOUT JUNIOR TOEFL

plan, though. It's best for students who know they're going to eat in the cafeteria.

M: I see. What if I'm not sure?

W: We also have a stored-value card. That's good if you don't eat here as often, but you want the choice.

M: That sounds a little better, I think.

W: And finally, we've got a hybrid card that gives you 10 meals per week, plus stored value.

M: I see. Can I think it over?

남: 방금 수강 신청을 끝냈는데요, 밀플랜을 신청하라고 여기로 보냈어요. 어떻게 하면 되는 거죠?

여: 아, 온라인으로 신청할 수 있어요. 내 사무실로 가죠. 어떤 종류의 밀플랜을 원하죠?

남: 어떤 종류가 있는데요?

여: 가장 인기 있는 것이 하루에 2~3회 카페테리아를 이용하는 거예요. 사용하지 않으면, 그냥 없어져 버려요, 즉 나중에 다시 못 사용한다는 거죠. 꼭 카페테리아에서 식사를 하는 학생들에게 적합하죠.

남: 그렇군요. 어떻게 될지 모를 때는 어떡하죠?

여: 선불카드(비용가치 저장형)도 있어요. 카페테리아를 자주 이용하지는 않지만, 가끔 이용할 때를 대비해두는 사람들에게 적합해요.

남: 그게 좀 더 낫겠네요.

여: 마지막으로, 하이브리드 카드가 있는데, 일주일에 10번의 식사를 할 수 있고, 선불 기능도 겸하고 있는 카드죠.

남: 알겠습니다. 좀 생각해보고 와도 될까요?

어휘 | use-it-or-lose-it 쓰지 않으면 사라져 버리는

Lectures

1. 1. (C) 2. Decay - (B) Interference - (A), (C)   **2.** 1. (C) 2. Frank Gehry - (C), (E) Norman Foster - (A), (B), (D)

---

1. 1. 강의의 주제는 무엇인가?

    (A) 우리는 왜 정보를 잊어버리는가?

    (B) 전화번호의 비밀

    (C) 단기 기억의 두 가지 종류

    (D) 새로운 정보에 매일 노출되는 것

2. 교수는 두 가지 형태의 단기 기억을 설명하고 있다. 아래의 각 보기가 어떤 형태의 특징인지 아래 표에 표시하시오. 각 보기에 맞는 칸에 클릭하시오.

	Decay	Interference
(A) 새로운 정보가 오래된 정보를 지우는 반동 과정		V
(B) 시간이 흐름에 따라 기억을 잃는 자연적인 과정	V	
(C) 오래된 정보가 새로운 정보가 간직 되는 것을 막는 순향 과정		V

P: Short-term memory is one of those things we often take for granted but have trouble living without. It enables us to retain small amounts of information, for limited periods of time. These are things we tend to forget quickly. Think about phone numbers, for example. Have you ever wondered why most of them are seven or eight digits long? That's the maximum number of items short-term memory can easily retain.

Several things can interfere with short-term memory. One is decay, which is simply, uh, the natural process of forgetting. Over time, memories fade away. This is something we have all experienced. Well, some scientists believe decay is the primary form of memory loss: it's like a, uh, natural erasing process, and it enables that part of our memory to be ready for... for the next bit of information we need to recall. Interference is a little different. This is when new information pushes old information out of short-term memory, replacing it. There are two forms of interference here: proactive and retroactive. When we remember something new and it erases something old, that's retroactive interference. We can't remember older bits of information. However, when old information stays stuck in short-term memory, keeping us from remembering something new, that is called proactive interference. Both decay and interference are natural cognitive events. They're just normal facets of our day-to-day existence as human beings.

P: 단기 기억은 우리가 당연시 여기는 것들 중 하나이지만, 이 단기 기억이 없이는 사는데 어려움이 많을 거예요. 단기 기억은 제한된 시간 동안 적은 양의 정보를 간직하게 해주죠. 우리는 이런 단기 기억을 빠르게 잊어버리는 경향이 있어요. 예를 들면, 전화번호를 생각해봐요. 왜 대부분의 전화번호가 7자리나 8자리 숫자로 이루어져 있는지 궁금해 한적 없어요? 바로 이 자릿수가 단기 기억이 쉽게 간직할 수 있는 최대의 숫자이기 때문이에요.

단기 기억을 방해하는 것에 여러 가지가 있어요. 그 중 하나가 퇴화(decay)인데, 무언가를 잊어버리게 되는 자연적 과정이에요. 시간이 흐르면, 기억들은 사라져가요. 우리 모두 경험하는 것이죠. 일부 과학자들은 퇴화가 기억력 감퇴의 주요 형태라고 생각해요. 자연적으로 기억이 지워지는 과정 같은 것이고, 이렇게 지워지는 부분에 우리가 기억할 필요가 있는 새로운 정보가 들어가게 되요. 간섭은 퇴화와는 조금 달라요. 간섭은 새로운 정보가 오래된 정보를 단기 기억에서 밀어내고, 그 자리를 대체하는 것이죠. 간섭에는 두 가지 형태가 있어요. 우리가 새로운 무언가를 기억하고, 이 새로운 기억이 오래된 기억을 지우면, 그걸 반동 간섭이라고 해요. 이 경우에 더 오래된 정보는 기억을 못하게 되죠. 하지만 오래된 정보가 단기 기억 속에 박혀서 우리가 뭔가 새로운 것을 기억하지 못하도록 할 때는 순향 간섭이라고 하죠. 퇴화와 간섭 모두 자연스런 인식 작용이에요. 인간으로서 우리가 매일매일 살아가면서 겪는 전형적인 한 단면일 뿐이죠.

어휘 | short-term 단기의 | take A for granted A를 당연시하다 | digit 숫자 | maximum 최대의 | interfere with ~를 간섭하다 | decay 퇴화 | fade away 사라지다 | erase 지우다 | recall 기억하다 | interference 간섭 | proactive 순향의 | retroactive 반동하는 | cognitive 인식의 | facet 면, 단면

2. 1. 다음 중 어느 것이 Frank Gehry에 관해 맞는가?
   (A) 영국인이다.
   (B) 본인이 설계한 교통 시스템으로 유명하다.
   (C) 그가 설계한 건물 외관은 주로 금속으로 되어 있다.

(D) 그가 설계한 건물들은 직각을 이루고 있다.

2. 강의에서, 화자들은 두 명의 현대 건축가에 관해 이야기 하고 있다. 아래의 각 보기가 누가 설계한 건물인지 아래 표에 표시하시오. 각 보기에 맞는 칸에 클릭하시오.

	Frank Gehry	Norman Foster
(A) 홍콩 국제공항		V
(B) 싱가포르 MRT 역		V
(C) 빌바오 구겐하임 미술관	V	
(D) 런던 30 세인트 메리 액스		V
(E) LA 월트 디즈니 콘서트 홀	V	

P: Now, I'd like to talk about two of the most noted contemporary architects, Frank Gehry and Sir Norman Foster. Some of their most recent projects have earned them considerable admiration and publicity. Actually, Gehry, who is Canadian, um, his buildings often become tourist attractions because of their unusual, innovative designs. Is there someone who can tell me about Gehry's buildings?

S: As far as I know, he made his name with the titanium-covered Guggenheim Museum in Bilbao, Spain, and the Walt Disney Concert Hall in Los Angeles.

P: Yeah, even his private home in Santa Monica, California, is something of a tourist magnet. His buildings are often oddly-shaped, with few or no right angles, and metal exteriors. Well, Foster, who is British, is well-known for such buildings as the new Hong Kong International Airport, which many surveys now rank as the best in the world. He's also designed transportation systems like, um, he designed the new subway system in Bilbao, Spain, which has a station down the street from Gehry's Guggenheim. Ah, there's also a station for the Singapore MRT. Like Gehry, Foster is known to design unusual buildings, such as the uniquely pickle-shaped 30 St. Mary Axe, in London. These two architects have given us some of the most unusual, thought-provoking, and controversial buildings in the world, and it will be exciting to see what surprises they have in store with their new projects.

P: 이제 저명한 현대 건축가인 Frank Gehry(프랭크 게리)와 Norman Foster(노먼 포스터) 경에 관해 이야기 해볼까 해요. 그들은 최근 작업한 프로젝트로 사람들의 감탄을 불러 일으키고 자신들의 이름을 널리 알렸죠. 사실 캐나다인인 Gehry가 설계한 건물들은 독특하고 혁신적인 디자인 때문에 관광 명소가 되는 경우가 많아요. 누가 Gehry가 설계한 건물에 대해 말해볼래요?

S: 제가 알기로는 Gehry는 외벽이 티타늄으로 감싸져 있는 스페인의 Bilbao(빌바오) 구겐하임 미술관(Guggenheim Museum)과 LA에 있는 월트 디즈니 콘서트홀을 설계하며 유명해졌어요.

P: 그렇죠, 캘리포니아주 Santa Monica(센타모니카)에 있는 그의 자택 역시 관광객들의 발길을 끌어들이는 곳이에요. 그가 설계한 건물들은 직각으로 이루어진 곳이 거의 없을 정도로 외관 모양이 이상하게 만들어진 경우가 많고 외벽은 금속 물질로 감싸져 있어요. 영국인인 Foster는 홍콩 국제공항을 설계한 것으로 유명한데, 이곳은 많은 조사에서 전세계 최고의 공항으로 뽑혔어요. 그는 교통 시스템을 설계하기도 했는데, 스페인 빌바오의 지하철 역시 그가 디자인했으며, Gehry가 설계한 구겐하임 미술관을 따라 걸어가다 보면 역이 나오기도 하죠. 아, 그리고 싱가포르 MRT 역도 있군요. Gehry와 마찬가지로 Foster는 독특한 건물을 설계하는 것으로 유명한데요, 런던에 있는 오이

어휘 | noted 저명한 | contemporary 현대의 | architect 건축가 | admiration 감탄 | publicity 널리 알려짐 | tourist attraction 관광 명소 | innovative 혁신적인 | titanium 티타늄 | survey 조사 | pickle 오이 | magnet 사람의 마음을 끌어들이는 것 | thought-provoking 시사하는 바가 많은 | in store 준비하여, 저장하여

Practice

1. (D) **2.** (A) **3.** (B) **4.** (A) **5.** (C) → (A) → (D) → (B) **6.** (C) **7.** (B)
8. Mentioned - (B), (D), (E) Not Mentioned - (A), (C) **9.** (C) **10.** (D) **11.** (B)

[문제 1~5] 도서관에서 일어난 대화의 일부를 들으시오.

1. 학생이 도서관에서 필요로 하는 것은 무엇인가?
(A) 도서관 카드를 받아야 한다.
(B) 책을 대출해야 한다.
(C) 리포트를 써야 한다.
(D) 정기 간행물 기사를 구해야 한다.
해설 | 학생은 온라인 정기 간행물 서비스를 이용하고 싶어 한다. 리포트 작성을 위해 정기 간행물 기사를 찾고 있다. 정답은 보기 (D).

대화의 일부를 다시 들으시오. 그러고 나서 질문에 답하시오.
남: 네, 온라인 정기 간행물 서비스를 이용하고 싶어요. 리포트를 쓰는 중인데요, 정기 간행물 기사 5개를 찾아야 해요. 그런데 뭘 해야 할지 잘 모르겠어요. 교수님이 안내물을 나눠주셨는데요, 뭐가 뭔지 하나도 모르겠어요!
여: 걱정 말아요. 찾는 것을 도와줄게요.

2. 여자가 이것을 말할 때 의미하는 것은 무엇인가 : 🎧
여: 찾는 것을 도와줄게요.

(A) 학생에게 절차를 설명해 줄 것이다.
(B) 학생과 함께 다른 곳으로 갈 것이다.
(C) 학생은 다른 곳으로 가야 한다.
(D) 학생은 나중에 다시 와야 한다.

해설 | 정기 간행물 기사를 어떻게 찾아야 할지 몰라 곤란해하는 학생에게 사서가 걱정 말라며 도와주겠다고 했다. 사서는 학생이 서비스를 이용하는 방법을 설명해줄 것이다. 정답은 보기 (A).

3. 학생에 관해 추론할 수 있는 것은 무엇인가?

(A) 이번 학기에 리포트를 쓰느라 바빴다.

(B) 이번 학기에 도서관에서 책을 빌린 적이 없다.

(C) 당장 정기 간행물 기사가 필요하지는 않다.

(D) 도서관 카드를 사용해보기도 전에 잃어버렸다.

해설 | 학생은 신입생으로 학생증을 발급 받은 지 아직 얼마 안되어 학생 카드가 도서관 이용을 위해 활성화 되어 있지 않은 상태다. 활성화 되어 있지 않다는 것은 학생이 아직 도서관에서 대출을 해본 적이 없음을 암시한다. 정답은 보기 (B).

4. 도서관에서는 발행된 지 1년 이상 된 정기 간행물을 어떻게 하는가?

(A) 컴퓨터로 읽힐 수 있는 형태로 바꾼다.

(B) 분리된 장소에 모두 보관한다.

(C) 다른 도서관으로 보낸다.

(D) 새 책을 들여 놓기 위한 공간 확보를 위해 폐기한다.

해설 | 발행된 지 1년이 넘은 정기 간행물은 디지털화 하는 작업을 한다고 했다. 즉 컴퓨터로 내용을 볼 수 있게 만드는 것이다. 정답은 보기 (A).

5. 여자는 정기 간행물 데이터베이스를 이용하는 절차를 설명하고 있다. 각 단계를 순서대로 배열하시오.
보기를 표의 해당되는 빈 칸으로 드래그하시오.

	정기 간행물 데이터베이스 이용
1	(C)
2	(A)
3	(D)
4	(B)

(A) 온라인 데이터베이스에서 기사를 찾기

(B) 정기 간행물 담당 직원에게 목록을 갖다 주기

(C) 도서관에서 사용하기 위해 학생증 준비

(D) 기사 목록을 프린트하기

해설 | 먼저 사서가 학생의 신원을 확인해야 하고, 그 후에 학생이 데이터베이스에서 원하는 간행물을 찾아보고, 목록을 인쇄한 후 사서에게 가져다 주면 된다. 따라서 정답은 (C) → (A) → (D) → (B)의 순서이다.

🎧 [Questions 1~5] Listen to part of a conversation at a library.

W: Hi, are you looking for something in particular?

M: Yes, I need to use the online periodical service. I'm writing a paper, and I need to find five journal articles, but I don't know what to do. My lecturer gave out an instruction sheet, but it's all so overwhelming!

W: No worries. I'll walk you through it. First, you need to have your campus ID card activated for library use. Have you done that?

M: No, I'm a freshman. This is my first semester. I just got the card a few weeks ago.

W: All right, if you'll give it to me, I'll put it in the card reader and confirm your details. It'll take less than a minute... thanks, uh, so is this your dorm room and your phone number? Is the e-mail address correct?

M: Yes, so can I use it to get the journal articles now?

W: Not yet. You can check out books now, but journal articles are a little more complicated. Uh, you have to look them up in our database, print out a list.

M: A list?

W: Yes, and then bring it to the periodicals desk. After that, we'll handle it. But that's only for journals that are more than one year old. Until that time, we keep them here, and we have to get the copy for you.

M: Oh, I see. That sounds really complicated.

W: Well, you see, we digitize them when they're one year old, to save space. Then we recycle them. So if it's a new article, you'll get the journal here. If it's older than that, you get an electronic copy. It's better for the environment that way.

M: OK, I get it. Can I ask you one more?

W: Sure. What is it?

M: So what happens if another library has the journal, but this library doesn't?

W: Ah, in that case, let the person at the periodicals desk know. We'll either have a copy of the article scanned and sent directly to you by e-mail, or we'll arrange an inter-library loan of the journal. But we can usually do it by e-mail.

M: That sounds really efficient. Thanks a lot!

Now get ready to answer the questions. You may use your notes to help you answer.

Q. 2 Listen again to part of the conversation. Then answer the question.

> M: Yes, I need to use the online periodical service. I'm writing a paper, and I need to find five journal articles, but I don't know what to do. My lecturer gave out an instruction sheet, but it's all so overwhelming!
> W: No worries. I'll walk you through it.

What does the woman imply when she says this :
W: I'll walk you through it.

여: 안녕하세요, 특별히 찾고 있는 게 있나요?

남: 네, 온라인 정기 간행물 서비스를 이용하고 싶어요. 리포트를 쓰는 중인데요, 정기 간행물 기사 5개를 찾아야 해요. 그런데 뭘 해야 할지 잘 모르겠어요. 교수님이 안내물을 나눠주셨는데요, 뭐가 뭔지 하나도 모르겠어요!

여: 걱정 말아요. 찾는 것을 도와줄게요. 먼저, 도서관 이용을 위해서는 학생증을 사용 가능하도록 해야 해요. 그렇게 했나요?

남: 아뇨, 전 1학년이에요. 이번이 첫 학기거든요. 몇 주 전에 학생증을 받았어요.

여: 그랬군요, 학생증을 나한테 주면, 카드 판독기에 학생증을 넣어서 학생의 정보를 확인하도록 할게요. 1분도 안 걸려요... 아, 이게 학생의 기숙사 방 번호와 전화번호인가요? 이메일 주소도 정확한

어휘 | periodical 정기 간행물 | lecturer 교수, 강사 | give out 나눠주다 | overwhelming 압도적인, 굉장한 | freshman 신입생 | card reader 카드 판독기 | complicated 복잡한 | recycle 재활용하다 | electronic 전자의 | inter-library loan 도서관 상호 대출 | efficient 효율적인 | digitize 디지털화하다

[문제 6~11] 영문학 강의의 일부를 들으시오.

6. 강의는 주로 무엇에 관한 것인가?
(A) 영어의 역사
(B) 셰익스피어 비극
(C) 셰익스피어가 영어에 미친 영향
(D) 풍부한 영어 어휘

해설 | 셰익스피어의 등장으로 급격히 바뀐 영어 어휘에 관해 주로 이야기 하고 있다. 강의의 첫 머리에 주제가 드러나 있다. 정답은 보기 (C).

7. 다음 중 어느 것이 16세기 이전의 영어에 관해 맞는가?
(A) 상급 교육의 기본 과목이었다.
(B) 프랑스어와 라틴어보다 더 적게 쓰였다.
(C) 일상어가 아니었다.
(D) 문법 규칙이 모두 정해져 있었다.

해설 | 16세기 이전에는 프랑스어와 라틴어가 위세를 떨치던 시기로 영어 사용자는 별 존중을 못 받았고 영

어 문법 규칙도 정립되지 않았다고 하였다. 영어가 프랑스어와 라틴어보다 더 적게 쓰였음을 알 수 있다. 정답은 보기 (B).

8. 강의에서, 교수는 영어가 세계어로 부상하게 된 사건들을 언급하고 있다. 아래의 각 보기가 이러한 사건들에 속하는지 아래 표에 표시하시오. 각 보기에 맞는 칸에 클릭하시오.

	Mentioned	Not Mentioned
(A) 라틴계의 영향력 약화		∨
(B) 다른 국가들과의 관계	∨	
(C) 문학 작품의 인기		∨
(D) 외국을 지배하는 것	∨	
(E) 다른 국가와의 전투	∨	

해설 | 영어가 급격하게 팽창하게 된 이유로 언급된 것은 영국의 세계적 위상 강화, 외교 및 전쟁, 식민 정책 등을 통한 다른 국가들과의 접촉 등이다. 따라서 정답은 보기 (B), (D), (E).

9. 교수가 셰익스피어에 관해 암시하는 것은 무엇인가?
(A) 셰익스피어는 서민 계급 출신이었다.
(B) 셰익스피어는 고전 문학을 좋아하지 않았다.
(C) 셰익스피어는 여러 외국어를 할 줄 알았다.
(D) 셰익스피어는 영향력 있는 작가가 되기를 원했다.

해설 | 셰익스피어가 만들어 낸 수많은 단어들은 다른 언어에서 차용하거나, 고전 문학에 쓰인 단어들을 재활용하거나, 단순 실험을 통해 만들어졌을 수도 있다고 하였다. 다른 언어에서 차용했다는 부분을 통해 셰익스피어가 외국어를 구사할 수 있었을 거라고 유추할 수 있다. 정답은 보기 (C).

강의의 일부를 다시 들으시오. 그러고 나서 질문에 답하시오.
'옥스퍼드 영어 사전(Oxford English Dictionary)'을 보면, 이 사전에 실려 있는 많은 단어들의 첫 용례로 셰익스피어의 작품에 나오는 대사를 인용하고 있는데, 이 뛰어난 사전의 편집자들조차도 이런 방침을 재고하기 시작했어요. 셰익스피어의 문학 작품들은 오늘날까지도 남아있지만, 그 외 상당수 작가들의 작품은 그렇지 못하기 때문이죠.

10. 교수가 이것을 말할 때 암시하는 것은 무엇인가 : 🎧
셰익스피어의 문학 작품들은 오늘날까지도 남아있지만, 그 외 상당수 작가들의 작품은 그렇지 못하기 때문이죠.

(A) 옥스퍼드 영어 사전에는 셰익스피어가 그의 희곡에서 만들어냈던 많은 단어가 실려 있다.
(B) 옥스퍼드 영어 사전 편집자들은 셰익스피어가 이 사전에 실린 일부 단어들을 처음으로 사용한 사람이 아니라고 생각한다.
(C) 셰익스피어의 작품은 다른 작가들의 작품보다 더 유명했기 때문에 지금까지 남아있다.
(D) 다른 작가들이 옥스퍼드 영어 사전에 실린 일부 단어들을 처음 사용했을지도 모른다.

해설 | 당시의 다른 작가들이 옥스퍼드 영어 사전에 실려 있는 단어들을 셰익스피어보다 먼저 사용했을 수도 있는데, 그들의 작품은 셰익스피어의 작품과 달리 후대에 남아있지 않기 때문에 셰익스피어가 이러한 단어를

처음 사용한 것으로 인식되고 있다는 것이다. 정답은 보기 (D).

강의의 일부를 다시 들으시오. 그리고 나서 질문에 답하시오.
어찌 됐든 우리 중 누구도 셰익스피어가 우리에게 남겨준 단어와 구절이 없다면, 영어가 지금의 모습과는 달리 매우 초라한 언어로 존재하고 있을 것이란 사실을 부인할 수 없죠. 셰익스피어가 말한 것처럼, '끝이 좋으면 다 좋은 거죠(All's well that ends well).'

11. 교수가 이것을 말할 때 의미하는 것은 무엇인가 :
셰익스피어가 말한 것처럼, '좋으면 다 좋은 거죠!'

(A) 다른 작가들의 기여도 고려되어야 한다.
(B) 셰익스피어가 영어에 기여한 부분은 결과적으로 좋은 일이었다.
(C) 셰익스피어가 실제로 영어에 미친 영향은 거의 끝났다.
(D) 셰익스피어의 대사는 더 널리 쓰여야 한다.

해설 | 우리가 현재 쓰고 있는 많은 영어 단어들을 셰익스피어가 만들어낸 것이든 아니든 셰익스피어가 영어에 끼친 지대한 영향은 아무도 부인할 수 없다고 말하고 있다. 끝이 좋으면 다 좋다는 것은 결과적으로 보면 잘 된 일이란 것이다. 정답은 보기 (B).

P(M): *To be, or not to be; that is the question.* You probably know that this line comes from a Shakespeare play, *Hamlet*, but you might not realize the true extent of his influence on the English language. The sixteenth century was a time of great change for English. Prior to that, the language had not enjoyed much respect: it was the language of commoners, not of educated people. French and Latin were considered the languages of prestige. The rules of English grammar were not yet standardized. However, the arrival of Shakespeare helped to change all that, and numerous words from his body of work became standard English vocabulary.

Um, when we think about Shakespeare and his contributions, it's important to keep the events of the times in mind. While he was working, Shakespeare was thought to have coined about 1700 words. This meant, well, he was responsible for the creation of more words than all the other living writers in English combined. However, the English language was expanding rapidly at this time in its history. England itself had evolved into a political power, and contact with other nations like, uh, through diplomacy, war, colonization, and so on — was bringing many new words into the language. So if you think about the wider context, Shakespeare might not actually have invented these new words. They might have been in use at the time. But Shakespeare's writing was so influential and... and so far-reaching that the credit has been given to him, whatever his role might have been.

Today, when linguists and scholars of literature look at Shakespeare's influence on the language, they come to different conclusions. Some of them suggest about as many as 20,000 new words can be attributed to him: he borrowed them from other languages, recycled them from classical literature, or just experimented. Others believe the number is only half that — maybe 10,000. The *Oxford English Dictionary* often quotes a line from Shakespeare as the first known usage of many words, but even the editors of that respectable dictionary have started to reconsider this policy. Shakespeare's literature has survived, but the work of many other writers has not. It could be that these words were in wide use back then. It would be difficult to draw a strong conclusion one way or another. Whatever the case may be, no one can deny that English would be a much shabbier language today if we were to lose the words and the phrases Shakespeare gave us. Well, like he said, *All's well that ends well*.

Now get ready to answer the questions. You may use your notes to help you answer.

Q. 10 Listen again to part of the lecture. Then answer the question.

The Oxford English Dictionary often quotes a line from Shakespeare as the first known usage of many words, but even the editors of that respectable dictionary have started to reconsider this policy. Shakespeare's literature has survived, but the work of many other writers has not.

What does the professor imply when he says this :
Shakespeare's literature has survived, but the work of much other writers has not.

Q. 11 Listen again to part of the lecture. Then answer the question.

Whatever the case may be, no one can deny that English would be a much shabbier language today if we were to lose the words and the phrases Shakespeare gave us. Well, like he said, All's well that ends well.

What does the professor imply when he says this :
Well, like he said, All's well that ends well.

P: '죽느냐 사느냐, 그것이 문제로다.(*To be, or not to be; that is the question*)' 여러분은 이 대사가 Shakespeare(셰익스피어)의 희곡인 '햄릿(*Hamlet*)'에 나오는 말이란 걸 알고 있을 겁니다. 하지만 셰익스피어가 영어에 끼친 영향의 진정한 본질에 대해서는 잘 모르고 있을지도 몰라요. 16세기는 영어의 세계에 있어 큰 변화의 시기였어요. 16세기 전에는 영어를 사용하는 것이 그리 큰 관심과 존중을 받지 못했어요. 영어는 교육 받은 사람들이 아닌, 서민이 사용하는 언어였으니까요. 프랑스어와 라틴어가 명성을 뽐내고 위신을 세우는 언어로 여겨졌죠. 문법 규칙도 표준화되지 않았죠. 하지만, 셰익스피어의 등장으로 모든 것이 변하게 되었고, 그의 작품 속에 등장하는 수많은 단어들이 표준 영어 어휘가 되었어요.

우리가 셰익스피어와 그가 영어에 기여한 바를 생각할 때는, 그 당시의 시대상황을 염두에 두어야 해요. 셰익스피어가 작품 활동을 하면서 약 1700여 단어를 만들어냈다고 하죠. 이는 영어를 사용하는 모든 현존 작가들이 만들어낸 단어 수를 합한 것 보다 더 많은 어휘를 만들어냈다는 말이기도 해요. 하지만, 영어는 그 당시에 급격하게 팽창하고 있었어요. 영국은 세계 정세를 이끌고 있었고, 외교나 전쟁, 식민화 등의 방법을 통한 다른 국가들과의 접촉으로 영어에 새로운 단어들이 많이 등장하게 되었어요. 따라서 더 넓은 정황을 살펴보면, 셰익스피어가 실제로는 이 모든 새로운 단어를 만들어내지는 않았을 수도 있어요. 그 당시에 이미 쓰이고 있는 단어였을 수도 있죠. 하지만, 셰익스피어의 작품이 상당한 영향력을 가지고 있었고 파급 범위도 매우 넓었기 때문에 셰익스피어에게 당시의 새로운 단어들을 만들어낸 공이 돌아가는 거죠. 그의 역할이 무엇이었든 간에요.

오늘날, 언어학자들과 문학자들이 셰익스피어가 영어에 끼친 영향을 연구하면서, 서로 다른 결론을 제시하고 있어요. 그들 중 일부는 최대 20,000여 개의 새로운 단어가 셰익스피어의 머리에서 나왔다고 말해요. 다른 언어에서 차용하고, 고전 문학에 쓰인 단어들을 재활용하고, 단순 실험을 하기도 했다는 얘기죠. 또 다른 이들은 셰익스피어가 만들어낸 단어가 그 절반인 10,000여 개 밖에 안 된다고 하죠. '옥스퍼드 영어 사전(*Oxford English Dictionary*)'을 보면, 이 사전에 실려 있는 많은 단어들의 첫 용례로 셰익스피어의 작품에 나오는 대사를 인용하고 있는데, 이 뛰어난 사전의 편집자들조차도 이런 방침을 재고하기 시작했어요. 셰익스피어의 문학 작품들은 오늘날까지도 남아있지만, 그 외 상당수 작가들의 작품은 그렇지 못하기 때문이죠. 셰익스피어가 처음 사용했다고 하는 이 단어들이 이미 그 당시에 널리 쓰이고 있었을 수도 있어요. 어떤 식으로든 명백한 결론을 이끌어내는 것은 어려운 일일 거예요. 어찌 됐든 우리 중 누구도 셰익스피어가 우리에게 남겨준 단어와 구절이 없다면, 영어가 지금의 모습과는 달리 매우 초라한 언어로 존재하고 있을 것이란 사실을 부인할 수 없죠. 셰익스피어가 말한 것처럼, '끝이 좋으면 다 좋은 거죠(*All's well that ends well*).'

어휘 | play 희곡 | extent 범위, 정도 | commoner 서민 | prestige 명성 | numerous 수많은 | contribution 기여, 공헌 | coin 주조하다 | expand 확장하다, 팽창하다 | diplomacy 외교 | colonization 식민화 | context 정황, 문맥 | far-reaching 보급 범위가 넓은, 널리 미치는 | credit 공, 명성 | conclusion 결론 | quote 인용하다 | usage 용법 | editor 편집자 | one way or another 어떻게 해서든 | deny 부인하다 | shabby 초라한

Review

1. 1. You can usually <u>negotiate</u> <u>reasonable</u> <u>rates</u> for conferences.
2. Well, I'd <u>leave</u> <u>out</u> the information about your junior high school.
3. I've just finished registering for my classes, and they <u>sent</u> <u>me</u> <u>over</u> here to <u>sign</u> <u>up</u> <u>for</u> my meal plan.
4. You <u>ought</u> <u>to</u> use spell check before you <u>print</u> <u>this</u> <u>out</u> again.
5. Can you give me <u>any</u> <u>suggestions</u> like what to do and <u>what</u> <u>not</u> <u>to</u> do?

2. 1. Well, I guess / you want to decide / between using a hotel / and using the campus, / right?
2. Hotels will sometimes give discounts, though, / if you're holding an event / during the slow season.
3. I'll be leading a campus tour / for visiting parents / this afternoon, / but this is my first time.
4. You also want to wait / about five minutes / after the official start time, / in case anyone is still / on their way.
5. And finally, / we've got a hybrid card / that gives you 10 meals / per week, / plus stored value.

Chapter 7 Stance/Function

Office Hours

1. (B)   **2.** (A)

대화의 일부를 다시 들으시오. 그러고 나서 질문에 답하시오.

여: 네, 필요한 정보는 모두 수집해 놓았어요. 음, 강연에는 어떻게 가죠? 학교에서 버스를 대절하나요, 아니면 기차를 타고 가나요?

남: 그게 문제구나. 준비할 시간이 별로 없었기 때문에, 두 방법 모두를 생각해 보아야 할 것 같구나.

1. 교수가 이것을 말할 때 의미하는 것은 무엇인가 : 🎧

남: 그게 문제구나.

(A) 교수는 학생이 문제를 해결해야 한다고 생각한다.
(B) 교수는 교통편에 대해서는 아직 잘 모른다.
(C) 교수는 학생에게서 더 많은 정보를 원한다.
(D) 교수는 학생에게 질문을 하고 싶어한다.

M: Hey, how are you doing? So, do you have the list of names for Friday's trip?

W: I'm fine, thanks. And I do have the list. I still can't believe Mr. Dickinson is giving a lecture, and I'm going to see him. This never happens to me! Most of the English Literature majors are going, by the way.

M: Great. Did you get phone numbers and e-mail addresses? How about the classes they're going to miss? We need to print out enough permission forms.

W: Yes, I got all of that information. Um, how are we getting there? Is the school chartering buses, or will we take the train?

M: That's the question. We haven't had much time to plan this, so we might have to do both. I'll have my assistant look into it, and she'll get in touch with everybody. Thanks for making this list.

W: You're welcome!

Q. 1 Listen again to part of the conversation. Then answer the question.

W: Yes, I got all of that information. Um, how are we getting there? Is the school chartering buses, or will we take the train?

M: That's the question. We haven't had much time to plan this, so we might have to do both.

What does the professor mean when he says this : 🎧

M: That's the question.

남: 잘 지내고 있니? 음, 금요일 단체 견학을 갈 학생들의 목록을 작성했니?

여: 전 잘 지내고 있어요. 그리고 리스트는 다 작성했어요. Mr. Dickinson의 강연에 가서 직접 보게

된다니 아직도 못 믿겠어요! 이런 적은 한 번도 없었어요! 아, 영문학 전공생들은 거의 대부분 강연에 갈 거예요.

남: 잘됐구나. 전화번호와 이메일 주소도 모두 챙겼니? 학생들이 빠지게 될 수업은 어떻게 되었니? 동의서를 충분히 뽑아놓아야 해.

여: 네, 필요한 정보는 모두 수집해 놓았어요. 음, 강연에는 어떻게 가죠? 학교에서 버스를 대절하나요, 아니면 기차를 타고 가나요?

남: 그게 문제구나. 준비할 시간이 별로 없었기 때문에, 두 방법 모두를 생각해 보아야 할 것 같구나. 조교에게 한 번 알아보도록 할게, 그러고 나서 조교가 모두에게 연락을 해줄 거야. 목록을 작성해 주어서 정말 고맙구나.

여: 아니에요!

어휘 | permission 허가, 동의 | charter 전세 내다 | get in touch with ~와 연락하다

대화의 일부를 다시 들으시오. 그러고 나서 질문에 답하시오.

남: 음, 오리엔테이션이 많은 도움이 되긴 하지만, 꼭 참석하라고 강요할 수는 없지요.

여: 저희 오빠가 작년에 우등 프로그램을 졸업했고, 제가 오빠를 많이 찾아 왔었어요. 어쨌든 오리엔테이션에 참석하지 않으면, 불리한 점이 있을까요?

2. 여자가 이것을 말할 때 암시하는 것은 무엇인가 :

여: 저희 오빠가 작년에 우등 프로그램을 졸업했고, 제가 오빠를 많이 찾아 왔었어요.

(A) 이미 학교에 대해 많이 알고 있다.
(B) 오리엔테이션이 유용하다고 느끼지 않는다.
(C) 오빠와 함께 시간을 보내는 것이 더 중요하다고 생각한다.
(D) 오리엔테이션에서 얻게 될 어떤 정보도 놓치지 않을 것이다.

W: Professor Shulz, I'd like to ask about the honors program orientation for fall semester.

M: Sure. What's your question?

W: My family has been planning a trip that week, and it'll be our last chance to travel together for a while. Is the orientation required?

M: Well, it's very helpful, but obviously we can't require you to be there.

W: Um, my brother graduated from the honors program last year, and I've visited him a lot. Well, uh, will it count against me somehow, if I don't go.

M: No, we don't have the authority to tell you what to do before the semester starts. But the honors program is changing a few rules and requirements, and you need to know about them. Let me refer you to our person who's in charge of that.

W: OK, great, thanks for your time!

Q. 2 Listen again to part of the conversation. Then answer the question.

M: Well, it's very helpful, but obviously we can't require you to be there.

W: Um, my brother graduated from the honors program last year, and I've visited him

여: Shulz 교수님, 가을 학기 우등 프로그램 오리엔테이션에 관해 여쭤보고 싶은 게 있는데요.

남: 그래요. 궁금한 점이 뭔가요?

여: 그 주에 저희 가족이 여행을 계획하고 있는데요, 이번이 당분간 가족 모두가 함께 여행할 마지막 기회라서요. 오리엔테이션에 꼭 참석해야 하나요?

남: 음, 오리엔테이션이 많은 도움이 되긴 하지만, 꼭 참석하라고 강요할 수는 없지요.

여: 저희 오빠가 작년에 우등 프로그램을 졸업했고, 제가 오빠를 많이 찾아 왔었어요. 어쨌든 오리엔테이션에 참석하지 않으면, 불리한 점이 있을까요?

남: 그렇진 않아요. 우리가 학기 시작 전에 학생들에게 무엇을 하라고 말할 권한은 없어요. 다만 우등 프로그램의 규정과 요건이 일부 바뀌니까, 그런 것들에 대해 알아둘 필요가 있지요. 오리엔테이션 담당자에게 직접 알아보도록 해줄게요.

여: 네, 시간을 내주셔서 감사합니다!

어휘 | honors program 우등 프로그램 | count against ～에 대해 불리하게 작용하다 | authority 권한 | in charge of ～을 책임지고 있는

Service Encounters

1. (D) **2.** (C)

대화의 일부를 다시 들으시오. 그러고 나서 질문에 답하시오.

남: 와! 1등을 할 거라곤 예상 못했는데.

여: 그럴 자격이 충분히 있어요! 그런데, 청취자들이 요구한 것이 한가지 있어요.

남: 항상 발목을 잡는게 있다니까요. 그게 뭔가요?

1. 남자가 이것을 말할 때 의미하는 것은 무엇인가 :

남: 항상 발목을 잡는 게 있다니까요.

(A) 좋은 소식은 대개 사실이 아니다.
(B) 그는 여자가 한 말을 믿지 않는다.
(C) 그는 상을 타는 데는 관심이 없다.
(D) 좋은 소식 뒤에는 나쁜 소식이 따라오기 마련이다.

M: There's always a catch. What's the matter?

W: There was one consistent piece of feedback. You never give the titles of songs when you play them, and your listeners want to find those songs again after the show.

M: Well, it would interrupt the music. You know, I mix songs together, so it would take too long.

W: I see your point, but we need to come up with something. We are here for the listeners!

M: All right, how about... um, how about giving the list at the end of the show?

W: Uh, that's too long to wait. Why don't you post your play list on the station website?

M: I think that's a good idea.

Q. 1 Listen again to part of the conversation. Then answer the question.

M: Cool! I didn't expect to win.
W: You deserve it! Um, there's one thing, though.
M: There's always a catch. What's the matter?

What does the man mean when he says this :
M: There's always a catch.

여: 축하해요! 인기투표 결과가 나왔는데, 당신이 1등을 했어요. Jerry, 당신이 캠퍼스 최고의 인기 DJ이에요.

남: 와! 1등을 할 거라곤 예상 못했는데.

여: 그럴 자격이 충분히 있어요! 그런데, 청취자들이 요구한 것이 한 가지 있어요.

남: 항상 발목을 잡는 게 있다니까요. 무슨 일이죠?

여: 청취자들이 계속해서 보내주는 피드백이 있어요. 음악을 틀어줄 때 노래 제목을 알려주지 않는데, 청취자들은 쇼가 끝난 후 그 노래들을 다시 듣고 싶어하거든요.

남: 그렇게 하면 음악의 흐름이 끊길 거예요. 전 노래를 믹스하기도 하니까, 시간이 너무 오래 걸리게 될 거예요.

여: 무슨 말인지 알겠어요, 하지만 방도를 생각해야 해요. 우린 청취자들을 위해 있는 거잖아요!

남: 알겠어요, 음 쇼가 끝날 때 노래 목록을 알려주는 건 어때요?

여: 그럼 너무 오래 기다려야 하잖아요. 방송국 웹사이트에 노래 목록을 올려놓는 건 어때요?

남: 그게 좋겠네요.

어휘 | favorite 좋아하는 | catch 함정, 책략 | come up with ~를 생각해내다

대화의 일부를 다시 들으시오. 그러고 나서 질문에 답하시오.

남: 일대일 학습 시간이 많이 없어져서, 사람한테 도움을 받는 일이 거의 불가능해졌어요. 질문을 온라인으로 올려야 하는데, 시간이 너무 오래 걸려요.

여: 이해해요. 새로운 제도이고, 아직 오류를 잡아내는 중이에요.

2. 여자가 이것을 말할 때 암시하는 것은 무엇인가 :

여: 이해해요. 새로운 제도이고, 아직 오류를 잡아내는 중이에요.

(A) 다른 학생들은 문제를 제기하지 않았다.

Answer / Script / Explanation **63**

(B) 예전 제도가 새로운 제도보다 더 낫다.
(C) 컴퓨터 오류에 대한 불만 제기가 있었다.
(D) 튜터링 센터에 벌레가 널려 있다.

M: I need to talk to someone about the tutoring center. Can you help me with a problem?
W: Yes, what's wrong?
M: Well, the hours for one-on-one tutors have been cut back, so it's almost impossible to get help from a human being now. You have to submit questions online, and it takes too long.
W: I understand. It's a new system, and they're still working out all the bugs.
M: But I'm really having a hard time in my history class, and I'm a terrible typist. It takes too long to type my questions out, and it takes too long to get answers.
W: Yes, I know there are problems. Well, the tutoring center's budget was cut, but the IT department got more money. It was the best solution anyone could think of.
M: Well, it's not helpful!
W: I'm sorry, but all I can say is keep trying!

Q. 2 Listen again to part of the conversation. Then answer the question.

M: Well, the hours for one-on-one tutors have been cut back, so it's almost impossible to get help from a human being now. You have to submit questions online, and it takes too long.
W: I understand. It's a new system, and they're still working out all the bugs.

What does the woman imply when she says this : 🎧
W: I understand. It's a new system, and they're still working out all the bugs.

남: 튜터링 센터에 대해 할 말이 있어서 왔어요. 도와주시겠어요?
여: 그러죠, 무슨 일이죠?
남: 일대일 학습 시간이 많이 없어져서, 사람한테 도움을 받는 일이 거의 불가능해졌어요. 질문을 온라인으로 올려야 하는데, 시간이 너무 오래 걸려요.
여: 이해해요. 새로운 제도이고, 아직 오류를 잡아내는 중이에요.
남: 하지만 전 지금 역사 수업을 따라 가는 게 너무 힘들단 말이에요. 타이핑도 잘 못하고요. 질문을 타이핑 하는데도 시간이 오래 걸리고, 답변을 얻는데도 시간이 오래 걸려요.
여: 네, 문제가 있다는 건 저도 알고 있어요. 튜터링 센터의 예산은 삭감되었는데, IT 부서에는 예산이 더 배정되었어요. 그게 최선의 방법이었어요.
남: 하지만 전혀 도움이 안 되고 있어요!
여: 학생 상황은 안타깝지만, 계속 시도해보라는 말 밖에 해줄 말이 없네요!

어휘 I bug 오류, 버그 I typist 키보드 치는 사람 I budget 예산

 ALL ABOUT JUNIOR TOEFL

1. 1. (A) 2. (B)   **2.** 1. (B) 2. (D)

---

1. 강의의 일부를 다시 들으시오. 그러고 나서 질문에 답하시오.

여러분들은 영국 Elizabeth(엘리자베스) 여왕이 통치하던 황금시대가 영광과 모험, 사치로 가득 찼던 시대라고 생각하고 있을 겁니다. 아마도 여러분들이 보았던 엘리자베스 여왕이 나오던 영화 때문일 수도 있어요. 여왕과 여왕의 궁정, 사치스러운 의상과 보석, 호화스러운 연회들.... 하지만, 그 당시에 살고 있던 90%의 인구는 노동 계급인 농민 또는 매우 가난한 사람들이었다는 것도 기억해야 해요.

1. 교수가 이것을 말할 때 의미하는 것은 무엇인가:

하지만, 그 당시에 살고 있던 90%의 인구는 노동 계급인 농민 또는 매우 가난한 사람들이었다는 것도 기억해야 해요.

(A) 실상은 영화 내용과는 달랐다.
(B) 학생들은 영국의 황금시대를 더 잘 알아야 한다.
(C) 학생들은 엘리자베스 여왕이 통치하던 영국에 대해서는 아무것도 모른다.
(D) 노동 계급의 농민들은 사치스러운 생활을 누릴 수 없었다.

강의의 일부를 다시 들으시오. 그러고 나서 질문에 답하시오.

이러한 요인들이 복합적으로 작용하여 사람들은 도시로 몰려들었어요. 1590년대에는 몇 년간 흉작이 이어지자 상황이 더 악화되었습니다. 그 결과 농작물 가격도 올랐고, 빈곤에 시달리던 많은 사람들이 결국에는 절망에 못 이겨 필사적인 행동까지 하게 되었죠.

2. 교수가 이것을 말할 때 암시하는 것은 무엇인가:

그 결과 농작물 가격도 올랐고, 빈곤에 시달리던 많은 사람들이 결국에는 절망에 못 이겨 필사적인 행동까지 하게 되었죠.

(A) 식량을 직접 재배했다.
(B) 범죄를 저질렀을지도 모른다.
(C) 수도원에 머물렀다.
(D) 시골 지역으로 가야만 했다.

P(M): You may be led to think that the Golden Age of Elizabethan England was all glory, adventure, and extravagance. Maybe it's from the movies about the queen and her court, her luxurious costumes and jewelry, the sumptuous feast... but you should also remember that ninety percent of the population then were working class peasants or poor.

Of the many reasons for the poverty situation, some were actually triggered by Elizabeth's father, Henry VIII's, actions. Un, with the national conversion to the Church of England, moving away from Catholicism, he closed monasteries and nunneries. Before that time, they had been a refuge for the poor. This — along with the religion change — also contributed to the decline in Christian values. This meant charitable acts towards the poor were no longer seen as a duty.

As if that weren't enough, the population doubled — from two to four million — between Henry VIII and Elizabeth's reigns. At the same time, there were changes in the agricultural system that required less work for farmhands. This combination of factors drove people into the cities. The situation grew even worse in the 1590s, when there were several years of bad harvests. Prices of food rose as a result, and many starving people were eventually driven to acts of desperation.

So the Queen had to something... something that might possibly remedy the poverty situation. The Queen passed a series of Poor Laws, which first began in identifying and categorizing the poor. Next came a local law that a form of welfare that gave some of the landowners' money to the poor. So England under Elizabeth was quite different from the glorious, glamorous place we see in the movies.

Q 1 Listen again to part of the lecture. Then answer the question.

You may be led to think that the Golden Age of Elizabethan England was all glory, adventure, and extravagance. Maybe it's from the movies about the queen and her court, her luxurious costumes and jewelry, the sumptuous feast... but you should also remember that ninety percent of the population then were working class peasants or poor.

What does the professor mean when he says this :
but you should also remember that ninety percent of the population then were working class peasants or poor.

Q 2 Listen again to part of the lecture. Then answer the question.

This combination of factors drove people into the cities. The situation grew even worse in the 1590s, when there were several years of bad harvests. Prices of food rose as a result, and many starving people were eventually driven to acts of desperation.

What does the professor imply when he says this :
Prices of food rose as a result, and many starving people were eventually driven to acts of desperation.

P: 여러분들은 영국 Elizabeth(엘리자베스) 여왕이 통치하던 황금시대가 영광과 모험, 사치로 가득 찼던 시대라고 생각하고 있을 겁니다. 아마도 여러분들이 보았던 엘리자베스 여왕이 나오던 영화 때문일 수도 있어요. 여왕과 여왕의 궁정, 사치스러운 의상과 보석, 호화스러운 연회들.... 하지만, 그 당시에 살고 있던 90%의 인구는 노동 계급인 농민 또는 매우 가난한 사람들이었다는 것도 기억해야 해요.

이렇게 사람들이 가난에 시달렸던 많은 이유들 가운데 일부는 엘리자베스 여왕의 아버지인 Henry(헨리) 8세로부터 비롯되었어요. 가톨릭교회와 결별, 영국 국교회로 개종하면서, 헨리 8세는 수도원과 수녀원을 해산했어요. 그 이전에는, 수도원과 수녀원이 빈민들이 찾아오는 피난처 역할을

어휘 | glory 영광 | extravagance 사치 | court 궁정 | luxurious 사치스러운, 호화로운 | sumptuous 호화로운 | feast 연회 | peasant 농민, 소작농 | poverty 가난 | trigger 유발하다 | conversion 개종 | monastery 수도원 | nunnery 수녀원 | refuge 피난처, 도피처 | charitable 자비로운, 자선의 | duty 의무 | reign 통치 | harvest 수확 | starving 굶주리는 | desperation 절망, 자포자기 | remedy 구제하다, 제거하다 | remedy 구제하다 | welfare 복지 | landowner 지주

2. 강의의 일부를 다시 들으시오. 그리고 나서 질문에 답하시오.

여러분 중 상당수가 *Robert Peary*(로버트 피어리)라는 인물에 관해 들어보았을 거예요. *Peary*는 지구의 최북단인 북극점에 최초로 도달했다고 주장한 미국 탐험가였어요. 음, 그의 주장을 둘러싼 많은 비난이 있었어요. 그런 이유로, *Peary*는 유명하다기보다는 악명이 높다고 할 수 있죠.

1. 교수가 이것을 말할 때 의미하는 것은 무엇인가 : 🎧

   그런 이유로, Peary는 유명하다기보다는 악명이 높다고 할 수 있죠.

   (A) Peary는 매우 훌륭한 탐험가이다.
   (B) Peary는 약간 부정적인 쪽으로 유명하다.
   (C) Peary는 더 많은 존경을 받아야 한다.
   (D) Peary는 탐험과 관련된 모든 것에 대해 거짓말을 했다.

강의의 일부를 다시 들으시오. 그리고 나서 질문에 답하시오.

이런 것들이 논란의 쟁점이 되었지만, *Peary*가 그래도 북극 인접 지역까지는 발을 디뎠었다는 사실에는 의심의 여지가 없습니다. 그런 이유로, 어느 정도의 인정은 받을 만하죠.

2. 교수가 이것을 말할 때 암시하는 것은 무엇인가 : 🎧

   그런 이유로, 어느 정도의 인정은 받을 만하죠.

   (A) Peary는 최초로 북극에 도달한 사람으로 공식 기록되어야 한다.
   (B) Peary가 훈장을 받았다는 사실은 그가 존경 받을 만하다는 것을 보여준다.
   (C) 신뢰도와 관련된 문제 때문에, Peary는 역사에서 잊혀 져야 한다.
   (D) 논쟁의 여지가 있기는 해도, Peary는 중요한 탐험가로 기억되어야 한다.

P(W): Many of you have heard about Robert Peary. Uh, he was an American explorer who claimed to have been the first person to reach the North Pole, which is the northernmost point of the planet. Well, there was a great deal of criticism surrounding his claim. As a result, he might be more infamous than famous.

Peary had made several prior expeditions to the Arctic between 1886 and 1909, mapping out a portion of Greenland as he moved farther north. However, these expeditions would already be tainted by misinformation he had provided on several occasions. Let me give you an example here... um, he claimed to have discovered a place known as Crocker Land in 1906, but it was later proved to be non-existent.

Anyway, in 1909, he and twenty-three men set off for the North Pole from New York City. As planned, the support parties turned back one by one, and finally just six people were left. Then, these six set off from Bartlett Camp, at 87 degrees 45 minutes north latitude, and on April 6, he established Camp Jesup, which he claimed was within five miles of the pole.

Peary would eventually be given a Rear Admiral's pension, and he received many other honors for his achievements. But this overlooks his sloppy and perhaps dishonest record-keeping. There were also some major discrepancies in them, like how the surprisingly speedy journey from Bartlett Camp to Camp Jesup could have been possible. Well, this conflicted with other accounts of long, complicated detours to avoid ice floes and open water. These issues would become major points of contention, though there should be no doubt that Peary at least reached regions adjacent to the pole. And for that, he does deserve some recognition.

Q 1 Listen again to part of the lecture. Then answer the question.

Many of you have heard about Robert Peary. Uh, he was an American explorer who claimed to have been the first person to reach the North Pole, which is the northernmost point of the planet. Well, there was a great deal of criticism surrounding his claim. As a result, he might be more infamous than famous.

What does the professor mean when she says this :
As a result, he might be more infamous than famous.

Q 2 Listen again to part of the lecture. Then answer the question.

These issues would become major points of contention, though there should be no doubt that Peary at least reached regions adjacent to the pole. And for that, he does deserve some recognition.

What does the professor mean when she says this:
And for that, he does deserve some recognition.

P: 여러분 중 상당수가 Robert Peary(로버트 피어리)라는 인물에 관해 들어보았을 거예요. Peary는 지구의 최북단인 북극점에 최초로 도달했다고 주장한 미국 탐험가였어요. 음, 그의 주장을 둘러싼

 ALL ABOUT JUNIOR TOEFL

어휘 | explorer 탐험가 | the North Pole 북극점 | northernmost 가장 북쪽의 | expedition 탐험 | infamous 악명 높은, 불명예스러운 | map out 지도에 표시하다 | taint 더럽히다 | misinformation 오보 | occasion 경우 | non-existent 존재하지 않는 | Rear Admiral 해군 소장 | pension 장려금 | achievement 업적 | sloppy 조잡한 | discrepancy 모순 | detour 우회 | ice floe 유빙 | contention 논쟁 | adjacent to ~에 인접한

Practice

1. (D) **2.** (B) **3.** (C) **4.** (A) **5.** Suggested - (B), (D), (E) Not Suggested - (A), (C) **6.** (B)
7. (A) **8.** (D) **9.** (C) **10.** Mentioned - (A), (B), (C) Not Mentioned - (D), (E) **11.** (D)

[문제 1~5] 학생과 교수 사이의 대화의 일부를 들으시오.

1. 여자의 문제는 무엇인가?
 (A) 여자가 필요로 하는 자료를 도서관에서 찾을 수가 없다.
 (B) 교수가 반 친구들 앞에서 여자를 불공평하게 대우했다.
 (C) 여자는 프로젝트를 잘 해내지 못하고 있다.
 (D) 서점에 여자가 필요로 하는 교재가 품절이다.

해설 | 교수는 학생이 수업 토론에 잘 참여하지 않는 것 같아 학생을 불러 이야기 하고 있다. 학생은 교내 서점에 재고가 없어서 책을 구입하지 못해 읽기 과제를 제대로 해오지 못했다고 말하고 있다. 정답은 보기 (D).

2. 왜 서점에서는 필요한 것보다 더 적은 부수를 주문하는가?
 (A) 학생들이 헌 책을 사고팔도록 유도하기 위해
 (B) 너무 많은 책이 남게 되지 않도록 하기 위해
 (C) 책의 수요를 높게 유지하기 위해

(D) 높은 가격으로 책을 팔기 위해

해설 | 교수의 말에 따르면, 서점에서는 재고 수를 줄이기 위해 학생이나 교수들로부터 요청 받은 교재 수의 80%만을 주문한다고 하였다. 정답은 보기 (B).

대화의 일부를 다시 들으시오. 그러고 나서 질문에 답하시오.
남: 그래, 학생들이 서점에서 겪게 되는 문제를 나도 알고 있단다. 하지만, 필요한 교재 수의 80%만 주문하는 것이 서점의 방침이야. 그러니까 내 말은, 내가 강의 주교재를 50권 요청하면, 서점에서는 40권만 주문하는 거야. 그래서, 항상 부수가 모자라게 되는 것 같더구나.
여: 하지만 여긴 그냥 서점이 아니잖아요, 교내 서점이라고요!

3. 여자가 이것을 말할 때 의미하는 것은 무엇인가 :
여: 하지만 여긴 그냥 서점이 아니잖아요, 교내 서점이라고요!

(A) 일반 서점은 대학 서점보다 재고가 더 많은 것 같다.
(B) 일반 서점은 대학 고객에게 개방되어야 한다.
(C) 대학 구내 서점은 학생들이 필요로 하는 것을 제공해야 한다.
(D) 대학 구내 서점은 재고를 쉽게 팔아치울 수 있다.

해설 | 재고 수를 줄이기 위해 책을 적게 주문한다는 서점의 방침에 대해 학생은 교내 서점은 일반 서점과 다르기 때문에 영업 이익보다는 학생들의 편의를 더 고려해야 한다고 생각하고 있다. 정답은 보기 (C).

대화의 일부를 다시 들으시오. 그러고 나서 질문에 답하시오.

4. 교수는 대학 구내 서점에 관해 어떻게 생각하는가?
남: 예전에는 요청 받은 대로 주문을 했는데, 학생들이 수강을 철회하거나 다른 곳에서 헌 책을 사게 되면, 재고가 너무 많이 남았던 것 같구나. 게다가 요즘에는 새로운 책들이 매우 빠르게 출간되어서, 남아지는 책을 줄이길 원하지. 왜 그런 일이 일어나게 되는지 이해해둘 필요가 있어.

(A) 교수는 서점의 딜레마에 동정적이다.
(B) 교수는 서점이 요청 받은 모든 부수를 주문해야 한다고 생각한다.
(C) 교수는 서점이 예전에 더 효율적이었다고 생각한다.
(D) 교수는 서점의 현재 방침에 불만을 가지고 있다.

해설 | 교수는 서점이 재고가 남지 않도록 더 적게 주문하는 방침에 대해 왜 그럴 수 밖에 없는지 이유를 설명하고 있다. 정답은 보기 (A).

5. 대화에서, 화자들은 서점에 책이 모자라는 문제를 해결하기 위한 여러 대안을 논의하고 있다. 아래 표의 각 보기가 교수가 제안한 대안에 속하는지 표시하시오. 각 보기에 맞는 칸에 클릭하시오.

	Suggested	Not Suggested
(A) 학생이 자신의 책을 사용할 수 있도록 빌려주기		V
(B) 서점 매니저에게 전화를 하기	V	
(C) 수업 시간에 책을 함께 보도록 허락하기		V

| (D) 개별 과제를 하는 것으로 강의 방향을 바꾸기 | V | |
| (E) 교재의 필수적인 부분을 사진 복사하기 | V | |

해설 | 학생뿐만 아니라 다른 학생들도 책을 구입하지 못하고 있다고 하자, 교수는 서점 매니저에게 전화를 해서 주문이 빨리 이루어지도록 요청하겠다고 한다. 학생에게는 책을 가지고 있는 다른 학생에게서 책을 빌린 후 도서관에서 필요한 페이지를 복사하라고 한다. 학생이 비용 문제를 제기하자 개별 프로젝트를 좀 더 일찍 시작하는 가능성도 열어두고 있다. 정답은 보기 (B), (D), (E).

[Questions 1~5] Listen to part of a conversation between a student and a professor.

M: Jill, can I speak with you for a moment?

W: Sure, Dr. Wilkins. Is everything O.K.?

M: It's fine, but ah, I just noticed that you haven't really been participating in some of our discussions about the reading assignments. Are you not completing your homework? I mean, it's really important for you to do the assignments and for me to make sure that you understand the main concepts.

W: I'm sorry, but it's not my fault! I went to the bookstore late last week to buy the textbook. Well, I know the class had already started, but I didn't have any money right away. And, by the time I got my scholarship money, the book had been sold out. So, I put my name on a list to order a copy, but they said that it might take a while. I'm just waiting now...

M: Yes, I know the problems some students seem to have with the bookstore. But, it's their policy to order on 80 percent of stock. What I mean is, if I ask 50 copies of a title for my class, they actually only place an order for 40. So, they always seem to run out of copies.

W: But this is not just any bookstore — it's the campus bookstore!

M: I guess in the past, they would order the full amount and then when students dropped the course or bought their books used from another store, well, they were left with a lot of overstock. And textbooks these days seem to go out of date so fast, so they want to reduce the amount of leftovers that they have. You kind of have to see where they're coming from.

W: I understand, but it's not just me. There are a couple of other girls in the class who didn't get books, too.

M: Really? Well, let me make a phone call to the manager. I know him quite well. I will also try to get them to speed up their ordering process.

W: Thanks, Professor. I really appreciate it. It's not that I wanted to skip out on my work...

M: I know. But, we do have to keep on track with the syllabus, so another option for you might be to borrow a book from another student and make some photocopies of the pages you need at the library.

W: I don't mean to sound petty, but photocopies aren't cheap. It's already ten cents a page and then we still have to buy the book when it comes in. I'm not sure that I can afford to do both. Is there an alternative?

M: Well, I suppose we could start our independent projects early. That way, you could just focus on some Internet research for the next few days.

W: That sounds interesting. And cheap! We can use the computers on campus then?

M: That's the idea. Let's talk more about this in class tomorrow.

W: Sounds great. See you then.

Now get ready to answer the questions. You may use your notes to help you answer.

Q. 3 Listen again to part of the conversation. Then answer the question.

> M: Yes, I know the problems some students seem to have with the bookstore. But, it's their policy to order on 80 percent of stock. What I mean is, if I ask 50 copies of a title for my class, they actually only place an order for 40. So, they always seem to run out of copies.
>
> W: But this is not just any bookstore — it's the campus bookstore!

What does the woman imply when she says this :

> W: But this is not just any bookstore — it's the campus bookstore!

Q. 4 Listen again to part of the conversation. Then answer the question.

> M: I guess in the past, they would order the full amount and then when students dropped the course or bought their books used from another store, well, they were left with a lot of overstock. And textbooks these days seem to go out of date so fast, so they want to reduce the amount of leftovers that they have. You kind of have to see where they're coming from.

How does the professor seem to feel about the campus bookstore?

남: Jill, 잠깐 이야기 좀 나눌 수 있겠니?

여: 네, Wilkins 교수님. 별 문제는 없는 거죠?

남: 그래, 그런데 요즘 네가 읽기 과제 토론에 참여를 별로 안 하는 것 같더구나. 과제를 다 안 해오는 것이니? 음, 네가 과제를 다 해오고, 네가 중요한 개념을 이해하고 있다는 것을 내가 확인하는 것이 정말 중요한 일이야.

여: 죄송해요, 하지만 제 잘못은 아니에요! 지난 주 늦게 교재를 구입하러 서점에 갔었는데요. 강의가 벌써 시작되었다는 건 알지만, 책을 살 돈이 없었어요. 그리고 제가 장학금을 받았을 때는, 이미 책이 품절이었어요. 그래서 한 권을 주문하려고 명단에 제 이름을 올려놓았는데, 시간이 좀 걸릴 것 같다고 했어요. 그래서 지금 기다리고 있는 중이에요...

남: 그래, 학생들이 서점에서 겪게 되는 문제를 나도 알고 있단다. 하지만, 필요한 교재 수의 80%만 주문하는 것이 서점의 방침이야. 그러니까 내 말은, 내가 강의 주교재를 50권 요청하면, 서점에서는 40권만 주문하는 거야. 그래서, 항상 부수가 모자라게 되는 것 같더구나.

여: 하지만 여긴 그냥 서점이 아니잖아요, 교내 서점이라고요!

남: 예전에는 요청 받은 대로 주문을 했는데, 학생들이 수강을 철회하거나 다른 곳에서 헌 책을 사게 되면, 재고가 너무 많이 남았던 것 같구나. 게다가 요즘에는 새로운 책들이 매우 빠르게 출간되어서, 남아지는 책을 줄이길 원하지. 왜 그런 일이 일어나게 되는지 이해해둘 필요가 있어.

여: 이해는 하지만요, 저만 그런 게 아니에요. 같은 반에 책을 구입하지 못한 애들도 있어요.

   ALL ABOUT JUNIOR TOEFL

어휘 | fault 잘못 | sold out 매진된, 품절된 | policy 방침 | place an order 주문하다 | run out of 바닥나다, 다 써버리다 | overstock 재고 과잉 | go out of date 시대에 뒤떨어지다 | leftover 남은 것 | syllabus 강의계획서 | photocopy 사진 복사

[문제 6~11] 생물학 강의의 일부를 들으시오.

6. 강의 주제는 무엇인가?
(A) 동물의 분류
(B) 냉혈 동물
(C) 동물의 체온
(D) 온혈 동물

해설 | 냉혈 동물의 체온 조절 방법에 관한 강의이다. 정답은 보기 (B).
강의의 일부를 다시 들으시오. 그러고 나서 질문에 답하시오.
냉혈 동물이란 용어는 사실 엄밀히 말하자면 정확하지는 않죠. 이 말에는 파충류나 곤충류, 개구리, 물고기 등의 생명체는 항상 차갑다는 의미가 담겨 있습니다. 그럼 한 번 생각해본다면, 그 말이 뜻하는 건 무엇일까요? 어떻게 작용하는 걸까요? 많은 물고기들이 따뜻한 물에 서식합니다. 물고기가 항상 차갑다면, 체온을 어떻게 조절할까요? 단열이 아주 잘되어 있어야 하는데, 우리 모두 알고 있듯, 이는 대부분의 물고기에 해당되는 이야기는 아니죠.

7. 교수가 이것을 말할 때 의미하는 것은 무엇인가 :
단열이 아주 잘되어 있어야 하는데, 우리 모두 알고 있듯, 이는 대부분의 물고기에 해당되는 이야기는 아니죠.

(A) 냉혈이란 용어는 완벽하지 않다.
(B) 대부분의 물고기는 냉혈이 아니다.
(C) 모든 물고기는 찬물보다 따뜻한 물을 선호한다.
(D) 엄밀히 말하면, 냉혈 동물은 항상 차다.

해설ㅣ 항상 차갑다는 의미가 담겨 있는 '냉혈 동물'이란 용어가 정확하지 않다는 것을 보여주기 위해 물고기를 언급하고 있다. 정답은 보기 (A).

8. 다음 중 어느 것이 체온 조절의 유형이 아닌가?
(A) 저율대사
(B) 외부열
(C) 변온
(D) 저혈당

해설ㅣ 냉혈 동물의 체온 조절 방법으로 3가지 종류를 언급하고 있다. 바로 ectothermy(변온, 외부열)과 poikilothermy(변온), bradymetabolism(저율대사)이다. 따라서 아닌 것은 보기 (D)의 저혈당이다. 정답은 보기 (D).

9. 언제 냉혈 동물의 신진대사율이 느려지는가?
(A) 하루 중 가장 더울 때에
(B) 비가 내릴 때
(C) 추운 겨울에
(D) 어두운 곳에 있을 때

해설ㅣ 냉혈 동물은 외부 온도가 떨어져 날이 추울 때 신진대사율이 느려진다고 하였다. 따라서 정답은 보기 (C).

10. 강의에서, 교수는 냉혈 동물이 체온 조절을 하는 메커니즘의 예를 들고 있다. 아래 표의 각 보기가 이런 예에 포함되는지 표시하시오. 각 보기에 맞는 칸에 클릭하시오.

	Mentioned	Not Mentioned
(A) 물속에서 수심을 바꾸는 물고기	√	
(B) 겨울에 연못 바닥에 서식하는 거북이	√	
(C) 따뜻한 돌 위에서 햇볕을 쬐는 뱀	√	
(D) 동면하는 북극곰		√
(E) 뭍으로 나오는 고래		√

해설ㅣ 교수는 몸을 따뜻하게 하기 위해 햇볕을 쬐는 도마뱀이나 뱀, 한낮에 너무 뜨거운 햇볕을 피하기 위해 모래 속으로 파고 들어가는 사막 동물, 적당한 온도를 찾아 수심을 바꾸어 헤엄치는 물고기, 연못 바닥에서 겨울을 나는 거북이 등을 언급하고 있다. 정답은 보기 (A), (B), (C).

11. 교수가 포유동물에 관해 암시하는 것은 무엇인가?
(A) 파충류와 공통점이 전혀 없다.
(B) 동면하지 않는다.
(C) 추운 날씨를 견뎌낼 수 없다.
(D) 냉혈 동물이 아니다.

해설ㅣ 거북이가 연못 수면이 얼어 붙을 때에도 연못 바닥에서 겨울을 난다는 것을 언급하면서, 이 상태는 포유류의 동면과는 다르지만 상당히 유사하다고 하였다. 이 말을 통해 알 수 있는 것은 포유류는 거북이와 같은 냉혈 동물이 아니라는 것이다. 정답은 보기(D)

[Questions 6~11] Listen to part of a lecture in a biology class.

P(M): As we know from our discussion of body temperature, all living organisms have to stay within a certain range of temperatures to maintain life. For many years, we categorized animals two ways, as warm-blooded or cold-blooded. Today, we'll talk about the cold-blooded ones. The term cold-blooded is not technically accurate. It suggests that creatures such as reptiles, insects, frogs, and fish are always cold. And what would that mean, if you think about it? How would it work? Many fish live in warm water. If a fish were truly cold all the time, how would it regulate its body temperature? It would need to be very well-insulated, and as we all know, that is not the case with most fish. That should suggest that something else is going on.

Um, let's go further into the topic. There are three different systems of temperature regulation in cold-blooded organisms. The first is ectothermy, which means that the organism takes advantage of outside heat sources. The second is poikilothermy, which means that the organism's internal temperatures may vary. Usually this means that the animal adapts to the outside environment. The third system is bradymetabolism, which involves a very fast metabolic rate while the animal is awake and active, and a very slow rate during periods of inactivity. However, it's important to remember that few of the cold-blooded animals fit neatly into one of these categories. Many organisms use a combination of these systems.

One of the most common examples of thermoregulation would be a lizard or a snake sunning itself on a rock when it needs to warm up. On the other hand, to avoid overheating during daytime, the same reptile would seek shelter in a cool, dark place. Desert animals burrow under the sand to avoid the sun, and fish swim to either deeper or shallower waters to find the ideal temperature. Cold-blooded animals generally experience a decrease in their metabolic rate when the outside temperature drops. Many of these creatures become very sluggish, or torpid, in cold weather. Some are capable of withstanding very cold winters, and all their vital processes slow down to a near-death state until warmth and a new food supply are available. Turtles, for example, will spend the winter at the bottom of ponds, and will survive even when the surface of the pond is iced over. This state is not hibernation in the same way we see it in mammals, but it is very similar.

Now get ready to answer the questions. You may use your notes to help you answer.

Q. 7 Listen again to part of the lecture. Then answer the question.

The term cold-blooded is not technically accurate. It suggests that creatures such as reptiles, insects, frogs, and fish are always cold. And what would that mean, if you think about it? How would it work? Many fish live in warm water. If a fish were truly cold all the time, how would it regulate its body temperature? It would need to be very well-insulated, and as we all know, that is not the case with most fish.

P: 체온에 관한 토론으로 알게 되었듯, 모든 생명체는 생명을 유지하기 위해 특정 범위 내의 체온을 유지해야 합니다. 오랜 세월, 우리는 동물을 두 부류로 분류했죠, 바로 온혈 동물과 냉혈 동물입니다. 냉혈 동물이란 용어는 사실 엄밀히 말하자면 정확하지는 않죠. 이 말에는 파충류나 곤충류, 개구리, 물고기 등의 생명체는 항상 차갑다는 의미가 담겨 있습니다. 그럼 한 번 생각해본다면, 그 말이 뜻하는 건 무엇일까요? 어떻게 작용하는 걸까요? 많은 물고기들이 따뜻한 물에 서식합니다. 물고기가 항상 차갑다면, 체온을 어떻게 조절할까요? 단열이 아주 잘되어 있어야 하는데, 우리 모두 알고 있듯, 이는 대부분의 물고기에 해당되는 이야기는 아니죠. 그렇다면, 뭔가 다른 작용이 있다는 것이겠죠.

오늘의 토픽을 더 자세히 알아보죠. 냉혈 동물이 체온을 조절하는 방법에는 3가지 다른 시스템이 있습니다. 첫 번째가 ectothermy(변온, 외부열)인데, 외부의 열원을 이용한다는 뜻이죠. 두 번째는 poikilothermy(변온)로, 동물의 체내 온도가 바뀐다는 뜻입니다. 보통 동물이 외부 환경에 적응하게 되는 것이죠. 세 번째 시스템은 bradymetabolism(저율대사)으로, 동물이 깨어있고 활동적인 상태에서는 신진대사율이 상당히 빠르지만, 활동을 하지 않는 동안에는 신진대사율이 매우 느려지는 것을 말합니다. 하지만, 온혈 동물 중 이 세가지 범주 중 하나에 딱 들어맞는 것은 거의 없다는 것을 기억해야 합니다. 많은 동물들이 이 3가지 시스템을 복합적으로 이용하니까요.

체온 조절을 하는 동물 중 대표적인 예가 몸을 따뜻하게 해야 하면 바위 위에서 햇볕을 쬐는 도마뱀이나 뱀이겠죠. 반면, 한낮에 과열되는 것을 피하기 위해서는 서늘하고, 어두운 곳으로 몸을 피할 곳을 찾아요. 사막 동물들은 태양을 피하기 위해 모래 속으로 파고 들어가고, 물고기는 적합한 온도를 찾아서 더 깊은 곳이나 얕은 곳으로 헤엄치죠. 냉혈 동물은 일반적으로 외부 온도가 떨어지면 신진대사율이 느려집니다. 많은 동물들이 날씨가 추울 때는 매우 느려지고 휴면을 하게 되죠. 일부는 극한의 겨울도 견뎌낼 수 있지만, 날이 따뜻해지고 새로운 먹이 공급이 가능해 질 때까지는 생명 유지 작용이 거의 죽은 상태처럼 느려져요. 예를 들면, 거북이는 연못 바닥에서 겨울을 나고, 연못의 수면이 얼어붙을 때에도 살아 남아요. 이 상태는 포유류에서 찾아볼 수 있는 동면과는 다르지만 상당히 유사하죠.

어휘 | temperature 온도 | range 범위 | maintain 유지하다 | term 용어 | accurate 정확한 | reptile 파충류 | regulate 조절하다 | insulate 단열시키다 | take advantage of ~를 이용하다 | vary 바뀌다, 다양하다 | metabolic rate 신진대사율 | fit into ~에 들어맞다 | thermoregulation 체온 조절 | overheating 과열 | burrow 굴을 파다 | shallow 얕은 | sluggish 느린 | torpid 느린, 휴면하는 | withstand 참다, 견디다 | pond 연못 | hibernation 동면 | mammal 포유류

Review

1. 1. We need to print out enough permission forms.

2. We haven't had much time to plan this, so we might have to do both.

3. But the honors program is changing a few rules and requirements, and you need to know about them

4. It was the best <u>solution</u> anyone <u>could think of</u>.

5. It's a new system, and they're still <u>working out all the bugs</u>.

2. 1. No, / we don't have the authority / to tell you / what to do / before the semester starts.

2. Well,/ the hours for one-on-one tutors / have been cut back,/ so it's almost impossible / to get help / from a human being now.

3. You never give the titles of songs / when you play them, / and your listeners want to find those songs again / after the show.

4. My family has been planning a trip / that week, / and it'll be our last chance to travel together / for a while.

5. It's already ten cents a page / and then we still have to buy the books / when it comes in.

Book List 반석 도서목록

TOEFL

TOEFL myself Reading (Advanced Course)
Steven Oh, Michael Nolan, Richard Owell, Kevin Heiser / 국배판 / 376면 / 22,000원

iBT 시대를 알리는 최초의 iBT Reading 대비 교재. Reading 부분만 20회를 엮고 별권으로 해답과 해설을 실었다. 이 책의 특징은 전체가 영문으로만 되어 있다는 것. advanced reader들에게 필독서가 될 것이다.

TOEFL myself Listening (Advanced Course)
Steven Oh, Michael Nolan, Richard Owell, Kevin Heiser / 국배판 / 440면 / 29,000원
(별권 – Answer Keys, mp3용 CD 포함)

ETS에서 제시된 규정에 따라 편집되어 실제 시험과 같은 조건에서 자기 실력을 평가할 수 있도록 하였다. 본서는 12회분의 iBT Listening 문제를 제시하고 별권인 해설서에는 정답과 영문 해설이 들어 있다. 약간 높은 수준으로 만들어졌기 때문에 실제 시험에서는 더욱 좋은 결과를 얻을 수 있을 것이다.

iBT TOEFL myself Reading (Regular Course)
Steven Oh, Michael Nolan, Richard Owell, Kevin Heiser / 국배판 / 336면 / 22,000원
(별권 – Answer Keys)

iBT 토플을 준비하는 수험생을 위한 Reading 실전문제집. 본서는 ETS에서 제시하는 요구 사항의 형식과 유형에 충실한 최상의 수험서로서, 실제 TOEFL 시험과 똑같은 환경에서 시험을 치르게 된다. 어휘를 넓히고 모든 문제에 대한 이해력을 높여주기 위해 제시문에 대해 정답 및 한글 해설을 꼼꼼히 달았으며 정답부문에 Summary를 첨부했다. 본서는 20회분의 iBT Reading 문제 및 별책인 해설서로 구성되었다.

iBT TOEFL myself Listening (Regular Course)
Jessica Jung / 국배판 / 416면 / 25,000원 (별권 – Answer Keys, mp3용 CD 포함)

iBT 토플을 준비하는 수험생을 위한 Listening 실전문제집. 12회분의 iBT Listening 문제 및 별책인 해설서로 구성되었다. 새로운 iBT TOEFL 형식에 더 익숙해질 수 있도록 실제 미국 대학 강의내용 수준이나 학구적인 내용에 바탕을 두고 있으며 수험생의 어휘를 넓혀주고 모든 문제에 대한 이해력을 높여주기 위해 제시문에 대해 정답 및 한글 해설을 꼼꼼히 달았다. 뿐만 아니라, 지문에 대한 내용 이해를 돕기 위해 정답부문에 Summary(지문요약)를 첨부했다.

iBT TOEFL Reading (Prep–Advanced Course)
Steven Oh, Michael Nolan, Richard Owell, Kevin Heiser / 4×6배판 / 316면 / 21,000원
(별권 – Answer Keys, mp3용 CD 포함)

iBT에 출제되는 지문은 역사적, 과학적, 사회적 사실이 대부분이므로 여러 번 응시하면 내용이 비슷한 것을 만나게 된다. 따라서 영역별로 가장 많이 등장하는 내용을 엄선하였으므로 청취학습을 겸들이면 학습효과가 배가된다. 난이도는 고급자를 목표로 하는 중급자 수준에 맞추었다.

TOEFL Vocabulary & Reading
오규상 / 4×6배판 / 624면 / 19,800원 (mp3 파일 무료제공)

어휘와 독해를 묶은 회심의 역작. 모든 어휘를 테마별로 분류하고 독해지문 100편을 수록했다. 특히 34편에 달하는 미국 역사는 역사 교과서 한 권을 읽는 효과를 준다. 동의어 찾기 문제해설은 英英韓사전 방식으로 되어 많은 동의어를 익히는데 큰 도움이 된다.

Find TOEFL Vocabulary 1 · 2 with Listening & Reading
Steven Oh / 국배판 / 424쪽(1권), 432쪽(2권) / 각권 15,000원 (mp3용 CD 포함)

iBT TOEFL의 어휘, 청취, 독해를 한 권으로 마스터하려는 학습자를 위한 교재. 영역별로 실전에 가장 빈번히 등장하는 중요 어휘와 5천여 개의 어구를 모두 영영한 사전 방식으로 해설하였고 어휘학습 후 청취 문제를 접함으로써 청취 실력을 향상시킬 수 있다. 한 테마에 어휘와 그에 해당하는 다양한 독해를 수록하였으며 독해 지문을 청취와 병행하여 청취 실력을 동시에 올리는 학습효과를 누릴 수 있다.

Essential TOEFL WORDS 5000
임 공 / 신국판 / 432면 / 12,000원 (B + T : 15,900원)

토플 리스닝과 리딩에서 갈수록 비중이 높아져 가는 Lecture 분야를 공략하기 위한 필수어휘서다. 리스닝과 리딩에서 질문하는 토픽이 동일하다는 점에 착안하여 리스닝과 리딩 점수를 동시에 향상시킬 수 있도록 Lecture 빈출지문 40개를 엄선하고, 각 빈출지문을 청취하거나 독해할 때 반드시 알아 두어야 할 핵심문장과 핵심어휘를 정리하였다.

iBT Find TOEFL Reading
Steven Oh / 4×6배판 / 600쪽(별책 156쪽) / 22,000원 (mp3용 CD 포함)

iBT 토플에서 단기간에 고득점을 올릴 수 있도록 테마별 학습이 가능하도록 하였다. 지문별로 중요하거나 어려운 어휘는 영영한 사전식의 설명이 되어 있고, 원어민이 녹음한 mp3 파일이 제공되어 청취를 병행한 입체적 학습이 가능하다. 권말에는 Actual Test를 통해 실전 감각을 키울 수 있도록 하였다.

iBT Find TOEFL Listening
Rebecca Hardy, Naomi Kim / 4*6배판 / 368쪽 / 19,000원 (mp3용 CD 포함)

iBT Listening 출제경향을 분석하고 고득점을 얻을 수 있는 최적의 전략과 학습 방법을 제시하고 있다. 실질적인 청취력 향상을 위하여 Dictation 훈련에 중점을 두고 있다. 긴 지문 중 밑줄로 듣기 능력을 테스트해 나아가 보면 점점 자신감이 높아지는 걸 느낄 수 있다.

iBT Find TOEFL Speaking
Rebecca Hardy, Naomi Kim / 4×6배판 / 379쪽 / 15,000원 (mp3용 CD 포함)

본서는 iBT TOEFL Speaking 섹션의 출제경향을 철저히 분석한 후 고득점을 얻을 수 있는 최적의 전략과 학습 방법을 제시하고 있다. 다양한 출제 예상문제와 대화 상황, 강의 주제를 다루고 있으며, 문제의 이해와 답변 제시 등의 과정을 실제 시험 상황과 동일하게 훈련할 수 있도록 체계적으로 구성되었다. 4주 또는 6주간의 계획에 맞춰 학습하도록 하였고 권말에는 Actual Test를 수록하여 최종 점검이 가능하도록 하였다.

iBT Find TOEFL Writing
Jack Betts, Naomi Kim / 4×6배판 / 332쪽 / 15,000원 (mp3용 CD 포함)

iBT 체제로 바뀐 토플 Writing 섹션의 출제경향을 철저히 분석하고 고득점을 얻을 수 있는 최적의 전략과 학습 방법을 제시하고 있다. 다양한 출제 예상문제와 대화 상황, 강의 주제를 다루고 있으며, 시험을 단계적으로 공략할 수 있도록 난이도를 조정하였다. 자신의 생각을 명확하게 표현할 수 있도록 문제의 이해와 답변 제시 등의 과정을 실제 시험 상황과 동일하게 훈련할 수 있도록 체계적으로 구성하였다.

All About Junior iBT TOEFL Reading (Pre-intermediate)
Naomi Kim, Alan Hahn / 4×6배판 / 216쪽 / 12,000원

All About Junior TOEFL 시리즈는 토플을 전반적으로 다루고 섹션마다 모든 문제형식을 훈련시킨다. 최신 출제경향을 반영한 본 시리즈는 학습자들을 토플 학습에 자신감을 갖게 하고 고득점에 필요한 모든 것을 제공한다. Reading, Listening, Speaking, Writing 섹션은 수준별로 각 초급, 중급, 고급이 있다. 본서는 Reading 초급이다.

All About Junior iBT TOEFL Reading (Intermediate)
Naomi Kim, Alan Hahn / 4×6배판 / 232쪽 / 12,000원

All About Junior TOEFL 시리즈는 토플을 전반적으로 다루고 섹션마다 모든 문제형식을 훈련시킨다. 최신 출제경향을 반영한 본 시리즈는 학습자들을 토플 학습에 자신감을 갖게 하고 고득점에 필요한 모든 것을 제공한다. Reading, Listening, Speaking, Writing 섹션은 수준별로 각 초급, 중급, 고급이 있다. 본서는 Reading 중급이다.

All About Junior iBT TOEFL Reading (Advanced)
Naomi Kim, Alan Hahn / 4×6배판 / 268쪽 / 12,000원

All About Junior TOEFL 시리즈는 토플을 전반적으로 다루고 섹션마다 모든 문제형식을 훈련시킨다. 최신 출제경향을 반영한 본 시리즈는 학습자들을 토플 학습에 자신감을 갖게 하고 고득점에 필요한 모든 것을 제공한다. Reading, Listening, Speaking, Writing 섹션은 수준별로 각 초급, 중급, 고급이 있다. 본서는 Reading 고급이다.

SAT & IELTS

All about IELTS 실전문제집 3 (Reading—General module)
Lee Soo-Young, Julie Tolsma / 4×6배판 / 256쪽 / 13,000원

본 책은 IELTS Reading TEST (General Module) 5회분의 문제와 해설을 수록한 최종 마무리 테스트용 교재이다. 각각의 1회분은 42문항(4개 지문)으로 구성되었고, 실제 시험과 비슷한 최신의 출제경향과 문제형태를 반영했다. 특히, 섹션별로 다양한 지문(6주제)과 문제유형(7형태)을 제공하여 실전감각을 익히는 데 많은 도움이 된다.

TOEIC

처음부터 다시 시작하는 토익은 내밥 RC 입문편
Pat Jeon / 4×6배판 / 432면 / 13,800원

본서는 TOEIC Part 5, 6, 7을 위한 입문서로 기획된 책이다. 어휘력과 문법 실력을 동시에 공략할 수 있도록 하였으며 TOEIC 독해를 위한 전략비법 70, 1~2초 안에 정답 고르기 공략법 등으로 구성되었다. 강의용 및 독습자를 위해 강의식 해설이 수록되었고 실전모의고사 10회분 체험하기 프로그램이 포함되어 있다.

처음부터 다시 시작하는 토익은 내밥 LC 입문편
김형주 / 4×6배판 / 456면 / 15,800원 (B+T : 25,000원)

TOEIC Part 1, 2, 3, 4를 위한 입문서로 기획된 책이다. 뉴토익의 경향에 맞춰 각 파트별 문제 유형을 data화하여 분석하였고 각각에 대한 대비책을 제시하여, 수험생들이 실제 시험에 대한 적응력을 높이고 고득점을 얻을 수 있도록 하였다. 각 파트마다 실전 테스트가 수록되었으며 미국인과 영국인 네이티브 발음으로 녹음된 MP3 파일이 제공된다.

뉴토익은 내밥1 LC 실전문제집
Jason Kim, Jay Lee / 국배판 / 256면(별책 146면) / 15,000원(B+T : 25,000원)

뉴토익 수험자의 최종 마무리 테스트용, 네이티브의 말하기 스피드에 적응력을 기르는데 주안점을 두었으며 680점 이상의 중고급자에게 뉴토익 LC의 파트별 공략법을 제시한다. 10회분의 미니테스트인 Pretest가 있고 10회분의 정식 Actual Test가 수록되어 있다.

뉴토익은 내밥2 RC 실전문제집
남재조, 박영광 / 국배판 / 400면(별책 128면) / 16,000원(별책 포함)

최근 토익 RC 문제를 심층 분석하여 적중률 높은 문제를 엄선하여 12회로 구성하였다. 특히 종합적 사고를 기를 수 있도록 출제하였고 혼자서도 공부할 수 있도록 문제의 흐름을 상세히 설명하였다. Part 5, 6에 다채로운 테마의 지문을 수록하였으며, Part 7 장문 독해를 강화하였다.

토익은 내밥 Basic LC
김학용 / 4×6배판 / 446면 / 16,800원(mp3 파일 무료제공)

New TOEIC LC Section, 즉 Part Ⅰ, Ⅱ, Ⅲ, Ⅳ별로 최신 출제유형과 경향을 분석하였고 문제별 핵심을 파악하는 핵심 포인트를 제시하였다. 철저한 출제유형 해부에 따른 파트별 공략법이 제시되었으며 실전을 대비한 Model Test와 Actual Test를 통해 실제 시험에 대한 적응력을 키울 수 있다.

토익은 내밥 Basic RC
김학용 / 4×6배판 / 618면(별책 103면) / 16,800원

어휘 문법 독해를 일망타진하는 책! New TOEIC의 출제 유형을 철저히 분석하였으며 그에 따른 내용을 충실히 전달하고자 파트별 출제빈도와 그 유형을 표시해두었다. 어휘편에선 고득점으로 인도하는 토익 어휘 공략법을, 문법편에선 문장을 분석하는 문법 지식을 탄탄하게 쌓을 수 있도록 하였으며, 독해편에선 지문에 관련된 문제의 핵심을 파악하는 훈련이 가능하도록 하였다.

토익은 내밥 Xpeed 700 RC
김영진, 이희연 / 4×6배판 / 624면 / 16,500원

New TOEIC RC 단기 완성용 특강 교재. TOEIC 초급~중급자들이 단기간에 Part 5, 6, 7에서 고득점을 거둘 수 있도록 기획된 책이다. 각 파트별 출제유형과 출제경향에 대한 철저한 분석을 바탕으로, 단순히 문제풀이 요령을 익히는데 그치지 않고 기초 실력 배양까지 가능하도록 12주에 걸쳐 학습하도록 구성되었다.

토익은 내밥 Xpeed 700 LC
이희연, 김영진 / 4×6배판 / 464면 / 16,500원(B+T : 25,000원)

New TOEIC LC 단기 완성용 특강 교재. TOEIC 초급~중급자들이 단기간에 Part 1, 2, 3, 4에서 고득점을 할 수 있도록 기획된 책이다. 각 파트별 출제 유형의 철저한 분석과 더불어, 토익시험이 선호하는 단어와 중요 표현에 대한 반복 청취 훈련과 확인 학습을 할 수 있도록 구성되어 있다.

즉석 토익 VOCA
김학용 / A5 / 432쪽 / 12,000원

파트별로 유용한 어휘를 충분히 연습하도록 구성했고 파트1에서는 사진 문제의 핵심을 파악하는 연습을 시킨다. L/C와 R/C편의 어휘를 종합적으로 공부할 수 있도록 각 Part별로 출제 빈도가 높은 어휘를 실었기 때문에 어휘력 향상에 큰 도움이 될 것이다.

JUNIOR TOEIC RC
도성자 / 4×6배판 / 440쪽 / 15,000원

TOEIC을 처음 치르는 주니어들이 시험 준비 첫걸음을 디딜 수 있도록 구성되었다. 토익의 기본 유형 뿐 아니라 저자 고유의 〈문장 분석의 해법〉을 통해 영어 독해 전반에 대한 기본실력을 쌓을 수 있도록 하였다. 또 반드시 극복해야 할 문법과 독해 공략법을 꼼꼼한 〈강의식 해설〉로 구성하였다.

독해 · 어휘 · 문법 · 작문

3일만에 끝내는 Super 영문독해 핵심전략
오규상 / 4X6배판 변형 / 312면 / 9,500원

이 책은 영문 독해의 핵심 전략적인 비법을 제공한다. 우선 Reading Skill과 Reading Material에서 독해의 기본구조를 바로 잡고 꼼꼼히 기초를 다진다. 실전문제를 통해 자신감을 배양하며, 학습자에게 부담 없이 꾸며져 있어 읽다보면 독해실력을 검증해볼 수 있다. Part 4에서는 구문과 문법사항을 확인하며 술술 읽을 수 있게 꾸몄다.

3일만에 끝내는 Super 영문법
Ueda Ichizo / 4X6배판 변형 / 339면 / 9,500원

본서는 문법을 처음부터 끝까지 배우는 것이 아니라 문법의 중요사항을 엮어 단기간에 문법 전체의 핵심을 짚을 수 있도록 도와주는 기획서이다. 그리고 영작문 연습과 각종 숙어, 구문별 뉘앙스 설명으로 영어 실력을 특별히 한 단계 업레이드시킬 수 있다.

3일만에 끝내는 Super 영작문
Hironobu Takeoka / 4×6 변형판 / 272면 / 9,500원

영작을 쉽고 빠르게 마스터할 수 있도록 구성된 영작문 기본서. 영작을 위해 꼭 필요한 58가지 법칙과 빈출패턴 67문형을 제시함으로써 영작의 기본을 다질 수 있으며 자연스럽게 영작 실력을 업그레이드 할 수 있다

영어원론
김건태 / 4×6배판 / 540면 / 25,000원

영어 독해에 어느 정도 자신이 있는 중상급 이상의 영어 학습자를 위한 기획서. 이 책은 친절하고 풍부한 해설을 담고 있으며 문장을 설명하면서 그 문장이 왜 틀렸는지 알기 쉽게 설명해준다. 부자연스러운 문장과 좋은 문장을 나란히 비교하고 차이를 설명한 것을 꾸준히 읽음으로서 조금씩 영어를 보는 안목이 넓어질 수 있도록 도와준다.

반석 영문독해 **1** 사회과학편
편집부 / 4×6배판 / 352면 / 10,000원

TOEFL, 대학원, 국가고시 등에 고정적으로 인용되는 텍스트들을 사회과학 분야(경제학 · 경제사상, 사회학 · 사회사상, 정치학 · 정치사상)별로 엄선, 체계적으로 엮었다.

반석 영문독해 **2** 인문과학편
편집부 / 4×6배판 / 348면 / 10,000원

TOEFL, 대학원, 국가고시 등에 고정적으로 인용되는 텍스트들을 인문과학 분야(문학, 문학이론, 역사, 역사인식, 철학, 철학인식)별로 엄선하여 체계적으로 엮어놓았다.

반석 영문독해 **3** 자연과학편
편집부 / 4×6배판 / 368면 / 10,000원

TOEFL, 대학원, 국가고시 등에 고정적으로 인용되는 텍스트들을 자연과학 분야(과학기술의 현단계, 과학과 사회, 과학철학)별로 엄선, 체계적으로 구성하였다.

즉석 영단어 3000
오규상 / 국반판 / 496쪽 / 8,900원 (mp3용 CD 포함)

본서는 TOEFL, TOEIC, 공무원 시험 등 각종 시험에 출제되는 많은 어휘들 가운데 시험에 꼭 나오는 핵심어휘들만 모아 동의어, 반의어, 파생어와 함께 예문들을 엮어 놓았다. 이러한 단어만 확실히 익혀둔다면 시험에 나오는 어떤 독해지문이라도 읽어나가는데 어려움이 없을 것이다.

즉석 영숙어 900
편집부 / 국반판 / 464쪽 / 8,900원 (mp3용 CD 포함)

본서는 영어를 읽고 구사하는데 필요한 900개의 필수 숙어와 2,000개의 각종 시험 대비 기출 숙어로 구성되었다. 필수 숙어는 모두 Q&A의 짧은 대화로 이루어진 상황과 함께 제시되며, 토플, 토익이나 여타 시험에 자주 출제되는 문제를 수록하여 새로운 어휘를 확장할 수 있도록 편집했다.

와신상담 공무원영어 9급 (독해 · 어휘편)
박기혁 / 4×6배판 / 448면 / 15,000원

각종 공무원 및 공사시험을 위한 강의식 어휘 · 독해 교재. 어휘와 독해를 단번에 정복할 수 있도록 기출 유형을 철저하게 분석하였으며, 셀프체크에서 문제 해결 비법을 제시하여 문제풀이 능력을 업그레이드 할 수 있도록 했다.

와신상담 공무원영어 9급 (문법편)
박기혁 / 4×6배판 / 472면 / 15,000원

독학용 강의식 수험 영문법 교재로서 어떤 유형의 공무원 시험이라도 적용할 수 있는 기초적인 영문법을 총망라하였으며, 각종 수험 영어의 실전에 대비할 수 있도록 문법사항마다 문제풀이 비법과 영문법의 출제 원리를 체계적으로 분석한 기획서이다.

로그인 1318 영문법
윤상범 / 4×6변형판 / 328면 / 12,000원 (Tape 2개 포함)

필요없는 문법은 과감히 생략하고 수능 독해에 꼭 필요한 알짜 문법만을 구어체로 서술하였다. 반복하여 읽다보면 문장과 문법이 자연스럽게 습득되며, 각 장의 끝에 연습문제를 통해 자신의 문법과 독해실력을 평가해 볼 수 있다.

초급 Junior Vocabulary
이홍배 · 김덕중 · 서석봉 / 4×6배판 / 300면 / 8,000원

TOEFL · TOEIC을 비롯한 각종 영어시험 빈출 어휘 3,000개와 매 과마다 9가지 이상의 상이한 응용문제를 수록하였다.

중급 College Vocabulary
이홍배, 김덕중 / 4×6배판 / 494면 / 10,000원

TOEFL · TOEIC을 비롯한 각종 영어시험 빈출 어휘 5,000개를 엄선하여 수록하였고 매과 시작전에 어휘력 측정시험(Pretest)을 실시함으로써 자신의 어휘력 수준을 진단할 수 있다.

시험에 잘 나오는 영어문법
선명수 / 4×6배판 / 508면 / 15,800원

본서는 공무원을 비롯하여 대학원, 편입, 각종 자격시험 따위에 빈출되는 TOEFL 유형을 토대로 기획 및 구성되었으며, 어떤 유형의 시험에서라도 고득점을 올릴 수 있도록 영문법의 기초적인 원리와 개념을 실전적으로 접목

아주 쉽게 배우는 영문법
최희 / 4×6배판 / 431면 / 10,000원

문법을 알기 쉽게 설명했고, 예문을 회화와 실용영어 중심으로 구성하여 '회화 · 작문 · 독해'를 처음부터 끝까지 이 책 하나로 끝낼 수 있다.

처음 시작하는 영작 기술
간종현 / 4×6배판 / 304쪽 / 9,500원

누구나 만들 수 있는 짧고 간단한 문장으로 숨이 찰 만큼 길고 복잡한 문장을 어떻게 수월하게 만들 수 있는가를 보여주고 훈련시켜 준다. 간단한 문장을 확장과 연장의 과정을 통해 자유자재로 원하는 문장을 만들 수 있는 수준까지 끌어올릴 수 있다.

즉석 기초 영작문
장승재 / 4×6배판 / 348면 / 10,000원

어렵게만 느껴졌던 영작문을 초보 학습자들도 쉽게 다가갈 수 있도록 구성한 영작문 교재. 영작을 위한 핵심 문법을 근간으로 하여 쉬운 것부터 점진적이며 반복적인 연습을 통해 영어식 사고 방식을 체득할 수 있다.

회화 · 일반

즉석 비즈니스 영어회화 사전
정한석 / 국판 / 483면 / 15,000원 (B+T : 19,000원)

국내의 다국적 기업에 근무하거나 세계화 경제에 발맞춰 국제시장에서 활약하는 전문 기업인들을 위한 Daily Business 영어 회화 교재. 본문은 모두 11개의 단원으로 이루어져 있으며 각 단원은 주제에 따라 국제업무 환경에서 기업업무를 수행하는데 흔히 접할 수 있는 상황을 중심으로 한 다양한 대화로 구성되어 있다.

즉석 영어 회화 패턴 900
김수진 / A5 / 432쪽 / 10,000원 (mp3 파일 제공) 테이프 포함: 15,000원)

본서는 상황별 영어회화를 토대로 기초적인 표현에서부터 각종 질의응답의 요령까지 Basic Expressions를 통하여 영어회화에 자신감 있게 접근할 수 있도록 구성하였다. 본서는 60개 주제와 900개의 기본 문형으로서 기본적인 문장구조와 회화에 많이 쓰이는 어휘를 모두 실었다.

즉석 일본어 회화 900
봉영아 / A5 / 440쪽 / 10,000원 (mp3 파일 제공) 테이프 포함: 15,000원)

본서는 주제별, 상황별, 장면별 일본어 회화를 토대로 기초적인 표현에서부터 각종 질의응답의 요령까지 Basic Expression을 통하여 일본어 회화에 자신감 있게 접근할 수 있도록 구성하였다. 실용 일본어에서 빈출되는 900개의 패턴문형을 중점적으로 반복 훈련하여 일본어 회화를 정복해 보자. 본서의 기획 핵심은 Pattern Drill에 나오는 대체형 반복연습으로

取り(청해) 실력을 비약적으로 향상시키는 것과 여기 나오는 다양한 표현을 회화에서 직접 응용할 수 있도록 하는 것이다.

즉석 중국어 회화 900
김현철, 조길 / A5 / 439쪽 / 10,000원 (mp3 파일 제공) 테이프 포함: 15,000원)

본서는 주제별, 상황별, 장면별 회화를 토대로, 일상생활에서 겪는 기초적인 회화에서부터 비즈니스나 해외여행에 필요한 상황이나 장면에 적용할 수 있는 중국어 회화 표현 900문형 이상을 수록하였다. 총 60 Unit으로 구성되었으며, Basic Expression과 Pattern Drill에서 빈출 핵심 패턴문형, 묻고 답하는 요령에 의한 어휘력과 표현력 확장, 문형변화까지 폭넓게 다루었다. 또한 중국인 네이티브 스피커의 목소리로 녹음된 MP3 파일을 제공함으로써 중국 현지인들의 발음과 성조에 익숙해지도록 하였다.

즉석 일상 영어
이국호 / 국판 / 351면 / 9,500원 (B+T : 12,500원, mp3 파일 무료제공)

이 책은 영어 기초 정도의 실력을 가지고 회화를 막 시작하려는 학습자를 대상으로 하여 일상생활, 여행 등에 기본적으로 쓰일 수 있는 회화 표현을 중심으로 엮었다. 어떤 장면이나 상황에서도 영어 회화를 가능한 정확하고 다양하게 익힐 수 있도록 체계적으로 구성하였으며, 영어 초보자도 쉽게 접근할 수 있도록 한글로 영어발음을 표기하였다.

즉석 일상 일본어
이화승 / 국판 / 351면 / 9,500원 (B+T : 12,500원, mp3 파일 무료제공)

이 책은 일본어 기초 정도의 실력을 가지고 회화를 막 시작하려는 학습자를 대상으로 하여 일상생활, 여행 등에 기본적으로 쓰일 수 있는 회화 표현을 중심으로 엮었다. 어떤 장면이나 상황에서도 일본어 회화를 가능한 정확하고 다양하게 익힐 수 있도록 체계적으로 구성하였으며, 일본어 초보자도 쉽게 접근할 수 있도록 한글로 일본어발음을 표기하였다.

즉석 일상 중국어
이춘호 / 국판 / 351면 / 9,500원 (B+T : 12,500원, mp3 파일 무료제공)

이 책은 중국어 기초 정도의 실력을 가지고 회화를 막 시작하려는 학습자를 대상으로 하여 일상생활, 여행 등에 기본적으로 쓰일 수 있는 회화 표현을 중심으로 엮었다. 어떤 장면이나 상황에서도 중국어 회화를 가능한 정확하고 다양하게 익힐 수 있도록 체계적으로 구성하였으며, 중국어 초보자도 쉽게 접근할 수 있도록 한글로 중국어발음을 표기하였다.

넘버원 여행영어
이국호 / 4×6판 / 208쪽 / 7,000원

영어에 서툰 여행자가 해외여행을 자유롭게 즐길 수 있도록 도와주는 본격 Spoken Travel English 회화교재. 여행 시에 일어날 수 있는 수많은 돌발 상황들에 대처하기 위해 늘 휴대할 수 있도록 포켓북 사이즈로 제작하였으며, 영어에 서툰 여행자라도 자연스럽게 영어를 구사할 수 있도록 원어민 발음법에 따라 우리말로 표기를 달아두었다.

즉석 여행 영어
이국호 / 4X6판 / 336쪽 / 7,500원 (mp3 파일 무료제공)

현지에서 바로바로 활용이 가능하도록 원어민의 발음에 가깝게 한글 발음을 병기하였고, 상황별로 필요한 영어 표현은 물론 각종 정보가 가득한 여행 가이드북이다. 또한 네이티브의 정확한 발음을 익힐 수 있도록 CD가 포함되어 있으며 자료실에서 책 전문을 mp3 파일로 다운받을 수 있다.

즉석 여행 일본어
이화승 / 4X6판 / 336면 / 7,500원 (mp3 파일 무료제공)

현지에서 바로바로 활용이 가능하도록 원어민의 발음에 가깝게 한글 발음을 병기하였고, 상황별로 필요한 일어 표현은 물론 각종 정보가 가득한 여행 가이드북이다.

즉석 여행 중국어
송준호 / 4X6판 / 336면 / 7,500원 (mp3 파일 무료제공)

현지에서 바로바로 활용이 가능하도록 원어민의 발음에 가깝게 한글 발음을 병기하였고, 상황별로 필요한 중국어 표현은 물론 각종 정보가 가득한 여행 가이드북이다.

그들만의 영어표현 아주 쉽게 따라잡기
홍성은 / 크라운판 / 330면 / 11,000원 (mp3용 CD 포함)

미국의 초등학생은 잘 알지만 한국의 영문과 학생들은 잘 모르는 표현을 위주로 엮은 독특한 내용의 회화책. 재미있는 일러스트와 재치 있는 설명이 가득하고 슬랭도 과감하게 소개했다. 원어민들의 솔직한 표현과 헐리웃 영화를 제대로 이해하고 싶다면 일독을 권한다.

프리토킹에 강해지는 즉석 영어 회화
이국호 / 국판 / 560쪽 / 18,500원 (CD 포함)

영어회화를 약간 해본 사람이 원어민과 자유로운 대화가 가능하도록 다양한 표현을 담아 영어 회화사전식 구성을 취했다. 즉석에서 활용할 수 있는 필수적인 표현을 엄선했고 6,000개 이상의 방대한 회화 표현이 나오며 다양한 주제의 실용 회화가 가능하다.

프리토킹에 강해지는 즉석 일본어 회화
金롯츰 · 村上二郎 / 국판 / 656면 / 18,500원 (CD 포함, mp3 파일 무료제공)

이 책은 자연스러운 일본어 회화를 위해 언제 어디서나 즉석에서 사전처럼 바로 활용할 수 있도록 만들어진 기획서이다. 기본 회화, 실용 회화, 필수 문형의 세 파트로 구성되어 있으며 유창하고 자연스러운 회화를 위해 필수적인 관용적 표현 25,000문장을 수록하여 체계적으로 일본어 프리토킹에 대비할 수 있다.

프리토킹에 강해지는 즉석 중국어 회화
조요섭 · 김형준 / 국판 / 480면 / 15,000원 (mp3 파일 무료제공)

본서는 중국어 회화를 본격적으로 시작하려는 학습자를 대상으로 하며, 기본어법, 기본회화, 실용회화로 나누어 중국어 회화에 대한 모든 것을 총망라한 학습서이다. 어떤 장면이나 상황에서도 중국어 회화를 가능한 정확하고 다양하게 익힐 수 있도록 사전식으로 구성하였으며 즉석에서 바로바로 활용할 수 있도록 국내 최대의 중국어 8,000여 표현을 수록하였다.

캐티리의 병원 영어회화 첫걸음
캐티리 / 신국판 / 293면 / 10,000원 (Tape 2개 포함)

영어권 국가로의 이민, 여행 ,유학, 출장 중 위급하게 병원을 찾았을 때, 자신의 증상을 쉽게 표현하고 병원 의료진과의 대화를 보다 원활하게 할 수 있는 가이드 북으로, 실제 병원에서 일어날 수 있는 모든 상황들을 거의 다 수록했다.

대한민국 1% 영어고수로 가는 영어공부법
John Park / 신국판 / 256면 / 7,900원

본서는 영어를 잘 하고 싶은 한국인들을 위해 쓴 책이다. 오랜 세월 영어를 공부했음에도 불구하고, 영어가 잘 안되는 한국인들에게 정말 영어를 잘 할 수 있는 방법과 길을 제시해준다. 그리고 영어의 초급자부터 영어의 고수를 목표로 삼고 있는 중급자나 고급자까지를 대상으로 한다. 또한 현장에서 영어교육을 담당하고 있는 모든 분에게도 유용하도록 하였다. 이 책은 그냥 물고기를 주는 것이 아니라, 물고기를 잡는 방법을 알려주고 있다.

청소년이 꼭 읽어야 할 세계의 위대한 인물 사전
편집부 / 신국판 / 526면 / 13,500원

초·중·고생을 위한 세계위인 백과사전으로 사상가, 정치인, 예술가, 문학가, 경제인 등 일반인에게 잘 알려진 위인들의 숨겨진 비화나 성장과정에 대한 내용에는 인류 역사에 큰 영향을 끼치고 독창적인 개성으로 깊은 감동을 선사했던 101명의 위인들이 엄선되어 있으며, 지금까지 교양이나 지식 차원에서 알고 있던 내용도 포함되어 있을 수도 있겠지만 청소년들의 입장에서 꼭 알아두어야 할 인물들에 관한 개별적 정보도 얻을 수 있다.

영어비결
장승원 / 신국판 / 253면 / 8,900원

국내 최연소 토플 만점자 장승원의 영어공부 방법서이다. 토익보다 어렵다는 토플에서 만점을 받고 외고에 입학하기까지의 모든 과정을 14살이던 중학교 2학년 시절의 기억을 되살려 솔직담백하게 풀어썼다.

즉석에서 바로바로 활용하는 Make it 일어회화 사전
이춘승 / 4*6판 / 512쪽 / 12,000원(CD 포함), 15,000원(테이프 4개, CD 포함)

본서는 일본 현지에서 사용하는 정통 일본어 표현의 다양성을 만끽할 수 있으며, 여기서 익힌 표현을 상황에 따라 활용할 수 있도록 뉘앙스를 고려하여 기획된 일본어회화 사전이다. 누구나 쉽게 일본어회화를 익힐 수 있도록 기본표현부터 빈출 패턴 문형, 관용표현까지 핵심 표현을 폭넓게 실었다. 작은 판형으로 일상생활에서 일어나는 모든 주제의 대화를 수록하고 있다.

즉석에서 바로바로 활용하는 Make it 영어회화 사전
Steven Oh / 4*6판 / 496쪽 / 12,000원(CD 포함), 15,000원(테이프 4개, CD 포함)

본서는 미국 현지에서 네이티브들이 사용하는 정통 영어 표현의 다양성을 만끽할 수 있으며, 여기서 익힌 표현을 상황에 따라 활용할 수 있도록 뉘앙스를 고려하여 기획된 영어회화사전이다. 누구나 쉽게 영어회화를 익힐 수 있도록 기본표현부터 빈출 패턴 문형, 관용표현까지 핵심표현을 폭넓게 실었다.

즉석에서 바로바로 활용하는 Make it 중국어 회화 사전
김현철, 김춘희 / 4×6판 / 511면 / 12,000원(CD 포함), 15,000원(테이프 4개, CD 포함)

중국 현지에서 사용하는 표현을 상황에 따라 활용할 수 있도록 뉘앙스를 고려하여 기획된 중국어회화사전이다. 기본표현부터 빈출 패턴 문형, 관용표현까지 핵심표현을 폭넓게 실었다. 독자들이 정확한 발음으로 자신감 있게 학습할 수 있도록 mp3용 CD를 제공하고 있으며, 사이즈를 크게 줄여 휴대하기에 편리하도록 배려하였다.

어린왕자
앙투안 생텍쥐페리 / 이화승 역 / A5 / 한글판 136쪽, 영어판 136쪽 / 합본 9,500원 각권 5,000원

이 책은 묘한 매력이 있어서 본래 '어른을 위한 동화' 지만, 어린이가 읽으면 동화가 되고 어른이 읽으면 어른과 사회에 대한 비판이 된다. 그리고 작가가 이 책을 쓴 시대(1942년 경)를 더듬어 보고 비행사로서 작자의 인생관을 생각하면 이야기 내면에는 깊은 철학이 감춰진 것을 알 수 있다.

동물농장
조지 오웰 / 조혜정 역 / A5 / 한글판 120면, 영어판 160면 / 각권 5,000원 합본 9,500원

스탈린 치하의 소비에트 전체주의에 대한 풍자소설. 현대 사회의 전체주의적 경향이 도달하게 될 종말을 묘사한 조지오웰의 대표작으로서, 정치적인 면을 배제하고 우화로서 읽더라도 훌륭한 작품이다. 유명한 정치소설이라 난해한 소설이라고 생각하기 쉬우나 단순한 스토리에 분량도 짧아 쉽게 읽을 수 있는 책이다.

위대한 개츠비
스콧 피츠제럴드 / 이화승 역 / A5 / 한글판 271면, 영어판 143면 / 각권 5,000원 합본 9,500원

20세기 최고의 미국 소설이라는 명성 덕분에 국내 대학 영문과 교재로 오래 사랑받아온 작품. 완벽한 번역과 이해를 돕는 배경지도, 인물 분석을 더했다. 본서는 지금까지 나온 어떤 번역본보다 오류가 적다는 점을 자부한다.

안네의 일기
안네 프랑크 / A5 / 한글판 140쪽, 영어판 156쪽 / 각권 5,000원 합본 9,500원

꿈 많은 문학소녀가 남긴 생생한 감동. 안네는 아빠가 열세 살 생일선물로 준 일기장에 친한 친구를 대하듯 속마음을 털어놓는다. 유태인 탄압이 극심해지면서 8명의 '은신' 생활이 시작된다. 안네는 게쉬타포에 발각될 때까지 2년 여의 힘겨운 생활을 기록으로 남긴다.

변신
프란츠 카프카 / A5 / 한글판 104쪽, 영어판 112쪽 / 각권 5,000원 합본 9,500원

그 어떤 소설보다도 더 충격적인 묘사로 이야기는 시작된다. 평범한 월급쟁이 그레고르 잠자는 흉측한 벌레가 되어 누워 있는 자신을 발견한다. 그의 모습을 본 사람들은 모두 혼비백산하지만 가족들은 '혹시 그가 인간으로 돌아오지 않을까' 하는 기대를 품고 동거를 시작한다.

포우 단편선
에드가 앨런 포우 / A5 / 한글판 128쪽, 영어판 152쪽 / 각권 5,000원 합본 9,500원

〈검은 고양이〉는 인간의 잔혹성과 두려움의 전형을 보여준다. 최초의 추리소설 〈모르그 가의 살인사건〉에서는 독특한 구성과 분석을 구사하였다. 〈도둑맞은 편지〉는 포우의 뛰어난 지성이 드러난 작품이다. 일반적 추리소설과 달리 사건의 범인을 알려주고 이야기를 풀어가는 추리의 묘미와 재치가 흥미롭다.

청소년을 위한
반석 영한대역 시리즈
(영문판, 한글판)

위대한 개츠비

지금까지 번역된 개츠비는 위대하지 않았다!
스콧 피츠제럴드 저 | 이화승 역
「위대한 개츠비」는 20세기 최고의 미국 소설이라는 작품성 덕분에 오랫동안 사랑받아온 작품이다. 기존의 어떤 번역본보다 오류가 적다는 점을 자부한다.

안네의 일기

꿈 많은 문학소녀가 남긴 생생한 감동
안네 프랑크 저 | 이화승 역
꿈 많은 유태인 소녀 안네는 열세 살 생일선물로 받은 일기장에 속마음을 털어놓는다. 독일의 유태인 탄압이 극심해지면서 안네 가족 등 8명의 2년간 '은신' 생활을 기록으로 남겼다.

어린왕자

순수성을 잃어가는 어른들을 위한 동화
앙투안 생텍쥐페리 저 | 이화승 역
이 책은 묘한 매력이 있어서 본래 '어른을 위한 동화' 지만, 어린이가 읽으면 동화가 되고 어른이 읽으면 어른과 사회에 대한 비판이 된다.

변신

현대인의 불안감을 충격적으로 묘사한 걸작!
프란츠 카프카 저 | 이화승 역
평범한 그레고르는 어느 날 벌레가 되어 버렸다. 인간의 정신을 갖고 있지만 벌레의 몸으로 살아가는데 차츰 인간의 의식마저도 희미해져 간다.

동물농장

독재체제를 통렬하게 비판하는 예언 소설
조지 오웰 저 | 조혜정 역
모든 동물은 평등하다. 하지만 어떤 동물은 다른 동물보다 더욱 평등하다! 영국 농장에서 학대받는 동물들이 농장주를 타도하는 혁명을 일으킨다.

포우 단편선

추리소설의 아버지, 포우의 단편 미학!
애드가 앨런 포우 저 | 이화승 역
초기 작품 〈검은 고양이〉는 인간의 잔혹성과 두려움에 관한 전형적 단면을 보여준다. 최초의 추리소설 〈모르그 가의 살인사건〉에서 포우는 독특한 구성과 분석, 추리를 구사하여 세계인의 경탄을 받고 있으며, 문학의 새로운 장르를 개척하여 추리소설의 아버지라고 불린다.